What does it mean to forgive? The answer is widely assumed to be self-evident but critical analysis quickly reveals the complexities of the subject. Forgiveness has traditionally been the preserve of Christian theology, though in the last half-century – and at an accelerating pace – psychologists, lawyers, politicians and moral philosophers have all been making an important contribution to questions about and our understanding of the subject. Anthony Bash offers a vigorous restatement of the Christian view of forgiveness in critical dialogue with those both within and without the Christian tradition. Forgiveness is a much more complicated subject than many theologians recognize. Bash explores the relevance of the theoretical discussion of the topic to recent events such as the Truth and Reconciliation Commission in South Africa, post-Holocaust trials, the aftermath of 9/11 and 7 July, and various high-profile criminal cases.

# FORGIVENESS AND CHRISTIAN ETHICS

What does it mean to forgive? The answer is widely assumed to be self-evident but critical analysis quickly reveals the complexities of the subject. Forgiveness has traditionally been the preserve of Christian theology, though in the last half century – and at an accelerating pace – psychologists, lawyers, politicians and moral philosophers have all been making an important contribution to questions about and our understanding of the subject. Anthony Bash offers a vigorous restatement of the Christian view of forgiveness in critical dialogue with those both within and without the Christian tradition. Forgiveness is a much more complicated subject than many theologians recognise. Bash explores the relevance of the theoretical discussion of the topic to recent events such as the Truth and Reconciliation Commission in South Africa, post-Holocaust trials, the aftermath of 9/11 and 7 July and various high-profile criminal cases.

ANTHONY BASH is Rector of the Durham North Team of parishes and Honorary Research Fellow in the Department of Theology and Religion, Durham University. He is author of *Ambassadors for Christ* (1997) and a number of articles.

Christian ethics has increasingly assumed a central place within academic theology. At the same time the growing power and ambiguity of modern science and the rising dissatisfaction within the social sciences about claims to value-neutrality have prompted renewed interest in ethics within the secular academic world. There is, therefore, a need for studies in Christian ethics which, as well as being concerned with the relevance of Christian ethics to the present-day secular debate, are well informed about parallel discussions in recent philosophy, science or social science. *New Studies in Christian Ethics* aims to provide books that do this at the highest intellectual level and demonstrate that Christian ethics can make a distinctive contribution to this debate – either in moral substance or in terms of underlying moral justifications.

**New Studies in Christian Ethics**
*Titles published in the series*:

# FORGIVENESS AND CHRISTIAN ETHICS

ANTHONY BASH

CAMBRIDGE
UNIVERSITY PRESS

CAMBRIDGE UNIVERSITY PRESS
Cambridge, New York, Melbourne, Madrid, Cape Town, Singapore, São Paulo

Cambridge University Press
The Edinburgh Building, Cambridge CB2 8RU, UK

Published in the United States of America by Cambridge University Press, New York

www.cambridge.org
Information on this title: www.cambridge.org/9780521878807

© Anthony Bash 2007

First published 2007

Printed in the United Kingdom at the University Press, Cambridge

*A catalogue record for this publication is available from the British Library*

ISBN 978-0-521-87880-7 hardback

# Contents

# General editor's preface

This book makes a timely contribution to the series New Studies in Christian Ethics. It provides a nuanced and well-written account of forgiveness that takes fully into consideration a wide range of scholarly material in philosophy, psychology, law (Anthony Bash originally trained in law and practised as a solicitor before ordination), New Testament studies and theology. It makes important links with other books in the series, especially David Hollenbach's *The Common Good and Christian Ethics* and Jean Porter's *Moral Action and Christian Ethics*. And it fulfils well the two key aims of the series as a whole – namely, to promote monographs in Christian ethics that engage centrally with the present secular moral debate at the highest possible intellectual level and, second, to encourage contributors to demonstrate that Christian ethics can make a distinctive contribution to this debate.

The issue of forgiveness is certainly timely, as Anthony Bash demonstrates through the many examples that he takes, such as the process of Truth and Reconciliation in South Africa, post-Holocaust trials, the aftermath of 9/11 and 7 July, and various high-profile crime stories. He also shows that the virtue of forgiveness is much more complicated than is often realised either in society at large or specifically in churches. Pointing to philosophical, psychological and legal discussions of forgiveness he argues that in comparison many theological accounts of forgiveness are inadequate. Indeed, very few other recent theologians have shown a proper awareness of these detailed secular discussions of forgiveness.

Anthony Bash argues that forgiveness properly understood is a process, as psychological studies have suggested. He also sides with those philosophers who maintain that there are occasions when unconditional forgiveness is actually inappropriate, for example when the victim is dead or where forgiveness conflicts with justice. He concludes that, theologically, forgiveness is properly seen as a gift rather than as a moral duty. We do have such a duty, but it in turn is best seen as a duty to *strive* to forgive – believing, on theological grounds, that it is finally God who forgives unconditionally.

Readers of this thoughtful book are likely to come away more (deeply) confused about forgiveness than before. Theologically inclined readers may, I hope, be persuaded that secular accounts of forgiveness do need to be taken seriously. Others may be challenged by the book's theological foundations – forgiveness is an eminently theological virtue. This is indeed a challenging book.

ROBIN GILL

### A NOTE ON THE COVER IMAGE: THE ESSA CROSS

Towards the end of the last century Gert Swart was commissioned to make a cross for the Evangelical Seminary of Southern Africa (ESSA), a multi-cultural seminary drawing students from many countries in Africa. ESSA's campus, a small but significant example of urban renewal, is situated in the South African city of Pietermaritzburg, the capital of KwaZulu-Natal.

The complex symbolism of the cross was carefully selected to convey several messages including the suffering of many South Africans in the turbulent, violent years before the birth of our democracy, the suffering of countless others in what must be one of the bloodiest centuries in the history of the world, and, crucially, one of redemption, reconciliation and hope.

Gert used images of his hands, each with a finger on the trigger of a gun directed at the Lamb, to contextualise the cross – in a province known as the 'killing fields of Natal' in the 1980s – and as a comment on the complicity of each one of us in the brutal execution of Christ on the cross.

As people gathered to dedicate the cross on 11 September 2001 news was filtering through of the audacious and devastating attacks on the Word Trade Towers and the Pentagon. So it was that, while the USA reeled, a small assembly intimately acquainted with terror and tragedy exuberantly celebrated the arrival of the ESSA Cross, a beacon of hope on a dark day in a dark world.

GERT AND ISTINE SWART

# *Preface*

This book is about forgiveness.

The subject is no longer the preserve of only those within the Christian tradition. People within the disciplines of psychology, philosophy, law and politics, for example, are also talking and writing about forgiveness.

Most weeks there is something in the popular press that is germane to the topic of this book. It is rare that an academic book can engage with popular culture in this way without becoming journalistic.

The Christian tradition has a significant, coherent and sometimes critical contribution to make to academic and popular discourse on forgiveness. As this book will show, modern discussion about and reflection on forgiveness are impoverished without the contribution of Christian thinking. The fact that society may be 'post-modern' and 'post-Christian' does not mean that the Christian tradition has nothing to say about forgiveness. There remains a distinctive and important place for the Christian voice on the subject.

Modern discourse also has a contribution to make to Christian thinking. It forces theologians to rethink the content and forms of their categories of thought and to restate them for a modern audience that asks modern questions. It is urgent that theologians do that, if they are to engage coherently with the sorts of wrongdoing that have taken place in the last hundred years – wrongdoing that is probably unparalleled as to both its extent and its depravity. Modern thinking also has the incidental effect of highlighting what is distinctive in the Christian tradition and enables Christians to contribute better to the current debates.

Less obviously, forgiveness is also a relatively neglected topic in scholarly Christian writing. There have not been many books directly on the subject in recent years, yet forgiveness is rightly regarded as one of the central themes of the Christian gospel. This book seeks to help restore the omission and to further debate and discussion on forgiveness.

Books often have their genesis in the personal interests of their writers. My interest in this subject does not arise because I have been wronged in a particularly evil way. I have faced the normal 'ups and downs' of life and, like most people, have learned something about forgiveness pragmatically. I became interested in the topic as the subject of academic study in the summer of 2003 when, jointly with my wife, Dr Melanie Bash, I wrote a chapter of *Forgiveness in Context* (Watts and Gulliford 2004: 29–49). I became aware then of how much work remains to be done on this subject, and I also became aware of how deeply the topic was touching me personally. I may not have been carrying a particularly heavy burden of unforgiveness, but I began to realise then that I had been – and continued to be – unforgiving about some things. I have, since then, made some progress in this area; more progress has yet to be made.

I have been surprised, as I have talked to people about the contents of this book, how much they have wanted to disclose their own stories to do with unforgiveness, hurt and suffering. I suspect this book is timely to help people think in a measured way about forgiveness, to explore some of the complexities and issues that forgiveness raises and to learn to forgive responsibly.

I would like to thank a delightful conversation partner, Dr Geoffrey Scarre of the Department of Philosophy at Durham University, for the contribution he has made to help me formulate and hone my thinking about forgiveness. His gentle and measured approach and his sharp insights have been an unfailing source of stimulus.

To my friends and family who have read portions of this book as it was being written I would like to give thanks. Dr Joe Bouch has been, for over twenty years, a critical and loyal friend. I owe him an enormous debt of gratitude. Thanks are due also to Alan Brown, Professor Gyles Glover, Professor Peter Rhodes, Rowena Abadi, Dr George Boyes-Stones and the Reverend Dale Hanson who have read, offered advice or talked to me about portions of this book. I thank my father who, in his ninetieth year, has critically and carefully read the entire manuscript of this book. I am also grateful to Dr Stephen Cherry for reading a draft of this book and for his generous and insightful comments.

My thanks go to Professor Robin Gill, the editor of the series in which this book appears, and to an unnamed reader of an earlier draft of the book. I am grateful to them both for their comments and suggestions.

I wrote most of this book while I was Solway Fellow and Chaplain at University College, Durham. I am grateful to the College for the opportunity to engage in research and to explore some of the ideas contained in this book through conversations with students and academic staff and in the College chapel.

My three children, Hannah, Simeon and Matthias, have been surprised that I should have spent so long reflecting on forgiveness, a topic that seems to them self-evident in its scope, meaning and value. For them, the subject has been adequately explored in books such as *The Grumpy Day: Teddy Horsley Learns about Forgiveness*, one of a delightful series by L. J. Francis and N. M. Slee (Birmingham: Christian Education Publications, 1994). Another book on forgiveness (and one without pictures) is, in their view, unnecessary. They have also been quick to remind me to forgive, especially where they have been concerned. I hope that with the completion of this book they will find me less often at my desk in front of a computer screen.

The children have given my wife, Melanie, and me great joy, and brought many opportunities, within the context of happy family life, to forgive and to be forgiven. I dedicate this book to Melanie – my best friend and most loyal critic – and to our children, Hannah, Simeon and Matthias. It comes with much love and with many thanks to each of them.

# CHAPTER 1

## *Forgiveness and wrongdoing*

This book is about one kind of response to evil and wrongdoing – the response called 'forgiveness'. The aim of this book is to explore why, how and when a victim may forgive a wrongdoer for wrongdoing – in other words, what it means to forgive.

I stand within the Christian tradition. In writing this book, I have sought to engage with modern secular insights about forgiveness and to be in critical dialogue with those insights. I have also sought to look critically at the Christian traditions about forgiveness and restate some of them in the light of modern discourse.

In the following pages, I refer to someone who has been wronged as 'the victim' or less often (and only for stylistic reasons) as 'the wronged person' or words to that effect. The person who does the wrong I usually refer to as 'the wrongdoer'. The wrong that the wrongdoer does to the victim I call 'wrongdoing'. When I refer to 'wrongdoing' or use a similar word, I mean 'a *morally* wrong act or omission'[1] in contrast to an act or omission that is wrong but not also morally wrong. Where there could be ambiguity, I make the meaning plain.[2]

I appreciate that words such as 'victim' and 'wrongdoer' may be read as words with emotive connotations. I do not intend them to be understood that way. I have been unable to find words that convey a more neutral sense. I have, in addition, sought to use gender-neutral language whenever possible to avoid, for example, suggesting that typically victims are women, wrongdoers men or that God is male.

---

[1] The root of this definition is Aristotelian: see *Rh.* i, 10, 1368b5–10 (in Barnes 1984). There, wrong-doing is defined as injury voluntarily inflicted contrary to the written laws that regulate particular communities or to unwritten and universally acknowledged general principles.

[2] Not all wrong acts are morally wrong. For example, the law may treat it as wrong to break a speed limit, but it is not morally wrong to do so when taking a seriously ill child to hospital, particularly if the child's life is in danger.

POPULAR UNDERSTANDING

Ask anyone in the street if to forgive is good and worthwhile and the answer, almost certainly, would be 'yes'.

On a day-to-day basis, with the minor difficulties of life, it is not very difficult to forgive. If Jack lends Jill a book and Jill is careless and loses it, Jill may irritate Jack by her carelessness but, as they are siblings and as Jack wishes to retain a good relationship with Jill, Jack may well accept Jill's apology and then forget about the matter.[3] Similarly, one friend may unwittingly say some hurtful things to another, but for the sake of friendship the offended friend will forgive and not allow the hurt to stand in the way of the friendship.

Most people would also affirm – at least in principle, if not by their own practice – that *not* to forgive is both foolish and misguided. Popular understanding is that bitterness often comes from being unforgiving. It is also that being unforgiving can be emotionally corrosive and harmful to health. It does not take an astute observer of human behaviour to see that the effect of not forgiving or of being unforgiven can be dehumanising and personally diminishing. Both wrongdoer and victim may also become trapped in a pattern of behaviour that is personally and communally destructive. This can be expressed in terms of the thought of Lévinas: to forgive is to recognise that we are part of a matrix of social relationships, that we have responsibilities towards others because we are part of that matrix and that our wholeness and freedom are best expressed in the context of relationships with others.[4]

Of course, when it comes to forgiveness, most people fail to live up to their own standards, and (if they were to think about it) they know that they do not live up to God's standards. Whatever the nature of an act of wrongdoing, there will be some who find they are unable to forgive, who will feel guilty about this, and who will also feel guilty about having disagreeable – or even brutish – feelings towards those who have mistreated them. For Christians in particular, this can present additional problems, because Christianity emphasises the ethical ideal to forgive. If truth be told, forgiving the way people believe that Jesus forgave (unconditionally, unilaterally and lavishly) is immensely difficult and few seem able to do

---

[3] Here forgetting does have a moral basis: it is in response to the apology (which is often a covert appeal for forgiveness). One is unlikely to have forgiven if one simply forgets or buries the recollection of the wrong (Neu 2002: 31–3).

[4] The thought of Lévinas does not contribute to normative ethics and the determination of the moral worth of conduct. Rather, Lévinas offers an 'ethic of ethics' that identifies the responsibility of the self to others but not the ethical *content* of that responsibility.

it.[5] For some, revenge is an attractive alternative to forgiveness and they would rather retaliate than forgive.

Even if people fail to forgive, they still tend to hope that God will forgive them, either because God is merciful or because, if they try hard and intend to do well, God will show a sense of 'fair play' and forgive them. Alexander Pope expressed the relation between the human and divine conditions in this way: 'To err is human, to forgive divine.'[6] To put it unkindly, people think that God will forgive (because that is God's role) but they often will not (because that, sadly, is the human condition).

In this book, we will examine views such as these, so that we can think both ethically and Christianly about what it means to forgive. We begin with some initial thoughts about what forgiveness is, although it will not be until chapter 9 that we draw together the discussion in this book and reach a firm conclusion – as best we can – about what forgiveness is.

REVISITING FORGIVENESS IN THE TWENTY-FIRST CENTURY

A straightforward, popular dictionary definition of forgiveness is that it is an action or process that results in a person ceasing to be angry or resentful towards someone for an offence, flaw or mistake.[7]

That forgiveness is an action or process is self-evident. In almost every other respect, I take issue with the definition or wish to qualify it. For example, one implication of the definition is that one may 'forgive' another person if one forgets about, denies or even blames oneself for the offence, flaw or mistake. I shall argue that doing these is not to forgive. Similarly, if by mistake I bought you red roses thinking that you liked them, when I should have remembered that it was yellow roses that you preferred, you may, as a result, be angry – perhaps even resentful – that I had forgotten what you liked, but that does not mean that I have done something for which you should forgive me or for which I should seek your forgiveness.

I take as the starting point for discussion that forgiveness (whatever else it may also be) is *a moral response to wrongdoing*.[8] There are two elements to this starting point that need to be held in place: the first is that forgiveness

---

[5] Jones (1995) ascribes the capacity to do this as coming from the Holy Spirit who presses and shapes people to embody and so practise divine forgiveness.

[6] Alexander Pope (1688–1744), *An Essay on Criticism*, Part 2, line 525 in Audra and Williams 1961.

[7] This definition is based on the definition in the *Oxford Dictionary of English*, 2nd edition (Pearsall and Hanks 2003).

[8] See Lévinas 1969: 282f.: 'Pardon in its immediate sense is connected with the moral phenomenon of fault.' For Lévinas, ethics is not a matter of abstract principles or reason but the result of an encounter with something or someone other than oneself. The moral response becomes clear at the moment of the encounter.

is a moral response, and the second is that the response is to a morally wrong act.[9]

As for the first element (that forgiveness is a moral response), two observations may be made. First, not all moral responses to wrongdoing amount to forgiveness. For example, a victim who renews relations with a repentant wrongdoer in response to a moral principle (for example, that it is right to have relations with those who repudiate immoral behaviour) will not necessarily also have forgiven the wrongdoer (Hampton in Murphy and Hampton 1988: 41). Second, it does not necessarily follow that to forgive is always the right moral response to wrongdoing.[10] This is what Murphy in Murphy and Hampton (1988) argues: he suggests, for example, that one should not forgive if to forgive would not necessarily serve the public good or would result in an undesirable outcome.

That forgiveness is a moral response also has an important corollary. It is this: if the response to wrongdoing is not moral, the response cannot be forgiveness. Thus, if a *victim* implicitly or explicitly denies that the act in question is wrong, the response of the victim will not – and cannot – be forgiveness. It may be 'condonation' (Kolnai 1973–4: 96), excusing, pardoning, exonerating and so on[11] – but it will not be (according to Kolnai 1973–4 and most other commentators – see Worthington 2005: 557) forgiveness.

We turn now to the second element of our starting point that forgiveness is a moral response to wrongdoing, namely, that forgiveness is a response to a morally wrong act.

### MORALLY WRONG ACTS

Morally wrong acts range from what one might regard as relatively trivial (such as telling a lie to avoid embarrassment or breaking a promise) to acts – often referred to as 'evil' rather than 'moral wrongs' – of execrable

---

[9] Some suggest that forgiveness can sometimes be a one-way process or act on the part of the victim, not dependent on anything the wrongdoer does or does not do, and may occur even if the wrongdoer does not acknowledge the forgiveness (Holmgreen 1993: 341; Garrard and McNaughton 2002: 51, 53–9; Kolnai 1973–4: 9). This view will be explored later in this book.

[10] Lévinas (1969: 43) makes this point. What is right to do will depend on the situation and (in his view) will be the result of encounter (or a relationship) with something or someone other than oneself. He therefore rejects the idea of rigid or univocal moral principles and argues that the appropriate moral response in a situation is always the result of encounter. The result is more stringent and demanding than in any formal ethical code (Davis 1996: 54). The encounter produces the ethics, and not *vice versa*. Strictly speaking, therefore, Lévinas's philosophy is not about the contents of ethics, the norms or standards of moral behaviour (he calls these 'justice'), but about what is ethical.

[11] To pardon is to remit punishment rightly imposed on or due to a wrongdoer or to declare a person innocent of something of which the person has been pronounced guilty. See Horsbrugh 1974: 270 and Govier 2002: 54–61 further on the distinctions.

horror, cruelty and depravity, sometimes called 'dehumanising evil' (e.g., Wolfendale 2005).[12]

If an act is not morally wrong it is not forgivable (that is, 'able-to-be-forgiven') and forgiveness is not an appropriate response to such an act.[13] Three scenarios may arise. First, an act of which I may not approve but which is not morally wrong is not forgivable. (For example, if I do not like to see men wear ear studs, I cannot forgive my friend if he chooses to wear an ear stud. To wear an ear stud is not morally wrong, and no right-thinking moral philosopher would hold that it was. In such a case, it is I – and my social tolerance – that need to change.) Also not forgivable are morally innocent acts that have unintended but harmful consequences for a 'victim',[14] as in the case of a mistake or misfortune.[15] Lastly, if the victim is not aware of the wrong, the 'victim' will have nothing to forgive. If Jack steals from Jill's purse but Jill does not know, there will be nothing for her to forgive, even though Jack has done wrong. (Jack may consider that there is something to forgive, even though Jill does not know it, because, both in Jack's mind and objectively, he has done wrong.) If Jack later admits what he has done, there will then be something for Jill to forgive.[16]

To establish whether an act is right or wrong from a moral viewpoint, the act has to be critically evaluated in the context of an overarching moral

---

[12] Wrongdoing is certainly more than 'a breach of trust between two (or more) people' (Wilson 1988: 534).

[13] An act may also be unforgivable in two other circumstances: first, if there is no one to forgive it and second if there is no one to be forgiven. An example of the former is the case of murder: the victim will be dead and so cannot forgive. As to the latter, if a wrongdoer has died, there will be no one to receive the victim's forgiveness. However, if the wrongdoer died contrite, there seems to be no reason why the person wronged, when able, should not posthumously forgive the wrongdoer. Although there will be no possibility of a restored relationship, there is the possibility of letting go of the hurt, of inner healing for the victim and of psychological restoration. The person wronged can retrospectively embrace the repentance of the wrongdoer and experience the renewal that that will bring.

[14] Aristotle, *NE* iii, 1, 1110b30–1111a1 (in Rowe and Broadie 2002), calls this 'ignorance at the level of particular things' and so makes the action involuntary. See also *NE* v, 6, 1135a20–30 (in Rowe and Broadie 2002).

[15] In *Rh.* i, 13, 1374b5–10 (in Barnes 1984), Aristotle defines a mistake as 'an act . . . not due to turpitude, that has results that might have been expected', and a misfortune as 'an act, not due to wickedness, that has unexpected results'. In discussing what being wronged amounts to, Aristotle denies that such actions are unjust (and so actions for which people are morally responsible): see *Rh.* i, 13, 1373b1, 35 (in Barnes 1984). What is also important is how one interprets an action: a person may take something but the taking not amount to theft if, for example, the person believed they had a right to take the thing. In Aristotle's words, 'it happens that a man will admit an act, but will not admit the prosecutor's label for the act nor the facts which the label implies' (*Rh.* i, 13, 1373b35–40, in Barnes 1984).

[16] If a 'victim' does not suffer harm from an act that was *intended* to harm the victim, the victim may forgive the wrongdoer's wrongful intentions but not the act itself.

framework.[17] The framework may be derived from principles (whether from a supra-human moral being or power or from universally recognised social norms and laws) that underlie particular expressions of moral imperatives.[18] Even when we make appeal to an overarching moral framework, legitimate disagreement may remain about whether a particular action is morally wrong: the discussion in 1 Corinthians 8:1–13 and 10:23–11:1 about eating meat that has been used in idol worship is a case in point. Well-known also are views that the cultural climate of a former time affirms and even sustains but which a later generation recognises to be wrong. It is hard to attribute blame when people act strictly according to their consciences. Scarre (2003: 108, 110) gives the example of Aztec human sacrifice: it may today be 'morally repugnant, but it [is] hard to see it as wrong from [Aztec] viewpoint'. He also describes the persecution and murder of supposed witches in Europe in the middle ages. We may believe those who persecuted the witches to be wrong but they acted according to their understanding and with integrity of conscience for the supposed good of all. Those who adhered to and carried out Nazi political philosophy are, in my view, less excusable (*pace* Scarre 2003). As Milbank (2003: 2f.) says, many believed they were 'fulfilling the goods of order, obedience, political stability and peace' and 'articulated their defective desires . . . in terms of the promotion of racial health and excellence of humanity'. Even the aim to liquidate the Jews was expressed in terms that could be described as 'rational' (though perverse and flawed) and not out of 'the pursuit of evil for its own sake'. Even so, the moral and intellectual criteria of the time *could* have led people to condemn Nazi philosophy as odious and repugnant (as it did some) and there was a degree of culpable and wilful blindness by many who upheld Nazi philosophy.[19]

  Given that there are degrees of evil in wrongdoing and (as we shall see below) even degrees of responsibility for wrongdoing, one might have expected that there would be degrees of difficulty to forgiving, and that it would be easier to forgive a peccadillo than an egregious wrong or evil. In many instances that is true, but not always. When it comes to forgiveness, it seems to be that it is not necessarily the nature of the *act* that determines

---

[17] The question I am exploring is not 'What is right?' and 'What is wrong?' (and so I do not explore which expression of higher ethic we are following and whether we might agree that the act is moral or immoral) but '*If* we conclude that an act is morally wrong, *how* might we forgive it?'

[18] According to Aristotle in *Rh.* i, 13, 1373b1–10 (in Barnes 1984) there are two kinds of law: particular law (community-enacted rules, whether written or unwritten) and universal law (norms that are universally recognised). The aetiology of 'crimes against humanity' is that wrongdoing is an offence against the moral order from whichever ethical standpoint that moral order is looked at.

[19] See further on responsibility for actions, pp. 8–11 below.

whether people who have been wronged will find it difficult to forgive, but the nature of the *response* to the wrong. The initial, emotional response may be in proportion to the severity of the act, but not always. The response may be shaped by temperament, personal history, psychopathology, ethical outlook and social or cultural tradition. Wrongdoers take their victims as they find them, even if the victims have wafer-thin tolerance and are greatly wounded by the acts of wrongdoers.[20] It would not be right – tempting though it may be – for wrongdoers to say to their victims to buck up, get on and forgive. The victims may well believe they have much to forgive and find it hard to do so. There does come a point when to continue to harbour resentment about being wronged becomes excessive, misplaced and perhaps even obsessional – but that is for the victim to address, not the wrongdoer.

Wrongdoers with sensitive consciences will quickly realise that the effects of wrongdoing are not so contained and identifiable as they had hoped. Some wrongdoing *is* contained in its effects and forgiveness in such a context is about relations in an interpersonal context between a known wrongdoer and a known victim. In contrast, some wrongs will have consequences for the victim that the wrongdoer did not (and perhaps even could not) foresee, or the wrongs may affect many people besides the immediate victim. In the latter case, it is often not possible to identify all who have been affected by wrongdoing or how much they may have been affected. The consequences of wrongdoing may be, for example, social, cultural and political, and may affect more than one generation and in ways that have to do with loss of contingent possibilities. As Milbank (2003: 28; and see Derrida 2001a: 29f.) puts it: 'since an evil deed is contagious, it is impossible to know how far the consequences of even the simplest and most minor of misdemeanours extends'. Consider, for example, the consequences if Herod had succeeded in killing Jesus when he was a baby (see Matthew 2:16–23) or if Pharaoh, through the massacre of Jewish male babies, had succeeded in killing Moses when a baby (Exodus 1:15–22).

Of course, many people who are remotely and contingently affected by another's wrongdoing may not know that they have been affected in that way; but the wrongdoer – especially if the wrongdoer becomes contrite

---

[20] This is akin to the 'eggshell skull' principle in the law of tort, namely that, when it comes to compensation, a person (the tortfeasor) who is in breach of a duty of care to a victim must take the victim as the tortfeasor finds the victim, whether the victim is extraordinarily vulnerable or not. This principle, sometimes also known as the *talem qualem* principle, limits compensation to compensation for consequences that are reasonably foreseeable. For a review of the law, and the applicability of the principle to third parties, see White and Others *v.* Chief Constable of South Yorkshire and Others, 2 *AC* 455–511 (1999).

and penitent – may be all too aware. In the hypothetical examples above, who should forgive – and who can forgive? Those killed cannot forgive because they are dead; and many people will suffer contingent losses because someone has died. In the examples, those who have been affected by the wrongdoing – albeit indirectly – have something to forgive the wrongdoers but the wrongdoers may not be able to find those who can forgive them their wrongdoing.

Benn (1996: 378) raises the important question of how people can forgive if they are not directly victims of wrongdoing but are affected by it. The question is even more pressing if the victim has not, will not or cannot forgive the wrongdoer. Benn suggests that 'quasi-forgiveness' may be applicable here, that is when 'third parties, whilst not [at] all condoning what was done, overcome the indignation they feel on behalf of those directly wronged'. So the parents of a murder victim may eventually be able to express quasi-forgiveness (since the only person able to forgive is the murder victim); the relatives of a victim of a violent crime may be able to express quasi-forgiveness of the wrongdoer in the course of time. Benn rightly points out that this can only occur where to express quasi-forgiveness would not be disloyal to the victim. He also limits this to cases where the wrongdoer repents. A moving example of this concerns David Rice whose brother, Andrew, died in the attacks of 11 September 2001 in New York. David Rice tells of how he and certain other relatives of people killed were contacted by Madame al-Wafi, the mother of the surviving alleged hijacker, Zacharias Moussaoui. She wished to ask for forgiveness for her son's actions.[21] Mr Rice writes of how the meeting confirmed to him that to seek retribution was not an appropriate response to his loss; instead he sought to lay aside hatred and seek reconciliation.[22]

### WRONGDOERS

As for wrongdoers, there is a distinction, sometimes difficult to draw, between a person who is innately incapable of moral discernment (an obvious case is someone with a severe learning difficulty) and a person who may be hardened, naïve, self-deluded, unprincipled or morally incompetent. In the former case, the person is regarded as innocent (because not responsible

---

[21] Madame al-Wafi was, strictly speaking, not able to ask for forgiveness for her son's actions because, as I show in chapter 7, it is only wrongdoers who can ask their victims for forgiveness. Nevertheless, Benn makes a cogent case for 'quasi-forgiveness' and Madame al-Wafi's actions should be regarded as a request for quasi-forgiveness.
[22] Recounted in www.theforgivenessproject.com/stories/andrew-rice.

for his or her moral actions) and so not culpable; in the latter case, the person is immature but culpable.[23] Thus even when a person's moral reasoning may be overridden or even suppressed by weakness, indifference, selfishness and self-interest, greed or the refusal to engage, their culpability is not. In this category must be included those whose background, circumstances and personal histories predispose them to moral compromise. An example might be those from deprived and abusive backgrounds. The degree of culpability attributable to them may be diminished due to their circumstances, but they remain culpable nevertheless.

What of the responsibility of those who collude with wrongdoing that others commit? Obvious examples are the mistreatment of Jewish people before and during the Second World War and the oppression of black people in South Africa during the era of *apartheid*. In later years, when the wrongdoing had been exposed and recognised, the perpetrators tended to be portrayed as evil and unrepresentative – despite the fact that they had lived in and been supported by communities that knew – or could or should have known – of the acts of wrongdoing. Those who get on with the ordinary daily business and routine of living engage in collective self-deception that amounts to silent complicity. Such collusion does not exculpate them from a share in the guilt for the wrong. It amounts to moral blindness, founded on self-serving weakness and the desire for self-preservation. For it is all too easy to absorb society's justifying meta-narrative out of self-interest and to fail to respond critically to abuse of power and injustice. Such people are not innocent of moral fault.

Even the perpetrators of evil may come across as ordinary people who are as much colluding with the evil of others as themselves also perpetrating it. At his trial, Eichmann said that he did not personally have anything against the Jews and that he had not sought to be cruel. He appeared to be an ordinary person, little different from anyone else. His answer as to why he was one of the architects of Hitler's 'Final Solution' was that he was a soldier in a system that expected him to comply with its authority and that he was obeying orders. Arendt (1958: 49) observed that, the longer one listened to Eichmann, 'the more obvious it became that his inability to speak was closely linked to his inability to think, namely to think away from the standpoint of somebody else'. Scarre (2004: 6), in critical engagement with the subtitle of Arendt's book on Eichmann's trial, *Eichmann in Jerusalem. A Report on the Banality of Evil* (1968), rightly describes Eichmann – not the evil he committed – as 'banal' and says that

---

[23] See Aristotle, *NE* iii, 1, 1110b25–30 (in Rowe and Broadie 2002).

he was 'unimaginative, unreflective . . . with scant capacity for empathy'. In other words, Eichmann did not seem to think that what he had done was wrong, even though right-thinking people would think that it was.

It is easy to underestimate the power of a received ideology, and it takes a brave and intellectually unusual person to be critical and independent of the prevailing ideology. Those who collude remain morally culpable. As for Eichmann, possibly he was a child of his time, who had absorbed Nazi lies about the Jews. Even so, he was culpable – perhaps all the more so – because he vigorously carried out and initiated plans to implement the Final Solution and was one of the *architects* of the lies that others believed. He was not just an uncritical victim of the contemporary worldview. If he had reflected on the truth of what he believed and on the morality of his actions, he could *only* have realised that his actions were wrong. For these reasons, he was responsible for his actions and so culpable.[24]

It is worth adding that, in the day-to-day pattern of human life, it is sometimes simplistic to say that all the 'wrong' rests with the wrongdoer and all the 'right' with the victim. There is often wrong on both sides, and people are sometimes both wrongdoer and victim in relation to the same set of events. Both wrongdoer and victim may have to search their own consciences about forgiveness: forgiveness may be a mutual, not a one-way, process for them and the categorisation of the people involved as 'victim' and 'wrongdoer' will become considerably more nuanced.[25]

A wise observer of human beings will also recognise that people are capable of great evil.[26] Garrard (2003: 241) explores the fact that the innocent and guilty alike share a common nature and that people are 'morally mixed, not in the sense that some of us are almost entirely good, and some entirely evil, but rather in the sense that most if not all of us are capable of both good and evil'. We might add that, in some senses, people share in the wrongdoing that others do without themselves being personally responsible for it. Garrard (2003: 241) suggests that 'we are all inextricably implicated in, and shamed by, deeds of our fellow human beings [who are] the perpetrators [of wrongdoing], even though we do not endorse [the deeds] and are not responsible for them'.[27] (This latter point has been painfully illustrated by reports of abuses of human rights at the Abu Ghraib detention centre, abuses of a kind that many in the west assumed were – and could only

---

[24] See also Scarre 2004: 159–76.     [25] See Govier 2002: viii.

[26] The corollary to this is that *ordinary* people are capable of great evil: see Wolfendale 2005: 360f.

[27] Since only the perpetrators remain morally responsible, one wonders why she suggests that, since crimes against humanity are crimes against all humanity, they are, to some extent, forgivable by all humanity. See Garrard 2003: 232f., 239f.

be – committed by non-westerners.) Garrard's point is that we all share a measure of the same ambivalent humanity as those who do commit wrong and that each of us can participate in a sense of shame that human beings should have behaved in that way.[28]

## UNFORGIVABLE WRONGS AND UNFORGIVABLE PEOPLE

Some argue that there is a genus of wrongs that are unforgivable because of the nature of the wrongs themselves (e.g., Arendt 1958; Golding 1984–5; Lang 1994; North 1998; in Wiesenthal 1998, see Shachnow, Goulden, Telushkin, Langer and Ozick), that is, the wrongs are so reprehensible as to be beyond forgiving. If there are unforgivable wrongs, it also means that it is impossible to forgive those who commit unforgivable wrongs and morally wrong to attempt to do so. Jankélévitch (1986) has argued (particularly in relation to the Holocaust) that there is a duty not to forgive if the wrong is 'inexpiable' (not able to be expiated), irreparable, or where one does not know whom to blame or accuse.[29] Jankélévitch (1996: 567) also suggests hyperbolically that forgiveness 'died in the death camps' of the Holocaust.

Flanigan (1998: 98–102) says that what makes wrongdoing unforgivable is not the intrinsic nature of the act but its effect upon the victim. If the act amounts to an 'assault' on a person's fundamental beliefs that 'shatter[s] the injured's bedrock assumptions about life' (e.g., beliefs that shape identity, sense of self-worth, confidence in the rules of justice and the goodness of people), the act may be unforgivable. She acknowledges that different acts or events will affect people in different ways. Forgiveness *can* come, she says, when victims have 'cognitively restructured their bedrock assumptions so that their belief systems [are] intact' and reformulated them so that they create 'new assumptive sets'. Flanigan concludes that a person's capacity to forgive is inversely related to the degree of damage to their assumptive set: the greater the damage, the less likely a person will be to forgive.

Govier (1999: 68, 71) argues that no one is *absolutely* unforgivable. To think that they may be 'is to ignore their human capacity for moral choice

---

[28] Lévinas goes further and suggests that every human being has responsibility to others. The responsibility that *victims* have for others extends even to those who wrong them (see Hutchens 2004: 24f.). The difficulty with the idea of responsibility in the thought of Lévinas is that he would deny what the deontologist would assert, namely, that 'moral worth is determined by the right to judge *whether* to recognise an obligation to respond, such that one might not assist the other person at all because doing so might represent the transgression of a rule' (Hutchens 2004: 34).

[29] It may be, not that there is a moral duty *not* to forgive, but that the duty to forgive (if there is such a duty – see chapter 4) is in conflict with other moral duties or the best interests of the victim.

and change, which is the very foundation of human worth and dignity'. She also identifies a category of unforgivable wrongs: they are wrongs that are 'appallingly wrong acts that violate profoundly important moral principles'. Those who commit such wrongs are *conditionally* unforgivable if they do not acknowledge the wrong or offer restitution. Even so, Govier says that there is, even for heinous forms of wrongdoing, a place for *unconditional* forgiveness.

This analysis presents some difficulties. According to Govier, *all* types of wrongdoing are forgivable, whether or not the wrongdoer repents. It is therefore mistaken to regard a wrongdoer who does not acknowledge the wrongdoing to be 'conditionally unforgivable'. It is better to say that such wrongdoers are 'conditionally unforgiven' because their victims will not forgive them unless they repent and make restitution (and perhaps not even then). In fact, there is not a discrete category of 'unforgivable wrongs'. Govier is no more than distinguishing degrees of wrongdoing and saying that *any* wrongdoing may be forgiven, either after repentance and restitution or without repentance and restitution. It will depend on what the victims decide to do.

Wolfendale (2005) argues that believing a person to be unforgivable can cause victims to demonstrate the very moral qualities that they deplore in those who have wronged them. The belief implies that the wrongdoers are outside the moral community and inherently morally inferior. It also implies that the wrongdoers are incapable of moral change and of being responsible moral agents. What these beliefs fail to recognise, suggests Wolfendale (following Holmgreen 1993), is the wrongdoer's personhood and capacity for change. Wolfendale (2005: 358) rightly observes that such an unforgiving attitude 'is . . . similar to the moral outlook' of those who are guilty of dehumanising evil: just as the wrongdoers regarded their victims as having 'no claim to equal moral consideration and whose moral character is intrinsically and permanently inferior', so the victims treat those who violated them in the same way. To regard people as irreversibly morally inferior because of the wrong they have done is to fail to acknowledge that *all* people – even monstrous purveyors of evil – can sometimes change.

Forgiveness has *always* been hard in the face of the monstrous perversion of human cruelty and, as Milbank (2003: 54) rightly says, to deny that the crimes of the Holocaust (and, we could add, of any other expression of dehumanising evil) can be forgiven runs the risk of falsely glamorising and absolutising those crimes. The issue is not whether there is a genus of wrongs that are unforgivable. Neither is it whether victims have been particularly grievously affected or even whether the wrongdoers are especially vile. This is because forgiveness is the gift – the free choice – of the victim. Rather, the issue is whether the victim is able and chooses to forgive. It would be odd to preclude a victim from forgiving if the victim wanted to forgive and it would be stranger still if such a victim were told it would be morally wrong to forgive and be thereby denied the psychological benefits that are known to accrue to those who forgive. It would be for ever to insist that victims remain victims and not also forgivers.

### FORGIVING ONESELF FOR WRONGDOING

The idea of forgiving oneself for having done wrong is analytically complex, for in forgiving oneself one is both subject and object, both offender and forgiver.[30] The underlying question is whether it is meaningful to speak of forgiving oneself. Four different scenarios may arise:

### (a) The wrongdoer is repentant and the victim forgives

Repentance should result in the inner moral reordering of the wrongdoer, at least in relation to the wrongdoing. In this respect, it is a return to the shared moral values of the community and a recommitment to abide by them. The victim's forgiveness means that the victim has let go of unforgiving feelings and acknowledges that the wrongdoer has been restored to the moral community. If the wrongdoer accepts that forgiveness, the wrongdoer can live as someone restored to the victim and to the wider community. It is appropriate for the wrongdoer, now forgiven by the victim, to forgive himself or herself for having done the wrong.[31]

### (b) The wrongdoer is repentant and the victim does not forgive

Sometimes the wrongdoer may repent but will be unable to seek the forgiveness of the victim. A murderer cannot be forgiven because the victim is not alive to forgive the murderer: forgiveness is a matter of physical impossibility. From the Hebrew Scriptures, Joseph's brothers came to the point of realising that they had done wrong to attempt to murder Joseph and then to sell him as a slave (Genesis 42:21f.). They thought that their misfortunes were 'a reckoning for his blood' (verse 22). Implicit in their thinking is that they had forfeited the opportunity for Joseph to forgive them because they thought him to be dead.

---

[30] See Holmgreen 2002: 121–4, 131–3 on self-forgiveness.
[31] See footnote 13 above on forgiving a repentant (but deceased) wrongdoer.

Even when the victim does not forgive the wrongdoer (either from choice or because the victim has died), is self-forgiveness possible for the wrongdoer if the wrongdoer has repented, sought to put right what can be put right and sought the victim's forgiveness? The wrongdoer will have done everything possible for restoration and forgiveness but the *victim* will have denied the wrongdoer forgiveness. The effect of the victim refusing to forgive the wrongdoer may be *to lock the wrongdoer in the 'victimhood' of guilt and remorse*. To do this may be an abuse of the wrongdoer, in the same way that the former wrongdoing had been an abuse of the victim. If the wrongdoer does self-forgive, the wrongdoer may be spared that 'victimhood'.

Even so, there are logical difficulties to the idea that wrongdoers can give themselves gifts that others deny them. Two examples, one hypothetical and one actual, illustrate the problem.

The first (the hypothetical example) is where the wrongdoer repents but the victim refuses to engage with the fact that wrongdoing took place. Suppose Peter's mother-in-law is unwell and needs an operation to replace her hip. She attended her local NHS hospital and her consultant surgeon told her that the waiting list for operations of that kind was so long that she would do better to have the operation at her own expense in a private hospital. The surgeon said that he himself could perform the operation the following week at a nearby private hospital. The surgeon knew that what he said about the length of the waiting list was not true: though Peter's mother-in-law would have had to wait more than a week for the operation, it was likely that the surgery could have been performed at the NHS hospital within three to six months. The motive of the surgeon was to ensure that the number of patients waiting for surgery was as small as possible. He also took the view that those who could afford to pay for surgery privately ought to do so. In addition, he himself was short of money and the fee for the operation would have helped pay some urgent bills that had arisen on account of his profligate spending habits. Peter's mother-in-law had successful surgery at the local private hospital and was delighted with the outcome of the operation.

Two years later, as a result of meeting a wandering Galilean religious teacher, the surgeon realised that he had been wrong to mislead Peter's mother-in-law, and that he had profited from his lie (since he had performed the surgery privately). The surgeon decided to go to Peter's mother-in-law to apologise and to ask for her forgiveness. He was even willing to repay the fee for the operation. When he spoke to Peter's mother-in-law, she would have none of it. She said she was delighted with the outcome of the surgery and with her new-found mobility. She added that she shared the surgeon's view that those who could pay for surgery should, and had decided some years ago to spend her money while still alive on her own comfort and pleasure and not leave it to her daughter, Mary, and son-in-law, Peter, both of whom were associating with a religious figure of whom she did not approve. When the surgeon asked for forgiveness, she shrugged her shoulders and told him to stop being so sensitive and foolish and to get on with his work as a surgeon. 'What's the issue?' she asked. 'Everybody's doing what you did. I came to you to get better and now I am.'

What of the surgeon in this example? He knows that what he had done was deceitful and that he had profited from lying. He feels remorse and shame, and wants to put right the wrong he has done. He recognises that personal integrity, one's actions and one's moral framework should cohere, and that his do not. As a result, his conscience is troubled because he knows that what he did was wrong. His plea for forgiveness expressed his repentance and that he knew he had compromised truth, honesty and trust. But Peter's mother-in-law did not forgive the surgeon because in her view there was nothing to be forgiven. She *cannot* forgive the surgeon because in her view the surgeon's actions were not wrong. The view the surgeon takes of his actions and the view of his actions held by Peter's mother-in-law do not cohere.

In these circumstances, must the surgeon remain unforgiven, troubled by remorse and a guilty conscience? At this point, the poverty of Kolnai's view (1973–4: 99) that it is 'pointless' to speak of forgiving a repentant wrongdoer because there is nothing to forgive is evident: it fails to take account of the (new-found) moral integrity of the wrongdoer and the anguish that being unforgiven can cause.

In my view, there is a place for self-forgiveness if a victim unreasonably denies forgiveness to a repentant wrongdoer. In effect, the surgeon should say to himself, 'I have tried to put this matter right but could not. There is nothing more I can do. I shall now pay the fee I received to a charity, recommit myself to living in integrity, seek to put this behind me and move on.'

The attitude of Peter's mother-in-law means that the roles of victim and wrongdoer have now become reversed. Peter's mother-in-law's action has, in effect, unjustifiably maintained the surgeon in the role of wrongdoer (so that he now becomes the victim) and her refusal to forgive the surgeon arising from her perverse view of his actions puts her in the role of wrongdoer. Her refusal to forgive also violates the surgeon, because it precludes the surgeon from having a restored relationship with her.

'Self-forgiveness' in these circumstances is different from forgiveness given by a victim. It lacks the moral richness of an unconditional gift. It is a pragmatic response, made as a last resort, by a person who has been violated *by another's refusal to forgive.*[32]

When it comes to 'heinous wrongs', might not considering self-forgiveness underestimate the depravity of the wrongs committed and deny the true horror of the evil? In seeking self-forgiveness, might the wrongdoer be demonstrating a pathological degree of rationalisation and self-justification, of accommodation with evil, and a denial of personal responsibility? Many would say that self-forgiveness in a situation such as this is narcissistic, self-indulgent and sybaritic, typical of someone who does not feel the pain of authentic guilt and responsibility. Repentance does not entitle a person to mercy for wrongdoing: it is an expression of contrition that one has done wrong and it accepts the judgment 'guilty' for the wrongdoing. There is no acquittal except by the victim.

The case of Myra Hindley, our second example, illustrates the point. Hindley, together with Ian Brady, was convicted of the murder of two children in 1966 and of being an accessory to a third murder committed by Brady. Hindley was given a sentence of life imprisonment and was required to serve a minimum of twenty-five years (later extended to thirty years). The murders were regarded as particularly brutal and sadistic and caused enormous public revulsion at the time of the trial; the revulsion has not passed from public consciousness in the years following. In 1990, at the end of the twenty-five-year period, the then Home Secretary imposed on Hindley a 'whole life' tariff, meaning that she would be kept in prison for the whole of her life, without parole. Hindley appealed three times to the House of Lords for release from prison, arguing (as her parole boards had confirmed) that she was no longer a danger to the public and that she had acted under Brady's influence.

Hindley wrote an article, published in the *Guardian* on 18 December 1995, that set out that she accepted responsibility for her part in the murders but that she was 'repentant before Christ in the same way as Peter, after denying him three times, wept bitterly, repented and begged forgiveness'. She wrote of her 'redemption' both in a religious sense (implying that through faith she had been made a new person) and in a psychotherapeutic sense (that she understood the aetiology of her criminal behaviour). Hindley

---

[32] At p. 168 below, I argue that forgiveness given by a victim to a wrongdoer does not – and cannot – undo the past or free the wrongdoer from the consequences of what the wrongdoer has done. The surgeon's 'self-forgiveness' also does not undo his past wrong actions or free him from the moral consequences of what he has done.

died in November 2002, shortly before another House of Lords' ruling that would almost certainly have resulted in her release from prison.

Even if Hindley were a changed person who posed no threat to others and a person who had discovered the forgiveness of God (if not forgiveness of the parents of her victims), was it right for her to press vehemently and publicly for release? Is it not perhaps the case that true repentance means she would have accepted the justice of the sentence of life imprisonment for her crimes, rather than suggesting that because she was 'redeemed' and had atoned for her crimes she should be released? Does perhaps her insistence that she had acted under Brady's influence also suggest that she accepted rather less than full personal responsibility for her actions? The question of extending mercy to her was not hers to pose; neither was it right for her to seek it. Mercy is the gift of those who had sentenced her and of successive government ministers to extend on behalf of the Crown. The fact that she sought that mercy perhaps indicates a degree of self-justification and self-interest that true repentance should exclude.

Not every wrongdoer whose wrongs are heinous is without hope if the victim does not forgive, provided that the wrongdoer truly acknowledges and recognises the awfulness of the wrongdoing and its effects. Appropriate responses are repentance and contrition that are deep, thoroughgoing and rigorous. Such repentance acknowledges personal responsibility not only for the wrong done but also for the inner perversion that led to the wrong; the wrongdoer will strive to ensure enduring change. Not to repent because the wrongdoer is so overwhelmed by the depravity of the wrong may be a pathological response that may have the effect of reinforcing the victim's suffering. It may, however, help the wrongdoer reach a point of rediscovering self-dignity and self-respect (if not the peace of forgiveness).

### (c) The victim forgives but the wrongdoer does not repent

Self-forgiveness in these circumstances is impossible because the wrongdoer has not made a moral response to the wrongdoing. It is morally absurd (as well as an oxymoron) to seek to self-forgive without repenting. To attempt to self-forgive in such circumstances is a perversion of moral integrity, for the wrongdoer accepts the victim's forgiveness without acknowledging responsibility for having done wrong and without contrition or moral change. Those who do 'self-forgive' if they have not repented engage in an act of enormous selfishness and egotism that, at the expense of moral integrity, seeks to assuage a troubled conscience, denies responsibility, or indicates a person with a conscience that is pathologically self-absorbed and narcissistic. In such a situation, the victim will often suffer further violation that reinforces the hurt of the original act of wrongdoing. From the victim's point of view, it perpetuates the abuse of the original wrongdoing.

### (d) The victim does not forgive and the wrongdoer does not repent

'Self-forgiveness' in these circumstances is equally perverse and also impossible because the wrongdoer has not engaged morally with the wrongdoing. A wrongdoer who apparently self-forgives but does not repent denies, on the one hand, that wrong has been done but implicitly acknowledges the opposite, on the other. 'Self-forgiveness' here is marginally less pathological than in the previous example, because the wrongdoer does not accept the victim's forgiveness, the necessity for which the wrongdoer denies.

#### WRONGDOING AND PSYCHOLOGY

It is important to recognise (as I seek to do in this book) that wrongdoing – a morally wrong act or omission – is not only a question for moral philosophy. There is also a very important psychological aspect to wrongdoing, from the point of view of both the wrongdoer and the victim. One can go further and say that what makes wrongdoing and forgiveness such an important issue is that not only are they important topics of moral philosophy but also they are topics that affect people personally and emotionally. Reflection on these topics in the past has been principally *either* philosophical *or* psychological: in this book, I hope to combine the two and let each approach and inform the other.[33]

Many people experience powerful emotions after being wronged and these emotions make forgiveness a protracted and difficult process. Whether people come from faith traditions (Christian or otherwise) or no faith traditions, it seems to be a universal experience that it can sometimes be difficult to forgive others. The Reverend Julie Nicholson, an Anglican priest whose daughter was killed in a bomb attack in London on 7 July 2005,

---

[33] The philosophical grounding of such an approach is in part due to the influence of Lévinas, whose contention is that the relation between 'self' and 'other' is the proper context for ethical enquiry and that the 'self's' responsibility for the 'other' takes precedence over the 'self's' freedom and will. In other words, ethical enquiry has to be conducted in the context of relationships and of the responsibilities that those relationships assume, and to do this one sometimes has to be aided by psychological understanding. (See Hutchens 2004: 8, 12.)

resigned her post as vicar in March 2006 because she was unable to forgive the bombers who took her daughter's life. Nicholson said: 'It's very difficult to stand behind an altar and celebrate the Eucharist, the Communion, and lead people in words of peace and reconciliation and forgiveness when I feel very far from that myself.'[34] Forgiveness can sometimes be very hard,[35] and for some – whether religious or not – simply impossible.

Forgiveness is, as I have said, a moral *response* to wrongdoing,[36] and how (and whether) people respond to wrongdoing is in part conditioned by their psychological health. Richards (1988: 93f.) puts it this way: '. . . hard feelings toward those who mistreat us are not only natural but are called for, as expressions of aversion to the mistreatment'. But what of those who do not so react – or who remain trapped in such a reaction and cannot move on? An already under-confident person is unlikely to confront a wrongdoer. Suffering wrongdoing can be an emotionally degrading experience. Victims may consider that their status as human beings of worth, dignity and integrity has been impugned and that they have been treated as the plaything of the wrongdoer, to be used and abused at the whim of the wrongdoer. Victims abused in this way often find that their self-respect is undermined. As a result, they may blame themselves for the wrongdoing, be unable to confront the wrongdoer or deny that the wrongdoer's act is wrong at all.[37] Others will rage about the wrong they have suffered, sometimes many years after the event and long after the rage can apparently serve any useful purpose.

Hampton, in Murphy and Hampton 1988: 43–53, did combine psychological and philosophical insights. She distinguished 'demeaning acts' – acts that are insulting and express the wrongdoer's lack of respect but which do not undermine a person's sense of self-esteem and self-worth – from the more serious 'diminishing acts', which are acts that leave a person feeling degraded or devalued. In some cases, 'diminishing acts' may be so severe in their effects that the victim needs psychological therapy in order to recover.[38]

---

[34] Reported in *The Times*, 7 March 2006, pp. 6f. following a television broadcast on a BBC regional current affairs programme entitled *Inside Out* on 6 March 2006.

[35] See Weil in Miles 1986: 216f. – and Weil argues that victims need to change if they are to be able to forgive.

[36] See Scobie and Scobie 1998: Table 2 for an analysis of responses to wrongdoing.

[37] Psychological interventions can help people who have been wronged to rediscover and renew their self-respect in order to become ready to forgive: this seems to be the approach pioneered by Enright and the Human Development Study Group (on which, see chapter 3).

[38] See also Novitz 1998: 311–13.

The value of Hampton's approach is that it highlights the fact that an important element of forgiveness is how the victim perceives the wrongdoing. It is self-evident that not all people will react identically to the same wrong. Some may be mildly irritated, irked, even annoyed; others may feel victimised, violated and abused. Others may blame themselves or feel guilty. A number may respond with phlegmatic detachment, barely concerned about what has been done to them; others may become resentful, angry, vengeful or self-pitying. Loss of confidence and self-respect may ensue; so may anxiety and depression. Some apparently quickly forgive, but the 'forgiveness' is no more than a form of passivity.[39]

According to Hampton, what matters is the robustness of the victim's self-esteem rather than the nature of the act performed, and one person may be deeply 'diminished' by an act that another might pass off and barely notice. What is also important to note is that it does not follow that the greater the moral wrong, the harder it will be to forgive: the true issue here is not so much the act itself but how the victim perceives the act. (Not surprisingly, therefore, in such an analysis and as we have said above, acts that the 'victim' does not regard as morally wrong or of which the 'victim' is unaware are not forgivable because there is nothing to forgive.)

We have looked at wrongdoing from the point of the psychology of the victim. We turn now to wrongdoing from the point of view of the psychology of the wrongdoer.

Wrongdoers may do wrong in part due to their own psychological needs. For example, moral wrongs may take the form of an abuse of power, an expression of disdain or an act of calculated contempt or disrespect, the purpose of which is to disparage, humiliate, violate or degrade the victim. Sometimes wrongdoing discloses the egotism of the wrongdoer: the wrongdoer is so self-absorbed as not to care about the victim and the effect of the wrong on the victim. In the thought of Lévinas,[40] wrongdoing is (among other things) an exaggerated and distorted expression of one's own freedom as a human being at the expense of the victim's freedom. The victim is thereby subordinated to the wilful and abusive power of the wrongdoer and so is regarded as less than fully 'other' as a human being. People have responsibilities towards one another because they exist in a matrix of social relationships, and to wrong another is to disorder the matrix and to fail properly to exercise the responsibility that freedom brings. Sometimes,

---

[39] See Kant, *The Metaphysics of Morals* (1797) in Gregor 1996: 06:435.
[40] See especially Lévinas 1998: 13–38 and 91–101.

without psychological help, wrongdoers of this sort are unlikely to be able to recognise that their behaviour is morally wrong and that it is in part driven by morbid psychological desires.

Wrongdoers may respond in a variety of ways to their acts of wrongdoing. These responses may be outright denial that the events took place, that the victims suffered or that they were responsible. 'Reinterpretation' may also take place: this occurs when a wrongdoer distorts and diminishes the effect or significance of the wrong. Sometimes also, of course, a wrongdoer may repent, apologise and ask for forgiveness.

There are times when wrongdoers consider that the wrongs they have committed are so heinous that they 'should' not be forgiven. Perhaps this was the view of the prodigal when he came to realise his folly (Luke 15:11–32). Even so, the question whether a wrongdoer 'should' be forgiven is not for the wrongdoer to decide. Forgiveness is a gift from the victim to the wrongdoer: it can be sought or begged for, but it is the gift of the victim alone.

A relatively under-explored question is the effect of forgiveness on the wrongdoer. When a victim forgives a wrongdoer, the victim, in effect, gives the wrongdoer a 'new start'. Hampton in Murphy and Hampton 1988: 86f. correctly identified two of the benefits of forgiveness for the *wrongdoer* – benefits she described as 'perhaps the greatest good forgiveness can bring': the first is that the wrongdoer will be 'liberated' from the victim's 'moral hatred', and the second is that forgiveness may save the wrongdoer from 'the hell of self-loathing'.

Some wrongdoers, even after they have been forgiven, may continue in the 'hell of self-loathing', and may continue in this state for neurotic reasons, punishing themselves for the wrong they have done out of a sense of continuing guilt. They will be trapped in the 'victimhood' – to borrow and adapt Tutu's phrase for a different context – of shame, guilt and remorse for their *own* wrongdoing, even though the victim, by having let go of vindictive and other unforgiving feelings, will have released the wrongdoer from the victim's 'moral hatred'. Alternatively, a wrongdoer may accept forgiveness from the victim, and live as a forgiven person, letting go of guilt and remorse. Without this self-forgiveness, there cannot be a restored relationship and reconciliation. Just as the victim (usually) does not choose to be violated and has had to learn to overcome the violation, so the wrongdoer will have to cooperate with and participate in the gift of forgiveness that is given. To do so may be a further expression of repentance and contrition, and a way to demonstrate renewed respect for the former victim.

### THE NEXT STEP

We have now completed the exploration of what it means to do wrong and to be a wrongdoer. Before we can explore in detail what it means to forgive a wrongdoer and the wrong a wrongdoer has done, we will trace how thinking about forgiveness has been shaped and developed in the last two millennia.

# CHAPTER 2

# *Forgiveness then and now*

## FORGIVENESS AND RELIGIOUS PEOPLE

Until recently, forgiveness has principally been the concern of people of religious faith, and of Christian faith in particular.[1] In the past, politicians, philosophers,[2] lawyers, scientists,[3] psychologists and others have treated forgiveness as inconsequential for their work. They regarded forgiveness as a private matter, the concern of interpersonal relations and of those with religious faith, and irrelevant – perhaps even dangerous – for academic discourse and public policy.

Others have treated forgiveness not only as irrelevant but also as an unworthy moral ideal. They have regarded forgiveness as the antonym of justice, because forgiveness appears to free the guilty from blame and moral responsibility.[4] They think that forgiven wrongdoers evade accountability – they go, as it were, in one leap from being offenders to being forgiven, without acknowledging or coming to terms with what they have done, without engaging with how their actions violated their victims and without enduring a measure of retribution or punishment for the wrongs they committed.

Nietzsche (1844–1900) attacked the idea of forgiveness on different grounds. His view was that to forgive someone for wrongdoing fails to acknowledge the desire for revenge and the will to power that all people have, including victims. He regarded forgiveness as a sign of impotence practised only because victims were unable or unwilling successfully to seek

---

[1] For a summary of research on the importance of forgiveness to adherents in Christianity and Judaism (and briefly also to adherents of other faiths), see Mullet *et al.* 2003: 2–4. For forgiveness in other faiths, see Rye *et al.* 2000: 17–40 and Govier 2002: Appendix 1, 158–63. On the place of forgiveness and faith generally, see Lévinas 1998: 18f.

[2] Strawson (1968a: 6) wrote that 'forgiveness . . . is a rather unfashionable subject in moral philosophy'.

[3] For a long time forgiveness 'appears to have been considered insufficiently important [for] or amenable to scientific study' (Fincham 2000: 3).

[4] Enright and Fitzgibbons (2000: 267–76) address this.

revenge. Forgiveness is immoral, he argued: it exalts weakness, and renounces the violence that sustains power. It is also psychologically unhealthy because it means that people deny or repress – and do not face – the desire for revenge. In making a virtue out of such a necessity, Christianity glorifies weakness, insists people are content with being victims and so emasculates its disciples.[5] Kant (1724–1804) cruelly wrote that 'one who makes himself into a worm cannot complain afterwards if people step on him'.[6]

Despite these criticisms (which are addressed later in this book), forgiveness has had and continues to have an important place in religious discourse and in Christianity in particular. The idea of forgiveness is also embedded in Judaism[7] and is (at least) implicit in Islam,[8] Hinduism[9] and in some expressions of Buddhism.[10] Even so, there is no agreement between any of these faiths (and sometimes disagreement within these faiths) about what forgiveness is and how, when or why forgiveness should be practised (Gopin 2000: 54).[11] The writers who come from a religious tradition in the symposium contained in Wiesenthal 1998 clearly demonstrate the range of religious understanding on the subject. Despite the disagreements, 'forgiveness seems to have the status of a cultural universal – one of the small number of practices that, although varying in detail, appears in some form in all cultures' (Lang 1994). It is a moral ideal of which almost all people, religious and non-religious, are aware and which, to some extent, they seek to practise as a moral good.

The Christian view of forgiveness (which is further considered in chapter 5) is that forgiveness is an act of undeserved favour, imitative of the love that God has shown human beings (Ephesians 4:32; Colossians 2:13, 3:13) and offered in the confidence that to forgive is a moral good.

This approach to forgiveness is a development of what is in the Hebrew Scriptures where God, through grace, forgave (if at all) in response to repentance. In other words, repentance preceded forgiveness. There was

---

[5] Smith 1996: Essay 1, Sections 13f.     [6] Gregor 1996: 559.

[7] *Teshuva* (repentance: see Gopin 2000: 187–91), *mechila* (forgoing the other's indebtedness), *selicha* (forgiveness, a merciful act of the heart that extends compassion to the wrongdoer) and *kappara* and *tahora* (atonement and purification: the wiping away of sinfulness resulting in cleansing, granted by God alone).

[8] In Islam, Allah forgives those who turn to him in repentance; people are to forgive one another. See Gopin 2000: 82–4.

[9] In the festival of Mahasivaratri in the month of Magha, the focus is on austerity and (among other things) on forgiveness (*ksama*).

[10] See *Mahavagga* X.ii.3–20. See also the response of the Dalai Lama in Wiesenthal 1998: 129–30 and Kornfield 2002.

[11] See Tombs and Liechty 2005 for interfaith reflections on forgiveness and reconciliation.

no guarantee that God would necessarily forgive if a person repented. Forgiveness was a gift of grace, and God did not have to forgive except by God's own choice and volition. There is little emphasis on forgiveness or love as moral virtues for human beings to practise. God alone forgave sins – and this seems to have been the prevailing orthodoxy in Jesus' day (see Luke 7:49, Mark 2:7 and Luke 5:21) – though, according to all three synoptic writers, the 'son of man' had power to forgive sins (Mark 2:10 and parallels).[12]

Connected with – but distinct from[13] – the idea of forgiveness is reconciliation, also predicated as a moral good in the New Testament. Roberts (1995) regards reconciliation as the 'teleology of forgiveness', that is, reconciliation is the purpose or goal of forgiveness. Reconciliation means rebuilding and reconstructing a fractured relationship but it does not necessarily follow that the relationship will have returned to its former state. Acts may have taken place that, though they can be forgiven, prevent a return to the *status quo ante*. Some rightly say, for example, that parties to a marriage that has irretrievably broken down may forgive one another but still choose to end the marriage. When divorced, can the parties also be reconciled? The answer is 'yes', if here by 'reconciliation' we mean forgiveness coupled with a restored relationship *appropriate to the situation of the parties after they have forgiven one another*.[14] Anecdotal evidence can illustrate this point: I know of one couple who have divorced and of whom one has remarried. The former married couple now describe themselves as better friends than when married.

The New Testament urges both wrongdoer and victim to seek reconciliation. In Matthew 5:23f. Jesus insists that the *wrongdoer* should seek reconciliation and in Matthew 6:14f., it is a condition of divine forgiveness that the *victim* forgive (and by implication be reconciled to) the wrongdoer. In the case of unconditional forgiveness (that is, forgiveness of an unrepentant wrongdoer – see chapter 4 below), it is very difficult to see how there can be genuine reconciliation because the wrongdoer does not repent and acknowledge the wrong. Victim and wrongdoer may, on pragmatic grounds, work together for certain purposes – for example, as in South Africa – but this does not amount to genuine reconciliation. So-called reconciliation, particularly on a national scale, sometimes amounts to little

---

[12] See the discussion of these words at pp. 90–2, below.
[13] Cf. Wilson (1988: 534) who almost alone among commentators argues that forgiveness 'must' involve reconciliation.
[14] See the example in Benn 1996: 373, n. 3.

more than 'non-violent co-existence' (Govier 2002: 142). We consider this further in chapter 7.

Of all the world's religions, Christianity especially emphasises forgiveness, though, of course, forgiveness is not an innovation of Christianity. Christianity makes forgiveness central to Christian faith and *praxis*. What is new is that in Christianity to forgive, like to love, is to practise a surpassing moral ideal. True, the Hebrew Scriptures stipulated that people were to love their neighbours as themselves (Leviticus 19:18), but it was Jesus who made both forgiveness and love the identity markers of his disciples and it was Jesus who made forgiveness and love axioms of his restatement of the ethics of the Hebrew Scriptures.

Christian people have long been regarded as forgiving people (at least by profession), and to some extent that is true. Mullet *et al.* (2003: 16) have shown that, in a Roman Catholic context, social commitment to religion, such as church attendance (as opposed to 'mere personal beliefs'), promoted an enhanced willingness to forgive. The willingness to forgive among (Roman Catholic) religious people increased with age, probably because older people practise forgiveness as a problem-solving method they have learned in the course of life. Pargament and Rye (1998) have also shown that people who are religiously involved tend to place more value on forgiveness than their less religiously involved counterparts.

Mullet *et al.* (2003) have identified the following reasons to explain why religious people tend to be forgiving people. First, forgiveness is highly valued in many religions; second, religious texts contain role models of forgiveness; next, religion offers worldviews that help victims regard wrongdoers as human beings who remain members of the same 'family'; and, last, religious faith encourages forgiveness, despite uncertainty about how a wrongdoer may react. Research by others has shown that religious people are more attuned to the fact that they participate in 'universal finitude, frailty and guilt' and so should forgive and seek forgiveness (Pargament and Rye 1998: 68).

Religious people, and especially those in the Judaeo-Christian tradition, understand divine forgiveness to be the model for interpersonal forgiveness. Many also believe that expressions of forgiveness outside this religious context are derivative, subordinate and poor imitations of divine forgiveness. For example, even as late as the end of the twentieth century, Jones (1995) treated the biblical model of forgiveness he identifies to be the criterion by which to judge secular models of forgiveness. His starting point is that 'forgiveness is most adequately understood within a Christian theological framework – and more specifically, within the doctrine of the Triune God' which offers a model of 'self-giving love' (Jones 1995: xiii, 61).

Particularly in European traditions under the influence of the Reformation, reflection on forgiveness has principally been in relation to humanity's wrongdoing against God in the context of the doctrine of the atonement (e.g., Mackintosh 1927 and Taylor 1941; but cf. Lofthouse 1906). The view of Stendahl (1976) is that the emphasis on individual forgiveness in the post-Reformation interpretation of Paul and the gospel is a reflection of what he calls 'the introspective conscience of the west' rather than a reflection of what Paul himself writes. The emphasis on individual forgiveness, he suggests, reflects our own psychopathology and the western quest for relief from guilt.

## THE MODERN STUDY OF FORGIVENESS

The era of what may be termed 'the modern study of forgiveness' in the post-Reformation period began in 1718. In that year Bishop Joseph Butler (1692–1752) published *Fifteen Sermons* preached at the Rolls Chapel in London, of which the eighth and ninth sermons ('Upon Resentment and Upon Forgiveness of Injuries') concern forgiveness (see Gladstone 1995). Butler's description of forgiveness as the 'forswearing of resentment' is still widely quoted and is the basis of much modern work and discussion. It is, for example, Murphy's starting point in Murphy and Hampton 1988.[15]

In his discussion of forgiveness, Kierkegaard (1813–55) implicitly affirms grace, faith and love as the coordinates of forgiveness. He suggests that forgiveness is the antithesis (or mirror image) of creation (Hong and Hong 1995: 294–7). For just as Christians believe by faith that in creation God brings what is seen into existence from what is not seen, so forgiveness – also by faith – 'takes away that which does indeed exist' (Hong and Hong 1995: 294–5) and obliterates something that exists in such a way that it no longer exists. Both are expressions of divine grace – the one bringing about existence, the other removing it – and both are perceived by faith.

---

[15] Tara Smith (1997: 37) is among the few who reject this starting point. She regards forgiveness as 'a particular type of moral estimate[,] . . . the conclusion that one should understand and respond to another person's breach less harshly than would normally be appropriate'. Thus, Smith denies that resentment (a feeling or attitude) is pivotal. When it comes to forgiveness, she says that what matters is a judgment that the wrongdoing 'should not be treated as proof of a grave moral defect or an irredeemably bad character'. Smith is right to highlight the cognitive basis of forgiveness (without it, forgiveness can be limp); but forgiveness is more than a cognitive response to wrongdoing. As I argue in chapter 3, it involves a complex interaction of thoughts, feelings and behaviour.

Kierkegaard also emphasises that love should be the motivation for for-giveness and, reflecting 1 Peter 4:8, that love covers a multitude of sins (Hong and Hong 1995: 294, 314). The one who loves, he writes, 'by forgive-ness believes *away* what is seen' and 'believes away that which he indeed can see' so that 'what is seen is, by being forgiven, not seen' (Hong and Hong 1995: 295).

The main debates in the first half of the twentieth century were the-ological and particularly concerned the implications of the doctrine of the atonement. As in previous centuries, one question that was explored was whether God's forgiveness of human beings was provisional (as in the Parable of the Unforgiving Servant – Matthew 18:23–35) or whether it was unreserved and unconditional (as in some interpretations of the Parable of the Prodigal Son – Luke 15:11–32). Moberly (1901: 52, 56, 58), favouring the former view, argued that '[t]he only real forgiveness is the forgiveness of God, – reproduced in man just so far as man, in God's Spirit, right-eously forgives'. Forgiveness 'is never simply unconditional' but depends on 'forgiveableness', 'a condition in the personality of the forgiven'. 'For-giveableness' is the condition that arises from practising the forgiveness which is to come.[16] (Temple (1924: 267f.) also resorted to neologisms on this question. He said that 'forgiving-ness', that is, the victim's 'readiness to forgive', is 'always a duty'. Forgiveness depends not only on the victim's 'forgiving-ness' but also on the wrongdoer's repentance. It will, he argued, result when the wrongdoer 'is willing to accept the position of forgiven-ness'.) Mackintosh (1927: 242–3) declared that Moberly's view was 'a new legalism' and 'manifestly out of touch' with central parts of Jesus' teaching. Mackintosh held to 'the Lutheran truth concerning justification' that for-giveness is offered 'to all who will cast themselves on God' whom God puts not 'on probation' but 'accepts . . . just as they are'. Also debated in the earlier part of the twentieth century was whether forgiveness was dependent upon the wrongdoer's repentance (Redlich 1937) and whether forgiveness can be extended necessarily to include reconciliation (Taylor 1941).

From about the middle of the twentieth century, three significant changes began to occur.

---

[16] Thus '[p]resent forgiveness is inchoate . . .: it is the recognition . . . of something in the present, – but a something whose real significance lies in the undeveloped possibilities of the future; a something which is foreseen, and is to be realized, but which, in the actual personality, is not realized as yet'. It can be lost 'if the growth towards [its consummation] be broken, and the conditions necessary for it be rebelled against' (Moberly 1901: 61). 'Human forgiveness is to find its inspiration in man's experience of the forgiveness of God' (Moberly 1901: 63). 'Forgiveableness' is the result of 'a heart set upon personal righteousness' (Moberly 1901: 72) and is exemplified in love and the virtues that love produces, such as forgiving others and being penitent.

The first is that forgiveness ceased to be a matter that was principally the concern of those with religious faith. The reason for the change is probably that people became increasingly interested to pursue 'quality of life' issues – issues to do with well-being, psychological health and personal satisfaction – and forgiveness was regarded as one of those issues.[17]

The second is that forgiveness ceased to be a matter that was treated as concerning only interpersonal relationships: people began to see that wrongdoing concerned nations, groups and corporations as well as individuals.[18] People thought that if individuals did wrong and could be forgiven, so could nations. With this came the impetus for forgiveness to enter the public forum and to move from being primarily the focus of religious discourse and ethical reflection resulting from that. Forgiveness became a matter for nations as well as individuals.

The third is that, after the Second World War and the first use of atomic weapons in warfare, people realised that unless nations urgently addressed and resolved some of the issues of conflict that existed between them, wars – with suffering, destruction and death on a previously unimagined scale – were likely to result. Peace, seen as reconciliation between nations, was a necessity if assured destruction was not to result. To further this end, legal immunity for individuals acting on behalf of nations was to some extent lifted. Article 6 of the Charter of the International Military Tribunal that led to the 'Nuremburg trials' (1945–9) stipulated that alleged war criminals could be tried for three types of crime: crimes against peace, war crimes and crimes against humanity. The work of the United Nations Organization also resulted in further emphasis on 'human rights' and 'crimes against humanity' and has, as the preamble to its Charter states, the aim that peoples should 'practice tolerance and live together in peace with one another as good neighbours'.

These three changes meant that the idea of forgiveness began to be regarded as principally not a religious idea but a matter of secular, public discourse and practice. This has been dramatically and largely effectively illustrated in South Africa, for example, where the moral and political leadership of Nelson Mandela (buttressed also by the example and leadership of Archbishop Desmond Tutu) has helped promote a measure of public unity

---

[17] The reason Haber (1991: 1) gives is interest in the place of feelings in moral life. Worthington (2005: 1) attributes the genesis of research in the subject to the publication of Smedes 1984. Lamb, in Lamb and Murphy 2002: 3f., believes it is because of the directive approach of cognitive behaviour therapy that emphasises an individual's freedom to choose how to think about and respond to psychologically distressing events and feelings.

[18] Aristotle stated that wrongdoing affects communities as well as individuals: *Rh.* i, 13, 1373b20–5 (in Barnes 1984).

and public reconciliation in that country, particularly through the Truth and Reconciliation Commission. Even so, this public dimension to reconciliation is not without difficulties because the Commission promoted reconciliation without also insisting on forgiveness.[19] This is because the Commission and those who set it up assumed – erroneously in the view of many – that public reconciliation would 'trickle down' and promote personal reconciliation and forgiveness. Although both Mandela and Tutu promoted forgiveness and reconciliation in part out of their (Christian) religious convictions, discourse about forgiveness in the public realm has, in the main, tended to be deliberately kept secular so as to be accessible and acceptable to all people.

The idea of forgiveness has touched many aspects of public life. For example, the Forgiveness Project (www.theforgivenessproject.com) aims to promote reconciliation in prisons and schools. In 2004, the Project organised an exhibition entitled 'The f Word' (where 'f' stood for 'forgiveness'). The exhibition, which began to tour the UK in 2004, is a collection of twenty-four stories of reconciliation and forgiveness shown in words and images. The provocative title of the exhibition was chosen to highlight that, for many, the idea of forgiveness is shockingly offensive. In 2005 Latvia, Lithuania and Estonia, three Baltic states that were occupied by the USSR during the Second World War and subsequently annexed, sought an apology from Russia for the former USSR's actions. In the same year, actions by Christians during the crusades (1095–1291) came under renewed scrutiny and criticism following release of a film about the crusades called *Kingdom of Heaven*. Although people still recognise that it is difficult to forgive, forgiveness is not today regarded as 'the most unpopular' of virtues (cf. Lewis 1995: 110): rather, it is of accelerating public and personal interest and has become a 'globalised' idea, taking it out of the purely religious realm (Derrida 2001: 31) and making it both an individual and a corporate matter.

As one would expect, with the move of forgiveness into the public, secular arena came an enhanced interest in forgiveness in academic discourse, most extensively in philosophy and psychology and as an aspect of philosophical and jurisprudential reflection on 'restorative justice'. Even so, as Enright and North (1998: 4) rightly observe, articles and books on forgiveness are

---

[19] Thus the Commission in general recommended amnesties for those who made a full confession and accepted responsibility for racially motivated criminal acts under the *apartheid* regime. The Commission did not require wrongdoers to show remorse or contrition, repent or apologise. Of the 7,112 who fully disclosed their crimes under the *apartheid* regime to the Commission and applied for amnesty, 849 were granted amnesty: see http://news.bbc.co.uk/1/hi/world/africa/4534196.stm (accessed 9 January 2006).

still 'rare within academia, because explorations of forgiveness have been rare for almost sixteen hundred years'.[20] A search of the *Philosopher's Index* reveals 269 entries for the period 1940–2005, of which 132 of the entries (almost half) were published in the period 2000–5. Hieronymi (2001: 529) describes this as a 'small but sustained discussion of forgiveness' in the philosophical literature of recent years. Worthington (1998c: 1; and see Worthington 2005: 1) notes that there were only five scientific studies of forgiveness by psychologists before 1985, but between then and 1998 fifty-five studies were published.

Important articles by Downie (1965, on forgiveness as a moral virtue distinguishable from condonation and pardon), Strawson (1968a, on forgiveness requiring a belief that the wrongdoer is a culpable and responsible moral person who intentionally did wrong) and Kolnai (1973–4, on the morality of forgiving an unrepentant wrongdoer and on whether a repentant wrongdoer *can* be forgiven) marked the start of renewed interest in forgiveness among moral philosophers. In 1988, Murphy and Hampton published *Forgiveness and Mercy*, a seminal dialogue about forgiveness between Murphy (a legal philosopher) and Hampton (a political philosopher). Haber (1991) also produced an important book on the topic. For some time, there has been debate among philosophers about when, how and even whether Jewish people may 'forgive' Germany for its actions in the period 1933–45 (e.g., Garrard 2002).[21]

Philosophers have tended to argue that the concept of forgiveness is 'pre-eminently an ethical subject'. It is not, they suggest, primarily a religious subject but a subject concerned with relations between people and with how to deal with 'affront, injury, transgression, trespassing or offence' by one person against another (Kolnai 1973–4: 92; see also Haber 1991: 3, 7).[22] Minas (1975) went further and argued that it was logically impossible for God to forgive. Far from forgiveness being difficult or impossible for human beings because they lack divine attributes, forgiveness is possible and appropriate, she argued, only because human beings are *not* divine.

Psychologists, too, have made significant progress on the study of forgiveness. Psychological studies and books for clinicians continue to be published at an accelerating rate. In 2005 *Handbook of Forgiveness* was published under

---

[20] Enright and North (1998: 4) say their book is about 'interpersonal' forgiveness, that is, 'the kind of forgiveness that exists between people'. They distinguish this from the 'spiritual dimensions' of forgiveness, which they do not define but which appears to refer to the forgiveness God grants to human beings. In other words, the book is a social-scientific, not a theological, work.

[21] For a study on how contemporary members of one group may forgive the collective guilt of another group, see Wohl and Branscombe 2005.

[22] But not Adams 1991.

Worthington's editorship.[23] This book is a milestone in the clinical, medical and social scientific study of forgiveness and is likely to be a standard reference work on the subject, though in the first chapter Worthington acknowledges that there remains 'a fragile future for the scientific study of forgiveness' (Worthington 2005: 10).

Psychologists (and some from other disciplines) have rightly observed that the psychological health of those who do not or cannot forgive may be adversely affected. Many find it difficult to overcome anger, resentment and other negative emotions associated with having been wronged and so to be freed from being controlled by the memory of the wrongdoing and the wrongdoer (see Pargament and Rye 1998: 71–4). For some, clinical treatment is needed to ameliorate their condition. R. D. Enright and the Human Development Study Group (HDSG) at the University of Wisconsin-Madison have pioneered a model of forgiveness for use in 'forgiveness interventions' in psychological therapy. The model used shares many features with other models that are being developed by others in the field.[24] 'Forgiveness interventions' have been identified with positive therapeutic outcomes, namely improved psychological health for the forgiver (Kaminer *et al.* 2000).

In discussing social factors that influence forgiveness, psychologists have assembled some important data. For example, McCullough and Witvliet (2001: 450; and see McCullough *et al.* 1998) cite research showing that the context in which wrongs take place may play an important part in influencing forgiveness. Thus people 'are more willing to forgive in relationships in which they feel satisfied, close and committed' and probably one 'would not expect people to forgive perfect strangers in the same way they forgive their most intimate relationship partners'.

In addition, psychological research has shown that apologies influence forgiveness (Girard and Mullet 1997; McCullough *et al.* 1997 and McCullough *et al.* 1998). Several reasons help to explain this. First, an apology expresses the wrongdoer's acknowledgment of the wrong and of its consequences for the victim. It also communicates the wrongdoer's contrition and desire to put the matter right. The result is likely to be that the victim's feelings change towards the wrongdoer and the victim will view the wrongdoer more favourably. Lastly, an apology shows evidence of the intention to seek a restored relationship and so may promote reconciliation.

An example may illustrate the point. If you are my friend and I lend you a book that subsequently you lose, it may not be difficult to forgive

---

[23] An earlier important book is Enright and Fitzgibbons 2000.    [24] Wade and Worthington 2005.

you. I may be able easily to replace the book (you may even offer to buy a replacement for me) and I quickly accept your apology. If the book were out of print, of sentimental value and if it was your evident carelessness that resulted in the loss of the book, it may be harder to forgive you; but if you are a long-standing friend whose company I value, it would probably not take me long to forgive you. But if also you were to upbraid me for caring about the loss, suggesting that I valued the book more than my friendship with you, and if you were then also to make critical remarks about what you perceive to be my possessiveness, I may become dissatisfied with the friendship and so find it hard to forgive you. It may even be that I would wish to discontinue the friendship – or at least to put some distance between you and me for a time.

What is significant in these scenarios is the value the victim puts on the relationship with the wrongdoer (McCullough and Witvliet 2001: 450), the perceived degree of wrong and the wrongdoer's response to the wrong. Not surprisingly, therefore, the victim of a violent trauma, such as rape, will almost certainly find it very difficult to forgive the wrongdoer, and certainly more difficult than in the examples above about the loss of a book. It is a truism that, in general, people have more difficulty forgiving wrongs they regard as intentional and severe in their consequences (Boon and Sulsky 1997; Girard and Mullet 1997) than wrongs that they consider to be relatively slight.[25]

Other disciplines are now engaging with the idea of forgiveness. Forgiveness is one approach in business management (Kurzynski 1998; Aquino *et al.* 2003); its beneficial effects on physical health and well-being are argued[26] and its neurological effects on the brain identified (Farrow *et al.* 2001). Forgiveness is also the subject of 'self-help' books.[27] Many are now suggesting that forgiveness is a creative, transformative dynamic of human development and maturing, and this development has occurred as forgiveness has increasingly become an important subject of scholarly discussion and debate.[28] Exline *et al.* (2003) summarise the areas of academic discourse

---

[25] But see the discussion at pp. 6f., above.
[26] See Berry and Worthington (2001) who review the literature on the subject and show further evidence that unforgiveness can produce physical and mental health problems. See also Lawler *et al.* 2003, Witvliet *et al.* 2004, Worthington and Scherer 2004 and Lawler *et al.* 2005. For a critical appraisal of methods, see McCullough and Witvliet 2001: 452–4.
[27] For example, Macaskill 2002, a practical book based on the principles of cognitive behaviour therapy.
[28] For example, from 1997 the Templeton Foundation has made grants for the study of forgiveness; see also the Campaign for Forgiveness (www.forgiving.org) and the International Forgiveness Institute (established in 1994) (www.forgivenessinstitute.org), the work of which is described in Enright *et al.* 1998: 60f.

where forgiveness has become important; they also set out research agenda for forgiveness in social and personality psychology.

The Christian tradition has, in the second half of the twentieth century, also continued to contribute – albeit modestly – to the discussion of forgiveness (for example, Jones 1995; McFadyen and Sarot 2001). Much of the work has been in response to the secular agenda. There has been some interdisciplinary research: see, for example, Watts and Gulliford 2004, a collection of papers by Christian psychologists and theologians on forgiveness. Some who work in a secular context, such as in psychology or philosophy, are also self-confessed Christians. As a result, especially in a North American context, there has been some interchange between what they understand to be the Christian tradition on forgiveness and forgiveness as it is understood in secular disciplines (e.g., Hampton in Murphy and Hampton 1988).

CHRISTIANITY AND PUBLIC FORGIVENESS

Christians are also increasingly recognising and participating in aspects of public forgiveness. The contribution of Christians to the study and practice of forgiveness, reconciliation and peacemaking is undeniable. Appleby (2000: 7) has argued that religions now offer 'a new form of conflict transformation' that he calls 'religious peacebuilding', though not everyone agrees that forgiveness and reconciliation are 'a universally accepted method of peacemaking' for those outside the Christian tradition (Gopin 2000: 164).

I have already referred to the contributions of Nelson Mandela, former President of South Africa, and of the former Anglican Archbishop of Cape Town, Desmond Tutu, who chaired the Truth and Reconciliation Commission in South Africa. Tutu wrote an influential book on forgiveness as an instrument of public policy (Tutu 1999). Behind Tutu's thinking was the idea that 'to be a good Christian is to be proactive and generous in forgiveness' (Cherry 2004: 167). In South Africa, the contribution that people of religious faith have made to forgiveness as an expression of public policy has been seen, overall, to have produced favourable results and to have helped with the process of political and social reconciliation and reconstruction.

Another example of a Christian contribution to public forgiveness is the Woodstock Theological Center, an institute at Georgetown University, which the Society of Jesus established in 1974. It takes an ecumenical and independent approach on theological and ethical issues of public policy. It has published the proceedings of four colloquia under the series title *Forgiveness in Conflict Resolution* (1998) (and in particular reflected on conflict in Northern Ireland and Bosnia and on Truth and Reconciliation

Commissions). The colloquia sought to explore two issues: what 'forgiveness' means in the public forum, and how forgiveness may be used or be made useful in the resolution of public conflict.

More recently, under the initiative of the institute and using much of the work of the colloquia, the US Conference of Catholic Bishops published a book on the place of forgiveness in international politics as a way to peace (Bole *et al.* 2004). The authors sought to follow the plea of Shriver (1995: 7) to make forgiveness one of the 'ordinary political virtues'. The book also sets out how faith-based organisations, such as the World Conference of Religions for Peace and the Center for Strategic and International Studies, have sought to promote peace and reconciliation in a secular context by 'mining the peacemaking recourses of faith' (Bole *et al.* 2004: 142).

Some theologians question whether the social sciences should have *any* contribution to Christian discourse on forgiveness. For example, Jones (1995: 36, 50) wrote of the dangers of what he terms 'therapeutic forgiveness', by which he means a notion of forgiveness among Christians that is shaped more by secular disciplines (such as psychology) than by Christian theology. He observes that one effect of such an approach is 'trivialization' and increasing 'preoccupation with individual feelings and thoughts at the expense of culpability, responsibility, and repentance', which he understands to be contrary to an authentic Christian discourse on the subject. Jones is undoubtedly right to warn of these dangers if the result is that Christians 'have failed to appropriate psychological insights *critically*' – but that is not the same as saying that psychology and other social sciences have *no* contribution to make at all. Also voicing concern has been Murphy (2003: 73–86), a legal philosopher who is concerned about 'forgiveness boosterism' (the phrase is in the Preface to Lamb and Murphy 2002: x) in psychology, that is, a headlong rush to promote forgiveness by practitioners in the psychological disciplines without due regard for some of the moral and rational questions that philosophers address.

### THE NEXT STEP

We begin now a detailed study of the modern treatment of forgiveness in both secular and Christian disciplines. We consider first the important contribution that psychologists have made to the discussion.

# CHAPTER 3

# Forgiveness and psychological therapy

People sometimes suffer psychological trauma because they have been wronged. A victim of wrongdoing may be angry, afraid, hurt and resentful; as a result, the victim may feel violated.[1] Perceived wrongs may also make a victim feel violated. One issue that victims often have difficulty in coming to terms with is *why* they were wronged. The question has to do with making sense of – that is, finding out the reason for – what happened to them.[2] Those who already have low self-esteem (that is, a misplaced or diminished sense of self-regard, self-confidence and self-respect and an inaccurate perception of themselves as rational and relational human beings) may find it particularly difficult to forgive (Novitz 1998: 311–13) – or may 'forgive' all too easily out of a lack of self-respect.[3] With some types of wrongdoing, the victim may feel that the wrongdoer is implicitly communicating that the victim is worthless, a 'thing' (not a person) to be abused at will. Being wronged can be a psychologically destructive experience for a person, and can have harmful effects on the lives of others and even on communities.

Some people who have been wronged recover quickly and bear no lasting (psychological) scars. Though they may be more cautious in the future through the experience of the injury, they will have made, from a psychological point of view, a full recovery. Others may be troubled, distressed, resentful, bitter or jaundiced and may need psychological therapy[4] to help them recover from the effects of the injury. Those offering psychological therapy know that issues related to forgiveness are sometimes germane to

---

[1] Garrard and McNaughton (2002: 42) suggest that it is a mistake to suggest that this applies to all types of wrongdoing. They give the example of the theft of a car by a person unknown to the car owner and say that it would be odd for the car owner to feel resentment or slighted. But it is well known that many victims of crimes such as theft do feel violated (and so at the least also resentful).

[2] The technical term in psychological theory for this process is 'coping': see Pargament and Rye 1998: 60–4.

[3] Cf. Adams 1991.

[4] 'Psychological therapy' (or similar phrases) is what Lamb and Murphy (2002) mean by 'psychotherapy' in the book they edited entitled, *Before Forgiving: Cautionary Views of Forgiveness in Psychotherapy*.

their practice (Konstam *et al.* 2002). In recent years, psychologists, particularly in North America, have been developing models of therapy specifically designed to address issues related to forgiveness.

In the models adopted by many who promote the idea of 'forgiveness interventions' (see Table 1 in Wade and Worthington 2005), forgiveness is treated as a way to cope with wrongdoing and its effects. The result of a 'forgiveness intervention' is typically a diminution of unforgiving feelings towards the wrongdoer. This usually comes about through a psychological reordering of a victim's feelings and thoughts towards the wrongdoer. Forgiveness, so it is thought, is the means to better psychological health and so to the benefits that better psychological health brings.[5]

The models most widely used insist that forgiveness is more than an act of pure self-interest (Enright *et al.* 1998: 50, 59). Nevertheless, forgiveness is recognised to be an act that typically also has incidental personal benefits.[6]

Despite much recent work on the question, there is no agreed definition of forgiveness among those working in the field of mental health. Each contributor in Worthington 2005 was invited to 'begin by defining forgiveness as they understand it' (p. 10), indicating that there is no agreed definition among psychologists.

There are also only a few models that exist that explain the psychological processes involved with forgiving (Worthington 1998a: 322–8; Konstam *et al.* 2002: 55–9; Wade and Worthington 2005). E. L. Worthington at Virginia Commonwealth University in Richmond, Virginia (with his research team) and R. D. Enright and the Human Development Study Group (the HDSG) in the Department of Educational Psychology at the University of Wisconsin-Madison have carried out most of the work to create the theoretical models that are in use.

Worthington's 'Pyramid Model to REACH Forgiveness' (Worthington 1998b and Worthington 2001) sets out the steps to forgiveness, the letter of five of the steps forming the acrostic REACH. The steps are *recalling* the hurt, building *empathy*, giving an *altruistic* gift of forgiveness, *commitment*

---

[5] See p. 33, note 26, above.

[6] If forgiveness is motivated by self-interest and nothing more, it would not be forgiveness because it would not be a moral response to wrongdoing. Richards (1988: 79) offers this example: 'Suppose that I [change my feelings towards you] . . . as an act of mental hygiene. I am sick and tired of being so angry that my sleep is restless and my stomach upset. I resolve not to endure another day of it, and I manage, with professional help, to end this disruptive state of mind.' Richards concludes that such a process does not amount to forgiveness.

to forgive and *holding* on to forgiveness and maintaining the gains achieved. Another model is better known and more widely used. Enright and the HDSG (1996) have developed this model ('the HDSG model'). The HDSG model has been described as 'a major scientific contribution to the mental health field [and] . . . may be as important to the treatment of emotional and mental disorders as the discovery of sulfa drugs and penicillin have been to the treatment of infectious diseases' (Fitzgibbons 1998: 71). (In the light of the observations I make below, this is clearly an overstatement.) The model identifies forgiveness as a process that has cognitive, affective and behavioural outcomes and, as it currently stands, has twenty 'units' of psychological variables (Enright *et al.* 1998: Table 5.1, p. 53).

The HDSG model of forgiveness postulates a 'forgiveness triad' that consists of forgiving others, forgiving oneself and accepting forgiveness from others. According to this model, forgiveness is an internal process by which people, as a result of cognitive, behavioural and affective changes, come to a point where they can let go of the pain and hurt they feel as a result of having suffered an unjust injury. They can renounce anger and grudges, renounce the 'right to resentment and retaliation' and instead offer 'mercy to the offender' as a gift (Enright and Coyle 1998: 140).[7] The result, its supporters claim, will be better psychological health for the forgiver and will help free the forgiver from the 'control' of the wrongdoer.

Enright and Coyle (1998: 141f.) describe forgiveness as an 'interpersonal process' because, in their view, forgiveness involves the offer of 'mercy' to the wrongdoer, even though the offer of forgiveness does not depend on an apology from the wrongdoer or the wrongdoer recognising that wrong has been done. Forgiveness is thus unconditional and so 'a moral gift given to someone who does not necessarily deserve it' (Enright and Coyle 1998: 150 – and see also unit 15 of Table 1, pp. 144–5). Victims are to abandon hard feelings towards the wrongdoer and replace them not with neutral feelings but with positive feelings of compassion, goodwill, generosity and even love. Enright and Coyle distinguish this form of forgiveness, which they call 'genuine forgiveness', from 'pseudo forms and concepts similar to but distinct from it' which they suggest include pardoning, condoning, excusing, forgetting and denying (Enright and Coyle 1998: 140f. and, from a different perspective, see also Calhoun 1992: 78–80, on 'minimalist forgiving').

Like Taylor (1941) (but for different reasons and in a different context) Enright and Coyle distinguish reconciliation from forgiveness because the

---

[7] See also 'total forgiveness' in Baumeister *et al.* 1998.

wronged person who forgives may 'choose not to remain in a relationship' with the wrongdoer (Enright and Coyle 1998: 141 – and see Enright *et al.* 1998: 49). The basis of the approach seems to be this: forgiveness is 'one person's [the victim's] response to injury' whereas reconciliation is two people, victim and wrongdoer, 'coming together again': in other words, reconciliation comprises forgiveness (which according to Enright is unilateral and unconditional) *and* something else, namely, 'coming together'. Forgiveness is not dependent on the prior repentance of the wrongdoer: through the therapeutic intervention, the victim forgives unilaterally and without any expression of contrition by the wrongdoer. In light of this, it would be more accurate to say that 'interpersonal forgiveness' is, in fact, *intrapersonal* because such forgiveness, as Enright and Coyle describe it, is internal to the victim whereas what Enright and Coyle mean by 'reconciliation' involves, among other things, *interpersonal* forgiveness.

## A CRITIQUE OF 'FORGIVENESS INTERVENTIONS'

The work of Worthington and Enright and the HDSG is carefully nuanced and cautious. It is also still at the stage of being formulated and refined (Freedman *et al.* 2005: 394–9). I now wish to raise some questions about its philosophical underpinnings and express some points of disagreement. Not all the criticisms below apply only to their work; some are directed more widely to the idea of 'forgiveness interventions' generally and referred to in the literature on the subject. The context will make clear when I am referring to specific aspects of the work of Worthington or Enright and the HDSG.

A number of comments may be made at the outset.

First, forgiveness interventions tend to explore forgiveness as a psychological process internal to an individual. Communities and groups may engage in processes the outcomes of which are similar to forgiveness (see chapter 7). The nature of psychological studies in a North American context drives the individualistic focus, partly because North American society emphasises individualism and self-actualisation and partly because psychological therapy for forgiveness, as currently developed, is primarily concerned with how individuals forgive other individuals. Worthington 2005 seeks to correct the imbalance with four chapters by social psychologists on societal issues involving forgiveness. A great deal of additional work is needed to correct the imbalance.

Second, the intended outcome of psychological therapy for forgiveness is a decrease in levels of anxiety, depression, anger and resentment. In other words, the client's mental health and well-being will have improved. These outcomes, which Lamb in Lamb and Murphy 2002: 9 calls 'happiness', are measurable and demonstrable. Research evidence shows that these outcomes are being attained.

If these are the intended outcome of forgiveness therapy, might the basis of the therapy be no more than self-centredness and a means to improve the quality of the inner life without reference to the moral basis for doing so? Well-being and happiness may be legitimate outcomes for psychological therapy but, when it comes to forgiveness, they should not be the sole ends in themselves. In another essay, Lamb puts the issue clearly. She points out that, despite denials, those who advocate unconditional forgiveness as a 'gift' to an unrepentant wrongdoer are in effect offering no more than 'self-help' therapy. She says that, although therapists such as Enright (and others) 'vehemently disagree that forgiveness is *merely* a path to mental health',

this is an essential way in which they persuade others of its benefits; they cannot argue that it restores relationships (as in reconciliation) or persuades another to do better next time. As a gift, it has no strings attached. Without the self-help argument, they can only persuade a person to forgive because forgiveness is a virtue and because it helps society, but not because it will benefit the individual. (Lamb 2002: 157)

Third, Lamb wonders whether other forms of therapy for clients who are troubled by resentment and related feelings – forms that do not engage with questions to do with forgiveness – might produce the same outcome as therapists expect with forgiveness. Recent research in psychology also suggests that 'forgiveness interventions' may produce the same results *whichever* model of treatment is used, suggesting that the act of intervention (rather than the theoretical basis of the intervention) is what counts (Wade and Worthington 2005). Freedman *et al.* (2005: 400) attempt to answer this objection, probably rightly with the intention of not claiming too much for forgiveness therapy. They say, 'We do not think that those who study forgiveness are claiming that forgiveness is the only way to heal and effectively decrease anger and resentment' – and this is precisely the point Lamb is making. If the same outcome (decreased anger and resentment) can be produced by means other than through a forgiveness intervention, then 'forgiveness' in psychological therapy is no different from some of the outcomes in other types of psychological intervention.

If other psychological therapies can apparently produce the same outcome that forgiveness interventions produce, there is apparently nothing new that forgiveness interventions contribute. Disconcerting also is the fact that the same outcomes as psychological therapies produce – namely, decreased anger and resentment – can be produced if victims forgive as a moral response to wrongdoing. The issue at stake is the question of which route to the outcome is better. If the intended outcome is an increase in personal happiness and well-being through a decrease in anxiety, stress and depression, then psychological therapy for forgiveness is *one* of several options for the therapist. If the intended outcome is *also* successfully to have explored the moral issues that the wrongdoing raises and, if possible, to resolve them, then psychological therapy for forgiveness will not necessarily address all (or even any) of these. In this latter case, not only is there a better route to the outcome but also there is an outcome that is more far-reaching.

Next, Enright and the HDSG (1996: 109) warn that 'resisting the act of forgiving until the offender somehow changes is giving great power to the offender'. Because the victim will not have forgiven, the victim will not enjoy what Enright has identified to be the psychological benefits of forgiveness. Tutu (1999) describes this condition as being 'trapped in victimhood'.

That is sometimes undoubtedly true – but not always. Some people – even with therapeutic intervention – simply cannot or do not want to forgive an unrepentant wrongdoer. There is another way to respond that also denies the wrongdoer power and empowers the victim: it is to be angry and resentful, to affirm that one has value and counts, and not to acquiesce in the wrongdoer's violation (Murphy 2003: 81). Both courses of action – to forgive or not to forgive – affirm the integrity of the victim and do not amount to surrender to the supposed power of the wrongdoer. As Murphy rightly suggests, what is right depends on each situation.

A further point of concern with the idea of forgiveness interventions arises because the intervention does not involve dialogue and engagement with the wrongdoer and so runs the risk of being flawed from the outset. The model may enable victims to forgive wrongdoers as they *perceive* them, but not necessarily wrongdoers as they *are*. The therapeutic model does not involve engaging with wrongdoers, and so there is no way for wrongdoers to correct misimpressions, misunderstandings and mistakes or for victims to learn from them. Victims are dealing with mental representations of wrongdoers, not real people. In effect, victims are giving power to an internalised representation of wrongdoers – a psychological construct that may bear little or no resemblance to the wrongdoers as they are.[8]

---

[8] I am grateful to Dr C. J. K. Bouch for ideas contained in this paragraph.

This last point brings us to the central issue that is of concern with Enright's model. Forgiveness is best assured when it takes place in a relationship in which people talk through points of conflict and disagreement, identify what needs to be forgiven and then take appropriate action. Enright's model precludes this mature way of dealing with conflict and does not seek to integrate the wrongdoer into the therapeutic process. Its effect is to *prevent* the resolution of *interpersonal* difficulties by limiting forgiveness to being no more than an *intrapersonal* phenomenon in therapy. Of course, there are times when it may not be possible to engage with the wrongdoer – but to have a model that excludes the relational aspect of forgiveness is to limit the scope and effectiveness of the therapy and the supposed forgiveness.

We turn next to an important therapeutic tool of forgiveness interventions called 'reframing'. Reframing is an idea that has been developed by Enright and the HDSG.[9] A similar idea is implicit in Langer's discussion of the multiple meanings of behaviour (2001: 220–1) and independently has its origins in the concept of 'aspirational forgiveness' in Calhoun 1992.[10]

'Reframing' occurs when a victim begins to understand the wrongdoer in a wider context. It amounts to an attempt to understand why the wrongdoer acted in the way the wrongdoer did.[11] It is 'a matter of increasing the relevant data base regarding the offender; we might describe it as increasing the offender's narrative . . . Increasing the cosmic narrative can be as significant as increasing the relational narrative' (Yandell 1998: 43f.). The result is that the 'frame of reference' in which the victim understood the wrongdoer (e.g., 'this wrongdoer is a cruel misogynist who wronged me') may change and the victim begins to understand the wrongdoer and the wrongdoer's actions in a different 'frame of reference' ('this wrongdoer is unable to form respectful relationships with women because of psychological trauma in

---

[9] 'Reframing' is similar to Hampton's concept in Murphy and Hampton 1988: 84f. that forgiveness involves the victim's 'decision to see the wrongdoer in a new, more favourable light . . . [as] something other than or more than the character traits of which [the victim] does not approve'. Haber (1991: 13f.) disagrees with Hampton because (i) a person's behaviour is the only way to know with certainty whether that person is virtuous or not; (ii) we are deceiving ourselves if we see a wrongdoer other than as a wrongdoer. Haber's criticisms do not take account of the fact that what Hampton advocates can also include seeing and understanding the wrongdoer in a broader context and so appreciating that the wrongdoer is more than *just* a wrongdoer.

[10] Calhoun's idea is that the wrongdoer's actions must be seen in the light of the wrongdoer's life story.

[11] It is perhaps here that we find we can address what Milbank (2003: 51–6) asks, namely, how can wrongdoing be forgotten without also risking amnesia and complicity with the perpetrators? The answer is not that we undo the past but that it is undone through 're-narration' and so we come to 'a renewed understanding of the deluded motives of [the] violator' (Milbank 2003: 54).

the past'). When one reframes an action, one no longer sees the action as being culpable in the way one saw it initially.[12]

People do not often act perversely, irrationally or cruelly: there are usually reasons for their actions.[13] Understanding the reasons for a wrongdoer's actions – particular pressures the wrongdoer was under, the point of view or perspective of the wrongdoer, the psychological background of the wrongdoer – may, for example, go some way towards helping a victim to forgive because the wrongdoer's behaviour becomes explicable and so more easily forgivable. Langer (2001: 220) observes that behaviour 'makes sense from the actor's [that is, the wrongdoer's] perspective, or else it would not have occurred. I am right, and so are you.' Much of the bitterness and pain that wrongdoing causes can be ameliorated if the person who feels wronged explores *why* the behaviour made sense from the 'wrongdoer's' point of view – or accepts 'simply . . . that the behaviour in question must have made sense'. Reframing is of particular value where there has been no wrongdoing but a person believes that there has been wrongdoing and that he or she is a 'victim'.

Reframing sometimes enables a person who has difficulty forgiving a wrongdoer to change and to move towards forgiveness. North (1998: 26) adds that 'reframing . . . is also a way of *separating* the wrongdoer from the wrong which has been committed' so that the victim sees the wrongdoer not just as 'a bad person' but in a way 'that does justice to the complexity of the wrongdoer's personality'.

North (1998: 27f.) observes that reframing does not always enable a person to move towards forgiveness. There may be both moral and conceptual reasons why forgiveness remains impossible.[14] She writes that sometimes

it is that the reframing process, far from allowing us to separate the wrongdoer from his action, serves to reinforce the *identification* of the wrongdoer with his action. The more we understand, the more we come to regard the wrongdoer as culpable, as wholly and utterly bad . . . [T]he impossibility of forgiveness in such cases may be a *moral*, not just a psychological one.

At other times, she observes that a wrongdoer may be so evil and perverse as to be 'a sadist, a psychotic personality, the personification of evil, the devil in human form', and forgiveness is then 'a *conceptual* impossibility, because the wrongdoer is not "one of us", not of the kind to which concepts of love,

---

[12] Reframing is different from absolution. With absolution, the victim recognises the wrongdoer to be culpable for the wrongdoing but frees the wrongdoer from guilt for the action.
[13] Cf. McGinn 1997: 61–91.
[14] Richards (2002: 83–6) points out the drawbacks to reframing and shows how reframing can have the effect of pointing the victim to excuse, not forgive, the wrongdoer's behaviour.

compassion and forgiveness are applicable, not a person, but a monster'. In such a case the reframing process does not reveal 'anything other than a bad person' and there can be no forgiveness because the wrongdoer 'is so impenetrable in his moral corruption that we can find nothing to say in his favour'. Despite the aphorism *tout comprendre rend très indulgent* (often mistranslated 'to understand all is to forgive all'), 'it is simply not the case that superior understanding leads automatically to the acceptance of the foibles and crimes of others and oneself' and so to forgiveness (Neu 2002: 35).

The fundamental flaw with the idea of reframing is from a moral point of view. Reframing enables a victim to understand the wrongdoer and the wrongdoer's situation better – but understanding does not exculpate the wrongdoer from the morally wrong act or necessarily help the victim to forgive the wrongdoer.[15] It may even make forgiveness more difficult because it may appear to excuse the wrongdoer ('he hit you because his father hit him') and so fail to address the fact that the wrongdoing was morally wrong, whatever the reason for it. Alternatively, it may reinforce the victim's view that the wrongdoer committed a morally wrong act. Richard McCann, the son of one of the murdered victims of Peter Sutcliffe (known as 'the Yorkshire Ripper'), offers an interesting example of reframing that no more than served to reinforce the identification of the wrongdoer with the wrongdoing. McCann recounted how when he discovered that Sutcliffe showed no remorse about his crimes, he realised that Sutcliffe 'was simply evil and no longer deserving of his time and energy'.[16] Far from promoting and facilitating forgiveness, reframing in this example appears to have made it less likely.

Lastly, one of the theoretical bases of forgiveness interventions is 'the moral principle of beneficence, which may include compassion, unconditional worth, generosity, and moral love' towards the wrongdoer (Enright and Fitzgibbons 2000: 29). Beneficence (according to a dictionary definition) is a quality in an individual to do with doing good or being generous, and so is probably a moral attribute rather than a moral principle.

The principle of beneficence is not a term widely used in moral philosophy[17] and I have not seen the term used there in relation to forgiveness.

---

[15] This is the flaw in the argument of Smith (1997: 37) that forgiveness is the result of re-evaluating a wrongdoer so that one responds 'less harshly than would normally be appropriate'.

[16] See http://news.bbc.co.uk/1/hi/magazine/4522173.stm (in anticipation of a television broadcast on BBC One, Tuesday 10 May 2005 at 22.35 BST entitled 'One Life: The Ripper Murdered my Mum') (accessed 10 May 2005).

[17] An example is Murphy 1993.

Aristotle uses the term to refer to the motives of a benefactor.[18] More recently, the term has become an important element in medical ethics to do with issues in health care[19] and is now widely regarded as one of four culturally neutral moral principles that will apply whatever a person's moral, religious or political stance. In that context, beneficence (which is coupled with 'non-maleficence') aims overall to produce benefit, not harm, to patients and clients.

Beneficence is a wholly laudable attribute to cultivate because a beneficent victim will treat the wrongdoer as a human being. But in making beneficence a *guiding moral principle* when it comes to forgiveness Enright has introduced a serious flaw into the model of forgiveness. It is that the model is rendered unhelpfully dualistic because it does not engage with the wrongdoing, but only the wrongdoer (and even then without reference to the fact that the wrongdoer has done wrong). It shuts out the place for the victim to make a moral response to the wrongdoing and to integrate that response into the pattern of phenomena that is forgiveness.

It is also worth adding that the moral principles of beneficence and non-maleficence in medical ethics are only two of four widely accepted moral principles: the other two are respect for autonomy and justice. The 'scope' of the four moral principles is also important, that is, one must consider to whom one owes the moral obligations and to what extent one owes those obligations. In making beneficence a binding imperative, Enright is not inviting clients to give attention to the 'scope' of the moral obligation to be beneficent and forgive, which is both naïve and unsophisticated.

In addition, the four moral principles are termed *prima facie*, by which is meant that any one of the principles is binding unless it conflicts with another of the principles. In predicating his model on only one moral principle, Enright is elevating that principle to a binding imperative, without reference to other moral principles that may be relevant. It would be worth at least exploring in the explanation of models of 'forgiveness interventions' whether other moral principles apply. For example, in my view, justice is a relevant moral principle. I also wonder whether holding to a model that predicates forgiveness as the outcome does in fact respect the autonomy of clients: other outcomes are assumed not to be so beneficial (or perhaps not beneficial at all) to the client.

In closing, it will now be apparent that there are some serious flaws in current models of forgiveness interventions. For example, the HDSG

---

[18] *Nic.* ix, 7, 1167b15–1168a30 (in Rowe and Broadie 2002).
[19] Beauchamp and Childress 2001 (first published in 1979) and Gillon 1994.

model of forgiveness focuses on the wrongdoer without focusing on the wrongdoing as well. It fails to address the fact that the wrongdoing has violated the moral order as well as the victim. It is not that the models in use are entirely misconceived: it is that they omit important constituents of forgiveness as understood in other disciplines, such as moral philosophy.[20]

There *is* a moral dimension to forgiveness – an underlying supposition that to forgive is a moral response to a morally wrong act. To choose to forgive for therapeutic, pragmatic or psychological reasons is to choose a less than adequate way to forgive. To forgive requires more than simply a change of thoughts or feelings, the result perhaps of a clinical or pharmacological intervention: the change must also come about through moral engagement with the wrongdoer and the wrongdoing. When victims forgive for moral reasons, they do not have to compromise what they believe to be morally wrong. For example, I do not need to change my view that theft is wrong in order to forgive someone who steals from me. Even if I forgive a thief, I can maintain my view that stealing is wrong.

Forgiveness, then, is a moral issue with psychological implications; it is not a psychological issue with moral undertones. Psychological therapy can help people to explore how to make an appropriate moral response to psychological trauma but the therapy will not – and cannot – bring about forgiveness. At best, and this is very valuable, therapy can bring people to the point where they can choose to forgive or not to forgive.

I suspect that what forgiveness interventions seek to promote is not so much forgiveness as pardon. Horsbrugh (1974: 270) has explored the distinction. A pardon, he writes, is granted to a person (usually by a sovereign state) for a wrong done against the state whether or not the person pardoned is repentant or shows contrition or remorse. A pardon, as Horsbrugh describes it, is not forgiveness but a unilateral act of clemency to a wrongdoer.[21] It is typically given without reference to the moral condition of the recipient and given because the giver wishes to give it. A state may grant a pardon to celebrate a national event, such as the birthday of a head of state. In a similar way, individuals may choose to pardon those who have wronged them: this act, though akin to forgiveness, is not forgiveness as

---

[20] Dr Stephen Cherry has made the observation to me that a neglected aspect of wrongdoing is the hurt that a victim experiences. He observes that this is the starting point of Kroll 2000. I suspect that what forgiveness interventions primarily offer is therapy for the hurt a victim experiences and not therapy for forgiveness.

[21] Benn (1996) uses the term 'quasi-forgiveness' to refer to those who do not forgive the wrongs of another, for example because they were not wronged, but who were closely connected with the victim and who, in relation to the wrongdoer, have eliminated their own indignation and negative feelings. See also p. 8, above.

Horsbrugh understands it. With Horsbrugh's 'pardon', clemency is given unconditionally as an act of mercy. The model of 'forgiveness' in forgiveness interventions is Horsbrugh's 'pardon' – an unconditional act of mercy – with the addition of the victim having laid aside unforgiving feelings.

Having considered forgiveness and psychological therapy, we turn next to consider three affects of unforgiveness that psychological therapy seeks to address – resentment, vindictiveness and revenge – and to ask whether these affects are necessarily undesirable.

## RESENTMENT

Bishop Butler's starting point in his famous sermons on forgiveness in 1718 (Sermons VIII, IX, 'Upon Resentment, and Forgiveness of Injuries' in Gladstone 1995) was that forgiveness was 'forswearing resentment', and this remains the widely held view today.[22] Resentment is a pattern of thought, typically accompanied by anger. What Butler calls 'resentment' Strawson (1968a) has called 'reactive attitudes and feelings' and Murphy calls 'vindictive passions' – having the desire to hurt or hit back, the longing to get revenge or to punish, and so on. Without being resentful, there is nothing to forgive – but this should not lead us into thinking that to forgive is the *only* way to overcome resentment (Neu 2002: 26). Enright (in Enright and Fitzgibbons 2000: 29) recognises resentment to be the starting point for forgiveness: forgiveness takes place, he writes, when people 'willfully [that is, deliberately] abandon resentment and related responses (to which they have a right) . . .'. [23] (It is, though, questionable whether one has a 'right' to a particular reaction. What Enright probably means is that the resentment is not perverse.)

The HDSG model presupposes that resentment is an undesirable psychological state from which a person should be restored. However, it is not always the case that resentment is an undesirable psychological state. Though to forgive may demonstrate 'a highly admirable trait of character', there are occasions when to forgive shows 'flaws of character' (Richards 1988: 80): for example, were I to 'forgive' out of moral cowardice or low self-esteem, then forgiveness may not be the appropriate ethical response to wrongdoing. Resentment may be a normal and appropriate response to

---

[22] See, for example, Downie 1965, Horsbrugh 1974 and Murphy in Murphy and Hampton 1988. Haber (1991: 6f., 21) agrees but offers a more nuanced view, saying that forgiveness can take place even if the process of overcoming resentment has not been fully completed.

[23] I am not drawing a distinction between forswearing (or overcoming) resentment (Butler's starting point) and 'abandoning' resentment (Enright's starting point).

wrongdoing in such circumstances, affirming self-respect. Freedman *et al.* (2005: 400) rightly point out that even having vindictive thoughts can be as much an expression of self-respect as a unilateral act of forgiveness. Resentment can also be an expression of respect for morality and for what the wrongdoer should have been.[24]

The prayer of Elie Wiesel at the commemoration of the liberation of the death-camp at Auschwitz in 1995 perhaps most starkly represents an example of someone being resentful – and of being resentful in an overtly religious context. That resentment fuelled Wiesel's passion to ensure that those who designed, sustained and operated the systems that resulted in the Holocaust remained accountable for their actions. He prayed: 'Even though we know that God is merciful, still, we pray to you, O God: do not have pity on those who established this place. God of forgiveness, do not forgive the murderers of Jewish children . . . O God, O merciful God, do not have pity on those who did not have mercy on Jewish children.'[25] And is this prayer so different from the warnings of conflict that Jesus addressed to those who opposed him (for example, Matthew 10:34–6, 23:1–36) or so out of keeping with the judgment that Jesus said would alight on those who violate the weak, the defenceless and the vulnerable (see, for example, Matthew 18:6f.; Mark 9:42; Luke 17:1f.)?

Enright and the HDSG (1996: 109) further observe that someone who refuses to forgive another because the other has not repented suffers not only because of the wrongdoing but also 'as he or she is obligated to retain resentment, along with its concomitant negative cognitions and perhaps even negative behaviors'.

This statement makes three assumptions. The first is that it is always better to forgive than to be resentful. This is not necessarily so, as I have argued.

The second is that negative behaviour may result from resentment. It is true that sometimes negative behaviour does result from resentment, but not always and not necessarily. What matters is what is morally right in each situation and for the people involved. Some forms of wrongdoing are deliberate acts, intended to violate and degrade the victim, and to refuse to forgive an unrepentant wrongdoer may be a morally, as well

---

[24] Haber (1991: 90) says that people should forgive only if it is consistent with self-respect.

[25] Published in Hebrew in the then Hebrew weekly newspaper in the United States, *Hadoar*, 3 February 1995: 3. One may wonder whether Wiesel in this prayer is not only resentful but also vindictive. Murphy sees resentment as part of a spectrum of 'vindictive passions' (see page 47, above) rather than as something distinct from vindictiveness. On balance, I do not think Wiesel is vindictive because he does not himself intend to take vindictive actions against the perpetrators of the Holocaust and (as I say of resentment on page 47 above) models no more than a pattern of thought characterised by anger.

as a *psychologically*, appropriate way of expressing self-respect and of not endorsing the wrongdoer's abuse.

Rather than promoting negative behaviour, resentment may instead promote morally virtuous behaviour. It may lead people, as it appears to have led Elie Wiesel, to want the following: to right a wrong, to defy and to repudiate the implicit message of the wrongdoing, to secure justice and to restore one's honour and self-respect. These are wholly commendable responses. They arise from care for the integrity of others or oneself, anger about injustice and the abuse of the weak and defenceless, outrage at the violation of the innocent and a passion to put right what is morally execrable. When wisely directed, these feelings and thoughts may lead to acts that are morally virtuous. In such circumstances and so long as the behaviour to which it leads is not destructive, resentment is a moral virtue.[26] The New Testament also seems to recognise this implicitly: in Ephesians 4:26 the writer recognises that one can legitimately be angry and not sin. By extension, one could say that one can be resentful also, and also not sin. What is abhorrent is passivity in the face of wrongdoing: this is an expression of defeat and of accommodation with wrongdoing. If resentment can be rightly channelled and adapted, it confronts, challenges and overcomes the destruction that evil can bring.

It is too simplistic to say that *all* resentment is wrong; it can be a legitimate response to evil and it seems to energise some people to passionate and courageous engagement with issues to do with justice and integrity. Resentful feelings can be the starting point for better things: they can be directed to summon the person who has them to vigorous, decisive, passionate and, most importantly, morally virtuous action. The danger of resentment (and the actions that result from it) is not the fact of being resentful but of acting irresponsibly as a result.

The third assumption is that an unforgiving victim will 'retain resentment'. This also is not always so and not necessarily so. Most people find that even if time does not 'heal', time dulls the fact and memories of the wrongdoing. They also find that it is hard to sustain resentment in the long term. For many there will also be growth and change.

One can go further and say that a headlong rush to condemn resentment and to urge someone to forswear it can have harmful effects on a victim. There may be good reasons why a victim may not *want* to forswear resentment. Some may not want to forgive because they believe that the

---

[26] See Murphy 2003, summarising his earlier work that resentment can be a legitimate response to wrongdoing. See also Hampton (who wrote as a political philosopher and as one within the Christian faith), that '[c]ongregations who refuse to follow their ministers' injunctions to forgive wrongdoers can sometimes . . . be right' (Hampton in Murphy and Hampton 1988: 12).

wrongdoer does not know that wrong has been done or appreciate the full extent of the trauma the wrong caused. It does not even follow that the contrition or repentance of another will result in the person wronged wanting to forgive: as Richards (1988) put it, ' . . . there needn't be a flaw in character in being unmoved by the change in the repentant person'. It may be, for example, that the person wronged disbelieves the sincerity of the wrongdoer, is fearful lest the wrongdoing recur or carries continuing physical harm that makes it hard to put 'closure' on the wrong that caused the harm. It may also be that the wrongdoer is not yet able to set aside thoughts and emotions arising from the violation of the wrongdoing.[27]

What of those who are not *able* to forswear their unforgiving and resentful thoughts and who find they are led into negative behaviour or an undesirable psychological state? Unforgiveness and resentment of this sort do not necessarily respond to rational discourse and can stubbornly contradict one's intentions.

A person may engage in a degree of self-help as a first step to forswearing resentment. There are things that one 'can do indirectly in order to ease . . . negative feelings' and to learn to cultivate the habit and practice of a forgiving disposition (Novitz 1998: 309). Novitz says that fostering an enduring form of pity or compassion eliminates resentment and can make forgiveness possible. He suggests, for example, the following: empathic thinking that understands the wrongdoer's point of view and compassion for the wrongdoer.[28] Barber *et al.* (2005) have shown that those who ruminated on wrongs and fantasised about revenge found it harder to forgive than those who did not.[29] To renounce certain lines and patterns of thought may help avoid the pitfalls of pathological rumination. Novitz's solution will undoubtedly help some but it will not necessarily help all, as he himself recognises. So, for example, if Peter drives negligently and grievously injures Paul, Paul may choose not to ruminate on the wrongdoing, may appreciate that Peter was rushing in his car to hospital to visit his ill mother and may feel enormous compassion for Peter's situation both when he drove the car and now that he lives with a guilty conscience of what he has done to Paul – but none of these means that Paul will necessarily be able to forgive Peter.

If self-help does not produce a successful outcome, cognitive behaviour therapy may be of value. This form of therapy attempts to address the complex relationship between thoughts, feelings and behaviour and can be

---

[27] Dr Stephen Cherry in personal correspondence draws the distinction between 'healthy' forgiveness and 'unhealthy' forgiveness. The distinction is based on the victim's reasons for forgiving.
[28] Hieronymi (2001) disagrees that resentment can be eliminated by pity or compassion.
[29] See also Thompson *et al.* 2005.

of significant benefit to many, but there are some who derive only limited or no benefit from this model of therapy. Thoughts and feelings do not change by performative utterances (*pace* Haber 1991). The capacity to lay aside one's unforgiving thoughts may have as much to do with one's personal history and psychological health as with one's maturity as a moral being – and some people are so damaged by the experience of wrongdoing that they simply cannot lay aside their thoughts and feelings, even with appropriate therapeutic help. Trauma focused therapy may help a significant number of victims of trauma but not all. Lomax (1996), for example, wrote about how The Medical Foundation for the Care of the Victims of Torture helped him to engage with and explore the psychological trauma that he experienced as a Japanese prisoner of war.

Even if cognitive behaviour therapy does not benefit those who have been led into negative behaviour or an undesirable psychological state, the principles of bereavement therapy may help them. The effect of wrongdoing is akin to some of the losses of bereavement – loss of hope, ruptured relationships, disappointment, regrets and so on. Durham (1990) makes the connection between facing loss in bereavement and letting go of resentment and even the desire for revenge.[30] If the victim does the 'grief work' properly, the victim will pass through the stages that a bereaved person goes through in the 'bereavement cycle' (Kübler-Ross 1970) and will resolve the grief, anger and even depression that may arise as a result of the wrongdoing and move on to invest in new things.[31] They will not compromise the truth that they have been wronged, but they will not be paralysed or trapped by it. Rather, they may eventually be able to practise love and compassion, even mercy, towards the wrongdoer – eventually pardoning and perhaps even, later on, forgiving. It is important to note that, just as in the loss of bereavement, what victims think and feel after being wronged and the losses they suffer do not go away. The feelings may, however, diminish in time and the victim can learn to live life around them.

### VINDICTIVENESS AND REVENGE

The desire to seek revenge seems to be innate in human beings, and there is certainly evidence that some primates (besides human beings) retaliate against other animals after being mistreated (see McCullough and Witvliet 2001: 446 for a bibliography of research). There is anecdotal evidence

---

[30] On forgiveness as bereavement, see Pargament and Rye 1998: 61.
[31] This model is taken up in McManus and Thornton 2006.

(e.g., Cose 2004) that the thirst for revenge and retaliation can sometimes result in actions that lead a person to growth and greater maturity, enabling victims to put closure on the issue for which they wanted revenge or retaliation. These actions can transform how a victim feels. Affinito (2002: 106f.) distinguishes vengeance – which she describes as 'an emotional reaction that, centering on the past, seeks only pleasure in witnessing the offender's pain' – from 'punishment', a tool to prevent the recurrence of undesirable behaviour. She presents clinical evidence to show that punishment is an effective response to wrongdoing.

Even so, one is left with disconcerting questions if one chooses the way of revenge and retaliation. For example, how does one measure the quantity of suffering that it is appropriate to inflict on a wrongdoer so that revenge is neither excessive nor too lenient – and who should inflict it? How does one know that retaliation appropriately corresponds to the wrong done – and, in a civilised society, does one necessarily want to carry out (albeit as retaliation) acts that may correspond to heinous criminal acts by a wrongdoer? How can one retaliate or take revenge on behalf of another person (such as a murder victim)? In the case of retaliation by a surviving relative or friend for murder, is it not logical that the murderer's life should be spared and that a person close to the murderer and who corresponds to the murder victim should be put to death? Thus if a daughter is murdered, should not the murderer's own daughter be murdered in like manner – and what is to happen if the murderer does not have such a daughter? Why stop at retaliation by only one person in such a scenario, since there are likely to be many people affected by the murder?

Murphy suggests that the desire to seek revenge and to be vindictive is a legitimate response to having been wronged. It is, he summarises from his earlier work, a way to defend the values of 'self-respect, self-defense, and respect for the moral order' (Murphy 2005: 35).

Taking as the starting point a typical dictionary definition, to be 'vindictive' is to have a strong or unreasoning desire to hurt or harm others in return for an injury or wrong suffered at their hands. Resulting from vindictiveness is retaliation (repayment in kind, or the return of like for like), retribution (recompense for evil done) and vengeance (an act of retribution or vindictive punishment). Vindictive thoughts may result in vindictive behaviour (retaliation, retribution and vengeance), but not necessarily.

At the outset, we can make two important observations about vindictiveness. The first is that vindictiveness, like resentment, can be a moral response to wrongdoing – but with this addition, the desire to hurt or harm the wrongdoer. Second, it is important to distinguish between vindictive thoughts and feelings (these are not morally wrong in themselves) and vindictive behaviour. Vindictive thoughts and feelings can be the starting point that leads to morally *virtuous* behaviour in the course of time. If someone presents in therapy with vindictive feelings, the therapist's task will be to explore the choices the client has and (if the client wishes) how the client can exercise choices that lead to morally virtuous behaviour.

Murphy (2003: 17) offers what he calls 'two cheers' for vindictiveness and an *apologia* for 'the rationality and moral legitimacy of the passion of vindictiveness itself'. He imposes limitations on pursuing vengeance and vindictive behaviour (Murphy in Murphy and Hampton 1988: 31f., 97–103). He gives as examples of 'moderate and proportional' retribution 'a few well selected (and hopefully hurtful) words or . . . actions no more extreme than no longer extending lunch invitations or rides to work' (Murphy 2003: 24, 33).[32] Murphy might be right about this in the social sphere concerning matters of minor wrongdoing that irk, though I doubt it; unaddressed is the question of what one might do when faced with gross moral depravity. The refusal to have lunch with the wrongdoer is not a sufficient response.

In favour of vindictiveness, we can say that it expresses a way to resist evil, to defend oneself and to affirm one's integrity. According to Lévinas (1968: 44), revenge and retribution are permissible if the offer of forgiveness is refused.[33] Even so, it is hard to see how vindictive thoughts can lead to morally virtuous behaviour, and I cannot produce an example.[34] It is also not morally virtuous in most circumstances to hurt or harm people, even if it is in recompense for wrongdoing. For these reasons, it is difficult to explain why, when Jesus cleared the Temple with a whip – no doubt the lashes from the whip hurt – those actions were not vindictive and in what sense they were morally virtuous (John 2:13–22).

I therefore cannot offer any cheers for vindictive behaviour. I offer a muffled and reluctant cheer for vindictive thoughts: they are the result of anger about wrongdoing and the violation of the moral order. When no longer vindictive, they can lead to what is morally virtuous.

## CONCLUDING REFLECTIONS

Questions to do with forgiveness are not new in psychological therapy. In some models of therapy, therapists respond to what clients wish to explore

---

[32] See also Affinito 2002: 106f. on the place of punishing a wrongdoer as a therapeutic outcome.
[33] This is how Ansorge (2000: 80) interprets Lévinas's words.
[34] I discuss the question of punishment at pp. 147–52, below.

and if clients bring issues to do with forgiveness into therapy, then therapists will explore those issues with them, working within the framework that their clients have (moral, cultural, religious, social, and so on) to help them address what they bring into therapy.

What is new is the place of the client (the victim) in therapy. According to Freedman *et al.* (2005: 401), there is a 'large difference between traditional therapies and forgiveness therapy: No therapy before forgiveness therapy has deliberately taken the spot-light off the client and pointed it straight at the offender. The client in forgiveness therapy must step outside of a primary self-focus toward a moral focus on the offender. As paradoxical as this seems for therapy, it works.' As Freedman *et al.* (2005: 404) acknowledge, 'a continued effort with larger samples' is needed to sustain the claims made for forgiveness therapy. Even so, the question that remains disputed is whether 'forgiveness' in such therapy is conditioned and shaped by considerations that a moral philosopher would recognise or whether it is something merely akin to forgiveness – pragmatic, psychologically useful and beneficial but ultimately not just.

What is also new is the *systematic and scientific exploration* of the theory and practice of forgiveness as an aspect of psychological therapy. Also new are the tools and models that people such as Enright and the HDSG, Worthington and others have developed to help those who want to forgive. Results indicate that some who undergo a 'forgiveness intervention' experience a decrease in anxiety and depression and their self-esteem improves (Enright *et al.* 1998). I have some reservations about the tools and suggest that, for the following reasons, they should be used critically and with caution.[35]

Some may see a 'forgiveness intervention' as the *principal* therapeutic method to be used with victims of wrong who have suffered psychological trauma. They advocate forgiveness as desirable for psychological health and well-being. But not every victim needs to forgive; and neither does every victim who is angry, resentful or has other unforgiving thoughts need to forgive. And certainly not every victim has to love a wrongdoer in order to forgive the wrongdoer (Richards 2002: 73–6). Good therapy will explore with clients a *variety* of ways of addressing the trauma, of which forgiveness (whether defined by psychological therapists such as Enright or by philosophers or theologians or others) *may* be one.[36] A recent study demonstrated among patients with substance abuse dependence that

---

[35] See also Richards 2002.
[36] This point is also made in a series of cogent examples by Richards (2002: 78–82).

forgiveness therapy was a successful *addition* to traditional therapies (Lin *et al.* 2004).

Connected to these therapeutic questions is a 'moral question' that Lamb raised in Lamb and Murphy 2002: 9: when is it moral to forgive – and when is it moral not to forgive? To forgive is to make a moral response about a wrongdoer and about the wrongdoing. To forgive is not to practise a psychological technique. Affinito (2002: 89) says, 'Forgiveness is not a technique, though procedures can be described to lay the groundwork for healthy, moral decision making. This is the essence of counseling, helping clients to arrive at practical and emotionally releasing decisions consistent with their moral base.' Therapists cannot properly explore forgiveness as a therapeutic tool without also exploring the answers to these questions.

The ethical issues that forgiveness raises are not straightforward.[37] Psychological models to do with forgiveness, if they are to be morally coherent, need to hold together (in what will be an uneasy alliance) several disparate elements. First, that the wrongdoing was *morally* wrong. Second, that unforgiving thoughts are a *morally* acceptable and appropriate response to wrongdoing. Third, that to forgive is voluntarily to make a *moral* response to a wrongdoer – a response that continues to hold that the wrongdoing was morally wrong but a response that shows the victim chooses to set aside the unforgiving thoughts and to offer the wrongdoer a new start. To 'forgive' another only to improve the quality of one's life so that one is no longer troubled by unforgiving feelings is no more than pragmatism and self-interest.

What comprises a voluntary and moral response to a wrongdoer that means one forgives? There is no straightforward or simple answer. It may be to recognise that both victim and wrongdoer share a common identity as human beings and that the 'family' of humanity is damaged through unforgiveness, that wrongdoing is common to all people (and so the victim is in fact morally little different from the wrongdoer), that the wrongdoer is sorry for having done wrong, that the victim wants to show love and compassion, that the wrongdoer has sought to make amends. All these may be reasons to forgive. They do not exhaust the possibilities. What matters for true forgiveness is that forgiveness is a moral, not a pragmatic, response to a wrongdoer.

Those who promote and practise therapeutic interventions also need to recognise that to forgive is only one of several moral responses to wrongdoing. To be resentful is another response and to have vindictive feelings is yet

---

[37] Puka (2005: 138–43) sets out the difficulties with forgiveness from a psychological viewpoint.

another. It may be, if one can think of moral responses according to a hierarchy, that to forgive is the most morally virtuous response to wrongdoing. (This would seem to be the Christian view of moral responses to wrongdoing.) What is important is that people respond morally and appropriately to wrongdoing and not that they respond morally in one particular way.

Lastly, there is not an agreed definition of forgiveness among psychological therapists and there is considerable unease about those definitions among philosophers (see Lamb and Murphy 2002). The value of forgiveness interventions is open to question if there is such disagreement about what forgiveness in an intervention might mean. The very lack of definition implies that there is no agreement about what forgiveness is, how to recognise forgiveness when it takes place and what the outcomes of a forgiveness intervention are.

Given that the HDSG model does not adequately address the question of the wrongdoing and the victim's response to the wrongdoing, we turn next to that question.

CHAPTER 4

# *Justice and forgiveness*

JUSTICE AND FORGIVENESS

Deeply embedded in the human psyche is the longing for justice. When wronged, human beings yearn for justice, even after the passage of many years.

There are many examples of this longing, and the following are two examples from the press out of many that could be picked. On 21 June 2005, an eighty-year-old former member of the Ku Klux Klan was convicted of the manslaughter of three civil rights workers in 1964. In reported comments after the conviction, some said that they had been 'hoping' for forty years that the arrest and conviction would take place; and others said that the conviction signified that the United States was 'ready to move on to the future'.[1] A month later and in another report, ten former Nazi officers from the 16th Panzer Grandier Division of the Waffen SS were given life sentences of imprisonment by an Italian court for killing 560 people in Saint'Anna di Stazzema, a Tuscan village, in 1944. The massacre was one of Italy's worst civilian wartime massacres. One survivor said that the trial had served to establish 'justice and truth' and that the survivors had 'waited sixty years for this'.[2]

What makes forgiveness difficult to practise comes from the fact that forgiveness is both a moral and a relational issue. It is also one that concerns justice. With forgiveness, it is necessary, on the one hand, to hold to the fact that wrongdoing *is* wrongdoing for which the wrongdoer is morally culpable and accountable. To fail to do so makes light of the wrong in *wrong*doing and the fact that the victim has suffered. This was the argument of Strawson 1968a: if victims do not resent the violation of their rights, they clearly do not take those rights very seriously.[3] It is also necessary, on the other hand, to unshackle both the victim and the

[1] www.timesonline.co.uk, 22 June 2005.   [2] Ibid., 23 July 2005.
[3] See also Smith 1997: 39f. on the relationship of justice and forgiveness.

wrongdoer from the relational consequences of the wrongdoing and, when appropriate,[4] to promote restored relations between them. To fail to do so is irreversibly to lock both wrongdoer and victim into a disordered relationship. To deny or to make light of moral culpability for wrongdoing is unjust; to pursue restored relations without addressing the wrongdoing is also unjust. Forgiveness without justice can be limp, effete and pitiable, giving force to Nietzsche's view that forgiveness is a sign of weakness (see pp. 23f., above). Lévinas (1990: 20) rightly says that a 'world in which pardon is all-powerful becomes inhuman' – and we might add, cruel and unjust. Forgiveness with justice – that is, forgiveness that addresses the moral and relational issues that wrongdoing raises – can be a uniquely powerful ethic for the transformation of people and human society that is neither weak nor morally irresponsible. I disagree with Volf (1996: 123) who argues that forgiveness 'enthrones' justice by 'drawing attention to violation precisely by offering to forego its claims'. He claims that 'we can pursue justice fully' only if we are able to forgive. An *offer* to forgo the claims of justice is not the same as forgoing those claims. Pursuing justice after forgiving is irrelevant because (to adapt the turn of phrase in Kolnai 1973–4) if one has forgiven, there is nothing left about which to seek justice. To my mind, Volf's proposal does not stand up to logical scrutiny.[5]

Some would say that the longing for justice and the ideal of forgiveness are in conflict.[6] For, on the one hand, 'justice' seems to demand that we should hold wrongdoers accountable for the wrong they have done and not allow them to 'get away' with doing wrong. Accountability, if it is to mean anything, includes punishment when appropriate.[7] A Lithuanian

---

[4] See chapter 2, pp. 25f.

[5] The root of Volf's view seems to be in the Jewish writings in the Talmud (on this, see Lévinas 1968: 63).

[6] The conflict has long been noted. God's justice and God's mercy (that expresses itself in forgiveness) are treated as distinct. Milton (1608–74), for example, in *Paradise Lost* (Book III, lines 403–10 in Fowler 1971) suggests a conflict. Thomas (2003: 222–5) distinguishes 'righteousness' ('the exemplification of the highest level of moral goodness') and 'justice' ('not the zenith of moral goodness'). He suggests that 'from the standpoint of moral goodness, it is possible that righteousness could counsel forgiveness, whereas justice does not'. The distinction is difficult to sustain from the New Testament since both words have the same etymological root in the *dikai-* word group and are expressions of the *same* underlying idea. Talbott (1993: 164–6) argues that divine justice requires forgiveness and is not in opposition to it. This conclusion is reached analogously with reference to human examples. It does not follow, however, that what is true of interpersonal forgiveness is also true of divine forgiveness.

[7] Compare Simone Weil whose view is that the victim who forgives must be disinterested, being neither concerned with his or her own interests nor intending to impose a debt of obligation upon the wrongdoer. To be like that, the victim must undergo 'decreation' of the self, a process of renouncing and purifying the self of egotistical interests. The pattern of decreation is the pattern of Christ's *kenosis* in Philippians 2:5–8. On decreation in Weil's thought, see Panichas 1981: 350–6 and Miles 1986: 51–3.

court surely made a morally flawed decision in March 2006 when it convicted Algimantas Dailide, an eighty-five-year-old man, of crimes against the Jews in the Second World War but imposed no sentence because it held that the man was too old and no longer represented a threat to society.[8] Whether pragmatism or compassion guided the court's decision on the sentence is irrelevant: a sentence of some sort, even if nominal, should have been imposed to demonstrate that Dailide had violated the moral order and remained both accountable and responsible for what he had done. 'Forgiveness', on the other hand, seems to urge that wrongdoers should be released from that accountability and that the record of the wrongdoing be erased. With Christian forgiveness, there is another complication: many would say that it should be offered unconditionally, as an act of grace. Justice and forgiveness here seem irreconcilable,[9] for how can one unconditionally release another from moral *responsibility* and moral *accountability* for wrongdoing while continuing to hold the wrongdoer morally *culpable* for the wrong? Equally, how can it be just *not* to punish a wrongdoer (one runs the risk of condoning or overlooking the wrong if one does not punish) but also how can it be forgiving *to* punish a wrongdoer? It is hard to justify that one has forgiven if one also punishes. The act must be taken seriously as wrong, and the wrongdoer must be taken seriously as a responsible and accountable moral agent.[10]

How do people deal with this dilemma? Sometimes victims are told on a day-to-day basis to forgive the wrongdoer and then to 'put away' or 'put behind' them the memory of the wrongdoing. In effect, they are told to 'forgive and forget' or to 'let bygones be bygones'.[11] To preserve the possibility of justice in the future and perhaps of punishment for the wrongdoer, they are also told 'not to forget' about the wrongdoing (e.g., Bennett 2003: 128). The aim of such well-meaning but contradictory advice is to help a victim get on with day-to-day living, without being snared by painful memories about the wrongdoing.

Some may benefit from this advice but most people will probably find it unhelpful, patronising and impossible to put into practice. Besides the

---

[8] *The Times*, 28 March 2006, p. 38. I disagree with Thomas (2003: 220f.) that 'moral outrage [about wrongdoing] seeks neither revenge nor punishment'. This may sometimes be so, but not *necessarily*.

[9] Cf. Garrard and McNaughton (2002: 51, 53–9), who argue that unconditional forgiveness is 'compatible with outright condemnation of the wrongdoing and a determination to fight against it'.

[10] Lévinas (1968: 64) clearly sees this dialectic but argues that when a victim engages with the needs of the 'other' (the wrongdoer), the victim will refrain from claiming the right to retribution and revenge and find 'a straight and secure passage without any hesitation'. This view is simply averred and it is hard to support it except as an aspiration.

[11] On this, see McGary 1989 and Thomas 2003: 208f.

logical absurdity of the advice, it can be criticised on psychological and ethical grounds in at least five ways.

First, and perhaps most importantly, such advice leaves the victim without justice and without hope of justice. It tells the victim to 'forgive' as a self-help tool in order to 'get on' with life. The elements of wrong in the wrongdoing – and also the injustice – are simply not addressed. Kolnai (1973–4: 97f.) puts it with characteristic clarity: such forgiveness 'threatens to collapse into condonation, which perhaps may sometimes be necessary but is an intrinsically bad thing and plainly at variance with the condemnation of wrong which appears [t]o be implicit in the genuine concept of forgiveness, an act supposed to contribute to the eradication of wrongdoing . . . rather than to the fostering of it'. Second, to be wronged is to be affronted and for the dignity of one's personhood to be compromised. As a result, victims may feel devalued and demeaned, and their self-respect undermined. To ask victims to 'forget about' the wrongdoing and injustice they have suffered can reinforce the hurt and communicate that the wrongdoing and its effects on the victim are not being taken seriously. Third, the advice does not encourage victims to deal with their anger and loss: failure to do this can lead in the longer term to depression and other mental illness. Next, a culture that favours forgiveness is a culture that may desensitise people to the evil of injustice and the folly of complying with oppression. Lastly, many wrongdoers think that what they have done does not matter or is not so important as the victim thinks. Those who urge victims to 'forgive and forget' may be seen by the victim as (probably unwittingly) colluding with the pathology of the wrongdoer.[12] In short, 'forgiving unrepentant people for inexcusable injuries seems repugnant, if not impossible' (Calhoun 1992: 76).

Despite what Shakespeare (1564–1616) put in the mouth of King Lear ('forget and forgive'),[13] it is not that one forgets that wrong has occurred and so forgives; one can only forgive because there is something remembered – otherwise there would be nothing to forgive. One forgives when one's attitudes towards the wrongdoer, towards the effect the wrong has had and even towards the wrong itself change, and, because of the changes, one becomes able to forgive. If I am wronged, I may at first be angry, resentful and hate the wrongdoer. In course of time – perhaps with psychological help – I may cease to be so angry and even begin to feel sorry for the

---

[12] Dr Stephen Cherry made to me the observation that it is very unlikely that one can ever *intentionally* forget.

[13] *King Lear* IV.vii.84 in Craig 1964.

wrongdoer.[14] The result is that I become able to forgive the wrongdoer. If I forgive the wrongdoer, it may well be that the unforgiving feelings in relation to the wrongdoing disappear (hence the popular restatement of Lear's aphorism as 'forgive and forget') but not necessarily the memory of the wrongdoing itself. What is also important to note is that the changes the victim experiences are the result of a process of which forgiveness is only part, and one cannot attribute the whole of the change the victim experiences to the fact and act of forgiveness.

There are also genuine psychological difficulties that prevent many victims from reaching a point where they may 'forgive' an unrepentant offender. In such cases, a person who has been wronged may try to suggest to themselves that the wrongdoing was not so severe as it had seemed, that it would be 'Christian' to 'forgive and forget' and that others are in worse plights and 'therefore' it would be wrong to continue to reflect on one's own situation. This may be especially so if the victim is being told to 'move on' and 'get on with life'. What the victim may lose in such a scenario is truth (that the victim has been wronged), psychological integrity (that the victim is deeply hurt or injured) and self-esteem (that it is legitimate to feel hurt or injured by the wrongdoing), and the victim may experience guilt at being unable both to achieve the goals for which the victim longs and to heed the well-meaning (but foolish) advice the victim has been receiving. At best, the supposed 'forgiveness' is a sleight of hand, a self-administered therapeutic tool to recover peace of mind that in the long term will not promote or effect psychological health and well-being. Lomax (1996: 241) wrote of those who told him that it was time to 'forgive and forget': '[t]he majority of people who hand out advice about forgiveness have not gone through the sort of experience I had . . .'.

There is another way that people deal with the dilemma of justice and forgiveness and that is to distinguish between the wrongdoer and the wrong. A victim may seek to forgive an unrepentant wrongdoer, for example, while not forgiving the deed. In effect, the victim says, 'I forgive you but not the deed', a statement that involves a strong measure of dissociation between the person and the deed. This statement is based on Augustine's statement in Letter 211, paragraph 11 (Ramsey 2005) '*cum dilectione hominum et odio vitiorum*', popularly expressed as being that we should 'hate the sin but love the sinner'. Enright's model of forgiveness is implicitly built on such a distinction. Govier (1999: 66) expresses the approach in this way: 'That

[14] Thomas (2003: 212) expresses it this way: '. . . time is relevant to the diminishing of the psychological saliency of having been wronged'.

persons are distinguishable from their actions and are capable of choice, originality, deliberation, autonomy, and moral reform are key tenets of existentialism, humanistic psychology, and respect-for-persons ethical theory . . . The distinction between a person and his or her acts can be drawn, and can be argued to be central, from a logical and ethical point of view.'

Bennett (2003) offers a refinement of this view. He distinguishes between 'redemptive forgiveness' and 'personal forgiveness'. The former is where the *wrongdoer* repents of and atones for the wrong done. The effect is 'to wipe the slate clean' (to use Bennett's term). This is in contrast to 'personal forgiveness' where a *victim* chooses unilaterally to forgive. It is, he says, in effect 'to turn the other cheek' – and is 'compatible with continuing to condemn' the wrongdoing. Forgiveness of this sort accords, he believes, with the 'intuition' that such actions do amount to forgiveness in the sense that he means. Bennett acknowledges that some may regard this not as forgiveness but as 'the beginnings of a process which might eventually lead to (redemptive) forgiveness' (2003: 127, 9; 141).

I remain unconvinced by the attempt to distinguish the person from the deed. Though it is true that people are distinct from their actions, it is questionable whether people and their actions are so unrelated as to be *dissociated*. It is true that my bad actions do not mean that I am a (wholly) bad person, but the fact that I do bad deeds means that I am in part a bad person. If it were otherwise, I would not *want* to do wrong and I would not in fact *do* wrong. To deny that I am partly good and partly bad (and that this is the reason why sometimes my actions are bad and at other times they are good) is to fly in the face of plain common sense and of what I know about myself. As North (1998: 27) rightly observes, there may be some cases when it is 'extremely difficult to separate the wrongdoer from the wrong'. She suggests that this may be so in 'certain horrifying crimes where the wrong is of such magnitude as apparently to defy understanding'.

Finally, Fiddes (1989) takes another approach. Fiddes argues that forgiveness is unconditional and, when unconditionally given, implicitly confronts the wrongdoer with the wrong and so challenges the wrongdoer to repent and to accept responsibility. To forgive requires the victim empathically to engage with the wrongdoer and to endure the wrongdoer's anger and resentment when confronted by forgiveness. Fiddes says that forgiveness offered in this way does not condone the wrong and seeks to facilitate repentance.

Attractive though this solution is, it has two principal difficulties. The first is that there will be no justice for the victim if the wrongdoer does not repent. In such a case, the victim will sustain a double blow: the injustice of the wrongdoing and the injustice of being spurned by a forgiven (but unrepentant) wrongdoer. Second, there is a place for sustained 'moral hatred' towards some wrongdoers: even the example of Jesus, Hampton argues, supports this view. She cites Matthew 10:34–6 and writes that 'Jesus does appear to encourage us to sustain opposition to our moral opponents, and not to reconcile ourselves with them for as long as they remain committed to their bad cause.' Jesus judged some people to be '"rotten" beyond hope and fitted for the fires of hell' and that there are occasions when it is morally right to withhold forgiveness and 'in particular, when too much of the person is "morally dead"' (Hampton in Murphy and Hampton 1988: 149, 153). Fiddes' approach is to oblige victims always to forgive even if there are sound moral reasons not to forgive, and that, in my view, cannot be right, not least because (as I shall argue in the next chapter) to forgive is not a moral duty.

CONDITIONAL AND UNCONDITIONAL FORGIVENESS

The longing for justice is perhaps behind the debate as to whether it is possible to forgive 'unconditionally', that is, without the wrongdoer first having repented of the wrongdoing. We turn now to explore merits and demerits of conditional and unconditional forgiveness.

*The value of repentance*

Some say that there should be no forgiveness until the wrongdoer acknowledges and regrets the wrong, even if one waives one's right to punish a wrongdoer.[15] Others go so far as to say that forgiveness without repentance is morally irresponsible because it leaves the wrongdoer free not to accept that the action was wrong and so free to repeat the wrongdoing.

From a psychotherapeutic point of view, repentance has three elements (and see North 1998: Table 3.2, p. 30, which identifies nine stages in the process of repentance). It is, first, an unforced expression of contrition to the victim for the wrong; it is, second, an expression of contrition for incidental harm caused by the wrongdoing; lastly, it is critical moral self-appraisal and realignment to demonstrate that the wrongdoer has returned to the shared moral order and is committed not to repeat the wrongdoing. The last element means that the wrongdoer disapproves of the former behaviour

---

[15] So Lévinas 1968: 44 and Kolnai 1973–4, for example, but cf. Pettigrove 2004b: 192–6.

and accepts a moral framework – perhaps by acquiring a new moral principle or by recommitment to formerly practised moral principles – both to judge the former behaviour and by which to live in the future.[16] Just as forgiving can be a restorative and healing experience for the victim, so being forgiven can be a healing and restorative experience for the repentant wrongdoer: not only will the wrongdoer have been forgiven but also, by repenting, the wrongdoer will have repaired or restored an aspect of the wrongdoer's moral framework.

Certainly, there are drawbacks to forgiveness without repentance. Unconditionally forgiving a wrongdoer may deprive the wrongdoer both of the incentive and of the opportunity to right the wrong. Wrongdoing usually results from wrongful intentions by the wrongdoer. Unconditional forgiveness lets the wrongdoer escape accountability as a responsible moral agent. Without the wrongdoer acknowledging the wrong, there is the risk that the wrongdoer will not learn from mistakes – either denying that there were mistakes or being uncritical and complacent about what were mistakes.[17]

That is not all. To forgive unconditionally may be to leave the wrongdoer free to do wrong again. It is well known in psychology that people tend to repeat patterns of dysfunctional behaviour unless the behaviour is confronted and addressed. To forgive in this way may be to do the *wrongdoer* no favours and to reinforce the cycle of wrongdoing. It may even be to fail to take the wrongdoing seriously and perhaps to be seen as condoning it.

On the other hand, unconditional forgiveness is attractive because insisting on repentance before forgiving raises some very difficult issues. First, who determines how much repentance is necessary? Second, who determines how the wrongdoer is to demonstrate repentance? Third, who determines whether what is required of the wrongdoer is reasonable or not? Fourth, who determines when the preconditions for forgiveness have been met?[18]

There is also another drawback to insisting on repentance before forgiving: it assumes that fault is on one side only. Often, *both* parties may be at fault – and so both parties may need to repent and to forgive as part of a linked process. What is needed in such a situation, Govier

---

[16] Thomas (2003: 212) makes the important point that 'it is only with the passing of time that certain acts of repentance seem credible'.

[17] It is doubtful that forgiveness – whether conditional or unconditional – can *ever* be 'risk free and rational' (Calhoun 1992: 81).

[18] It does not follow, *pace* Wolfendale 2005: 352, that a victim has a moral *duty* to maintain feelings of resentment and hatred – and so be placed under 'a serious psychological burden' that 'can destroy one's quality of life and one's self-image' – until the wrongdoer repents.

(2002: viii) says, is 'mutual forgiveness', something that 'is barely mentioned in philosophical works on forgiveness'.

## Unknown wrongdoers

People do not always have a choice when it comes to forgiveness. Sometimes, if they are to forgive at all, they may *have* to forgive unconditionally because there can be no possibility of engaging with the wrongdoer or of justice. I offer the following example of unconditional forgiveness. I personally know the person concerned and the circumstances; I have changed some inconsequential details for the sake of the person concerned.

X was a Christian missionary and her home was burgled and then laid waste. She herself was grievously violated during the burglary. The burglary was committed by soldiers who wished to deter Christian missionary activities in the area and by people whose poverty was egregious. The wrongdoers have never been identified or tried. X was able to forgive the people concerned. She reasoned that she had always known that both burglary and physical violation were possibilities, that the motivation for the incident was not personally directed at her but arose largely from poverty and ignorance, that she had voluntarily entered the area knowing the risks, and that the risks were part of what she understood her calling as a missionary to be. In the following years, X has suffered post-traumatic stress disorder[19] about the incident from time to time, but she continues firm in her forgiveness, some forty years after the event. The friends that X has made in recent years are unaware of the incident in X's life and X no longer regards the event as significant for her on a day-to-day basis.

In a personal letter to me about the above paragraph, the person concerned wrote this:

It's not quite true to say I suffered over the years with 'post-traumatic stress disorder'. The amazing miracle to me was that I didn't. God seemed to heal so completely. Of course, for some years I was nervous about being in a room or house by myself at night. Even when I came on leave [to the UK] I didn't like all my outside doors here being glass. I used to imagine them being so easily broken into and had new extra locks put on. But the actual physical trauma was healed by the Lord's touch when we prayed [the Eucharistic prayer at a communion service] in church the next morning '. . . that our sinful bodies may be made clean by his body and our souls washed through his most precious blood . . .'. [God] healed the emotional scars, and miraculously gave me the gift to forgive straightaway.

---

[19] But see the extract from the personal letter in the paragraph below.

Several features of this account are important. First, X recognised that what happened to her was foreseeable and that she had voluntarily remained in post knowing that what did in fact happen had always been a risk. She had anticipated wrongdoing of that kind and had already reflected on how she might react if unfortunately it were to occur. This probably made it easier for her to forgive when the attack did occur. X also was pragmatic enough to realise that there never would be justice, in the sense that the assailants were unlikely ever to be identified and tried. She had probably also anticipated this outcome. Finally, X had never had a relationship with the assailants and was unlikely ever to have a relationship with them. This also would have made forgiveness easier for her.

Unconditional forgiveness of wrongdoers who are not known to the victim is rarely as happy in its outcome as in the case of X. Well known is the example of the late Mr Gordon Wilson who held the hand of his dying daughter, Marie, as he and she lay under the rubble caused by a Provisional IRA bomb in Enniskillen on 8 November 1987. Mr Wilson said on the day of the murder in a television interview, 'I have lost my daughter, and we shall miss her. But I bear no ill will. I bear no grudge. Dirty sort of talk is not going to bring her back to life.' He added, 'I shall pray for those people tonight and every night.' Though he did not use the word 'forgive', he was widely understood as referring to forgiveness in the interview.[20]

What is also important is that though Wilson 'forgave' the perpetrators of the atrocity, he was broken by the experience of the loss of his daughter. In the words of Bole *et al.* (2004: 65), 'Almost a decade after losing his daughter, Wilson still struggled with the original act of forgiveness, with the pain and grief that lay behind his choice to forgive. His ordeal sheds a somber light on . . . the limitations and ambiguities of th[e] whole endeavour of personal and social healing.' Wilson died a psychologically and physically broken man by the experience of the death of his daughter, and even though he 'forgave', he did not find peace and relief through his enormously courageous decision to eschew revenge and bitterness.[21]

### Unconditional forgiveness as a stimulus to repentance

By forgiving unconditionally, a victim may model an act of unconditional love and mercy that stimulates a wrongdoer into repenting (Hampton in Murphy and Hampton 1988: 84) and in consequence be important for the

---

[20] Reported in www.iraatrocities.fsnet.co.uk/enniskillen.htm, accessed on 23 August 2006.
[21] Equally, we do not know what Wilson would have been like had he *not* striven to 'forgive'.

further healing and restoration of the *wrongdoer*. Hampton (in Murphy and Hampton 1988: 86f.) adds that forgiving wrongdoers 'may enable [them] to forgive themselves by showing them that there is still enough decency in them to warrant renewed associations with them'.

This is of course true, and a famous example from the literary world is Jean Valjean's forgiveness of Javert in Hugo's *Les Misérables* (1862), (in Denny 1980). In the realm of public forgiveness, well known is the example of Nelson Mandela who in 1990 was released after twenty-seven years in prison in South Africa. He had been a leader in the African National Congress and imprisoned for holding that armed resistance to the South African *apartheid* state was necessary. When released, he did not receive an apology and he was not offered expressions of remorse or even regret. It would not have been surprising if he had emerged from prison angry and bitter and if he had used his enormous influence to promote revenge and violence. Instead, Mandela modelled and promoted forgiveness and reconciliation with courage and dignity, and strove for a united South Africa. He wrote (1994: 494): 'I knew that people expected me to harbour anger towards whites. But I had none. In prison, my anger towards whites decreased, but my hatred for the system grew. I wanted South Africa to see that I loved even my enemies, while I hated the system that turned us against one another.'

There is little doubt that Mandela's moral authority has made a very significant contribution to South African political history, to the peaceful abolition of the system of *apartheid* and to the emergence of 'the rainbow nation' in which black and white people could live and work together. As Govier (2002: 71) rightly says, 'One could hardly say a person had gone too far with forgiveness if it had helped prevent a major civil war. Anyone who would categorically reject unilateral forgiveness should remember that this [Mandela's stance] was a case of it, and these [peace, reconciliation and transition to black government without civil war] were its effects.'

Despite the example of unconditional forgiveness on the part of Mandela, many of the former oppressors both of Mandela and of those whom he represents have not repented. Mandela's model of unconditional forgiveness has promoted a degree of national peace and reconciliation but not necessarily repentance by some of the individuals involved – or if it has, the repentance appears to be selective. For example, the former President of South Africa, P. W. Botha, refused to appear before the Truth and Reconciliation Commission even when summonsed to do so. The former Law and Order Minister, Adriaan Vlok, contradicted some of the evidence to the Commission of former President F. W. de Klerk (who in August 1996 appeared before the Commission and asked for forgiveness for the years of *apartheid* rule). Despite de Klerk's earlier denials, Vlok testified that while in office de Klerk had known of illegal operations by the security forces against black opposition groups.

### The morality of unconditional forgiveness

Some say there are moral arguments in favour of unconditional forgiveness.[22] Holmgreen (1993: 341), for example, believes that unforgiving attitudes are morally objectionable. She says that 'the appropriate attitude to extend to all human beings – wrongdoers included – is an attitude of real goodwill' (1993: 349f.). Not to forgive assumes that a wrongdoer has not, cannot or will not change, and, in effect, this disrespects the moral integrity and personhood of the wrongdoer. She therefore argues that '. . . forgiveness is always appropriate and desirable from a moral point of view, regardless of whether the wrongdoer repents and regardless of what [the wrongdoer] has done or suffered' (1993: 341). For Holmgreen, forgiveness in these circumstances is an act of 'self-respect': true, victims must work through a process to restore their self-respect, but when (and only when) they have done so forgiveness is always appropriate, whether or not the wrongdoer repents.[23]

Others disagree and argue that if victims forgive wrongdoers unconditionally, they are acting *without* self-respect, apparently putting what they see as moral duty towards the wrongdoer before their own needs and expectations. Inadequate self-esteem and self-respect may sometimes drive victims to 'forgive' (Swinburne 1989: 85–7; Haber 1991: 88; Murphy in Murphy and Hampton 1988: 24–9). There are also times in personal relationships when people 'forgive' in order to avoid confronting painful issues. Such avoidance is not loving, healing or forgiving but something that is deeply destructive (even if it does not appear to be so). Murphy (in Murphy and Hampton 1988: 18 – and sharply attacked by Calhoun (1992: 83–6)) puts it this way: 'If I count morally as much as anyone else (as I surely do), a failure to resent moral injuries done to me is a failure to care about the moral value incarnate in my own person . . . and thus a failure to care about the very rules of morality.' Thus, the violation that the

---

[22] Within the Christian tradition, there is a strong emphasis on unconditional forgiveness: Fiddes 1989, Jones 1995 and Volf 1996; but cf. Swinburne 1989.

[23] See also Garrard and McNaughton 2002: 51, 53–9, Jones 1995: 255 ('we humans are forbidden to repudiate anyone ultimately') and Holmgreen 2002.

wrongdoing entails serves to reinforce that mistaken self-view. It may also suggest a pathologically compliant and quiescent response to wrongdoing. With a biting quip, Perelman (1970) entitled an article, 'To err is human, to forgive, supine.'

An example may make clear some of the issues involved. Jennifer Nicholson was one of fifty-six people killed on 7 July 2005 by a bomb in London. Jennifer's mother, the Reverend Julie Nicholson, publicly stated eight months later that she was not able to forgive those who killed her daughter.[24] In interviews published on 7 March 2006 she spoke of her rage at her daughter's untimely death and her rage at what she saw as evil choices by the bombers. She also suggested that the manner of her daughter's death and the motives of those who killed her rendered the killers 'unforgivable' by other human beings, though Mrs Nicholson recognised that there was 'potential forgiveness' by God in an after life.[25]

It would be only a foolish person who would say to Mrs Nicholson that her attitudes were 'morally objectionable', that she should extend 'goodwill' to her daughter's killers and she should show 'self-respect' by forgiving the killers (*pace* Holmgreen, above). To be angry is not a sin and to lack the capacity to forgive is also not a sin. Murphy's approach is surely the wiser approach, which recognises that unforgiveness can be a legitimate expression of resentment about wrongdoing and of 'care about the moral value incarnate in my own person . . . and the very rules of morality' (Murphy and Hampton 1988: 18).

### Unconditional forgiveness and the moral community

Another line of argument in favour of unconditional forgiveness comes from the view that human beings – wrongdoer and victim alike – share a common humanity. Forgiveness is an appeal to our solidarity with others and to concern for their well-being. Forgiveness in this context means that as members of the same human family we 'have a reason to overcome hostility, and seek each other's good' (Garrard and McNaughton 2002). In addition, no victim is immune from the possibility that he or she might do the same sort of wrong that the wrongdoer has done. All people share the same inclination to moral weakness and all people are capable of doing very great wrong. Not forgiving amounts to a denial of the shared humanity – and shared weakness – of wrongdoer and victim alike.

---

[24] See pp. 18f., above.
[25] www.timesonline.co.uk/article/0,,22989-2073010.html (accessed 17 March 2006).

The argument can be used to the opposite effect. Some argue that 'wrong-doing is a breach of trust between two (or more) people' and that this trust must be restored if there is to be true forgiveness. Restoration of trust is a bilateral process and involves the wrongdoer sincerely repenting of the breach of trust and the norms that go with it (Wilson 1988: 534; but cf. Benn 1996: 373 and North 1987: 505–7). Bennett (2003) argues that victim and wrongdoer are members of 'the moral community', and that the wrong-doer, by the misdeed, has violated the shared norms of the community. The appropriate response is for the community to withdraw recognition that the wrongdoer is a member of the moral community. This means 'that it [would be] no longer possible (or possible only in some extenuated sense) to involve [the wrongdoer] in any dialogue on questions of values or policies or responsibilities, and no longer possible to engage [with the wrongdoer] in a trusting relationship' (2003: 132). Readmission to the moral community will take place if the wrongdoer repents of and atones for the wrong done.

In distinguishing between 'redemptive forgiveness' and 'personal forgiveness' (see p. 62, above), Bennett does not explore whether a wrongdoer who has received the victim's 'personal forgiveness' will also be readmitted as a member of the 'moral community' by virtue of the victim's 'personal' forgiveness. If the wrongdoer is readmitted, then the 'moral community' is not taking the wrong and the wrongdoer seriously – and what would be different, from the point of view of the presence of the wrongdoer as a member of the moral community, if the wrongdoer were, in course of time, to repent and atone for the wrong? If the wrongdoer is not readmitted, what value has the victim's 'personal' forgiveness if the wrongdoer remains ostracised by the moral community but not by the victim?

### Unconditional forgiveness and power

Others have pointed out that not forgiving traps people, in the words of Tutu (1999), in 'victimhood'. They may remain dominated by memories of the wrongdoing and unable to forget about the injury and be disabled by the wrongdoers' abuse of power. Tutu (1999: 219) thinks that it does not matter if the victim's reasons for forgiving arise out of self-interest. Letting go of anger and resentment through forgiving can free a victim to grow and mature and to experience peace of mind. It amounts to 'abandoning your right to pay back the perpetrator in his own coin': this abandonment, though a 'loss', nevertheless, 'liberates the victim' (Tutu 1999: 219). Elizondo (1986: 70) puts it this way: 'The greatest damage of any offence – often greater than the offence itself – is that it destroys my freedom to be me, for I will find myself involuntarily dominated by the inner rage and resentment – a type of spiritual poison which permeates throughout all my being – which will be a subconscious but very powerful influence in most of my life.'

The corollary of this is that forgiving unconditionally denies to an unrepentant wrongdoer the power to stop the victim forgiving. According to his way of thinking, even the powerless have power to forgive and so initiate peace. Unconditional forgiveness may therefore, according to Tutu, initiate a process that can lead to restored relations. For this reason, victims of wrongdoings were pressed, during the hearings of the Truth and Reconciliation Commission, to forgive wrongdoers, even if the wrongdoers had not repented or shown signs of remorse. This was because Tutu, in particular, believed that to forgive was not only good for the psychological health of victims but also good for the future of South Africa.

There are serious drawbacks to the view that forgiving unconditionally denies an unrepentant wrongdoer power over the victim. Wrongdoing is often an expression of oppression or the misuse or abuse of power. Sometimes, if a victim forgives a wrongdoer, the victim will, in effect, be colluding with the abuse of power, and those who urge a victim to forgive may be colluding with and reinforcing not only the particular abuse of power but also structures that sustain that abuse of power. In other words, it would be immoral not to resist the abuse of power. Some might even say that to forgive in such circumstances would be to acquiesce in the abuse, to surrender to it and to discharge the wrongdoers from moral accountability to the victims.

These observations have been particularly explored in two contexts. The first concerns the abuse perpetrated against Jews in the Holocaust. Was the suffering so great and the abuse so horrific that to forgive would be tantamount to denying humanity's revulsion at the wrongdoing? There are many who hold that this is so. The second concerns women who have been physically and psychologically abused. Urging them to forgive may not be in their 'psychological and moral best interests' (Lamb 2002: 156). Forgiving can be a way of avoiding anger and of not confronting the wrongdoer; it may be to comply with stereotypical and oppressive patterns of behaviour that are systemically sustained.

Those who advocate unconditional forgiveness are suggesting – sometimes explicitly – that it *is* possible to forgive without also submitting to the power of the wrongdoer. To forgive in this way is to engage with a wrongdoer within an alternative framework – a framework that denies the wrongdoer's right to abuse and to be abusive but that does not repay in kind. It is much like Jesus at his trial before Pilate and the Jewish authorities: though Jesus was himself on trial, he insisted throughout that he was the one with true power (Matthew 26:53, 64). By his actions and responses, he yielded to the Jewish and Roman accusers without also yielding to the postulates they held about their power and authority. Though it is true that some who forgive unconditionally can do so without yielding to the abusive power of the wrongdoer, it is palpably evident that this is not always the case.

I have suggested that to forgive may be an expression of power, as well as a refusal to submit to the abusive power of the wrongdoer. A surprising example of unconditional forgiveness as an expression of power – perhaps even of the misuse of power – concerns the late Pope John Paul II. An attempted assassination of the Pope was made on 13 May 1981 by Mehmet Ali Agca, an escaped convict from Turkey. Shortly afterwards, John Paul II prayed in a broadcast from his hospital bed 'for that brother of ours who shot me, and whom I have sincerely pardoned'. Later, in 1983, John Paul II visited Mehmet Ali Agca in prison and after the visit again spoke of his forgiveness. We do not know whether Mehmet Ali Agca had asked to be forgiven.[26]

The act of forgiveness was a magnanimous act but one wonders whether it was in part shaped by the unequal balance of power between Pope John Paul II and Mehmet Ali Agca. Though the pontiff had been shot and grievously injured, he was not affected by oppressive structures of power but was a broker of power. One wonders whether he would have found it so straightforward to forgive if he had been an escaped convict who had been shot by the security forces of an oppressive country.

## Summary and example

In summary, it is difficult to make out a cogent case for unconditional forgiveness. With very few exceptions, examples of unconditional forgiveness are rare and usually ambivalent. The effect of forgiving unconditionally can be an expression of powerlessness, a sentence of injustice for the victim and an escape route for the wrongdoer from moral accountability and responsibility. It often fails to engage with the relational aspect of forgiveness and denies the wrongdoer the opportunity to understand the effects of the wrongdoing from the victim's viewpoint. In short, though occasionally

---

[26] Dr Stephen Cherry in personal correspondence has drawn my attention to the fact that 'we do not have the context of [the Pope's] struggle (if any) to come to the point of forgiveness – and so [the account of his forgiveness] is decontextualised / idealised . . . The end result is to generate guilt in those who . . . cannot do this and pressure on others to move to what I would called "unhealthy unconditional forgiveness".' (See p. 50, note 27 above, for Dr Cherry's distinction between 'healthy' and 'unhealthy' forgiveness.)

unconditional forgiveness may be the only form of forgiveness open to a victim (for example, where the wrongdoer has died or cannot be identified), it is usually better to approach forgiveness from a bilateral point of view. Doing so enables victims and wrongdoers to hold fast to the fact that wrongdoing is wrongdoing and that the wrongdoer is morally culpable and accountable for the wrongdoing. The result is that the victim is more likely to be unshackled from the effects of the wrongdoing – whether relational or psychological – and restored relations more likely to be re-established.

In his autobiography, Eric Lomax offers a striking example of bilateral forgiveness of this sort.

Lomax had been a Japanese prisoner of war and participated in the construction of the now notorious Burma–Siam railway that was intended to link Bangkok and Rangoon. Lomax was one of five British prisoners who were interrogated and tortured for possessing a radio and a map. One of the torturers was Nagase Takashi, an officer in the *kempeitai*, the military police, who was translator during a series of especially brutal interrogations at Kanchanaburi.

For nearly half a century, Lomax remembered the translator (whose name he did not know until 1989: Lomax 1996: 225f., 240–2, 255, 269) with hate and fantasised about doing to the translator what the translator had done to him. Lomax wrote:

The more I thought about it, and thought about it, the more I wished to do damage to the Kempei men if I could ever find them. Physical revenge seemed the only adequate recompense for the anger I carried. I thought often about the young interpreter at Kanchanaburi . . . [B]ecause of his command of my language, the interpreter was the link; he was the centre-stage in my memories; he was my private obsession . . . [He was] the only one with a face and a voice, the only one I had ever been able to endow with a personality across the years.

Lomax was eventually able to trace Nagase through a Japanese newspaper article published in 1989 and established that Nagase was apparently deeply repentant for his actions,[27] and in particular for his part in the torture of Lomax. Lomax continues: 'I felt triumphant that I had found [Nagase] . . .

[27] For example, Nagase built a Buddhist temple at the site of the bridge by the river Kwae, organised meetings to promote reconciliation (especially between Thailand and Japan), was active in pacifist causes and set up a charitable foundation for the survivors of the *romusha*, the Asian 'slave' labourers used by the Imperial Japanese Army to build the railway line. Lomax interpreted the actions of Nagase Takashi in Lomax 1996: 251–3 as expressions of profound penitence for his war crimes, and, later on, this helped Lomax to reach the point where he could forgive Nagase. However, Nagase's actions would almost certainly have been shaped by the Buddhist view that all sins are capable of being cancelled by good works and that it is possible to build up a store of merit by one's good works that cancels the negative effect of one's sins and demerits. Two of Nagase's actions, namely building religious monuments and meritorious interpersonal acts, are particularly noted for building up one's store of merit. On the quest for merit in Buddhist thought, see Fürer-Haimendorf 1979: 180–9.

[but] [i]n my moment of vengeful glory, triumph was already complicated by other feelings. This strange man was obviously drawn on in his work [of repentance and atonement] by memories of my own cries of distress and fear.' Lomax traces his own doubts about the genuineness of Nagase's repentance and admits that, in 1989, 'I was not inclined to forgive, not yet, and probably never.' He considered murdering Nagase – and, after deciding against that, sought to 'make Nagase suffer fully for the consequences of his actions' by surprising him at a meeting. In course of time, Lomax found out more about Nagase (partly through reading Nagase's autobiography) and began to realise that Nagase's repentance was almost certainly genuine. After reading a letter addressed to his wife from Nagase, Lomax wrote, 'In that moment I lost whatever hard armour I had wrapped around me and began to think the unthinkable: that I could meet Nagase face to face in simple good will. Forgiveness became more than an abstract idea: it was now a real possibility.'

In 1995, Lomax and Nagase did meet. Nagase expressed to Lomax his deep remorse and the remorse had been amply demonstrated by Nagase's actions in the half century after the ending of the Second World War. Lomax did not regard the meeting itself or the passing of time as a sufficient expression of forgiveness. Nagase's longing for Lomax to express forgiveness meant that Lomax needed formally to express his forgiveness. 'I could no longer see the point of punishing Nagase by a refusal to reach out and forgive him. What mattered was our relations in the here and now, his obvious regret for what he had done and our mutual need to give our encounter some meaning beyond that of the emptiness of cruelty. It was surely worth salvaging as much as we could from the damage to both our lives.' In a private encounter in Tokyo, Lomax read out to Nagase a letter expressing his forgiveness, thereby expressing formally his irrevocable and irreversible decision to forgive.

ATONEMENT

The idea of atonement attempts to take seriously moral responsibility for the wrongdoing and attempts to put right both the fact and the effect of the wrongdoing. It is, in effect, an attempt to give justice to the victim.

In the philosophical literature on the subject, views about forgiveness without atonement vary from its being morally wrong or inappropriate to its being permissible or desirable (Garrard and McNaughton 2002). Swinburne (1989: 81–4) sets out what he believes to be the four elements of atonement: repentance, apology, reparation (restitution or compensation for the harm done) and penance (doing something extra, such as offering a 'costly gift' that goes beyond reparation in recompense for the wrong).[28] Some argue that it is just to forgive where there has been 'atonement' for the wrong.

Kant's view is that neither forgiveness nor full atonement is possible.[29] Once wrongdoing has taken place, no amount of pleading for forgiveness (even of God) and for mercy can undo the violation of the moral laws on which the universe is predicated. The only hope is to make amends for one's sins and to live rightly in the future. Only then will there be a change of heart such that people become 'new' (echoing the idea of re-creation in 2 Corinthians 5:17). The former, sinful person will still be punished for the wrongdoing – but the new person will not. A repentant person who asks for forgiveness is, according to Kant, asking the impossible because the person who committed the wrong no longer exists and because the effect of wrongdoing cannot be reversed. There can, therefore, *never* be atonement, forgiveness or restoration.

Kant is right that human forgiveness does not – and cannot – undo the past or free people both from the consequences of what they have done[30] and from what Arendt (1958) calls 'the predicament of irreversibility'.[31] In this sense, the wrongdoing remains unforgivable. For the same reasons, human atonement also cannot undo the past or free people from the consequences of what they have done. It may express remorse, regret, penitence and contrition. As Bennett (2003) suggests, atonement may ameliorate the consequences of the wrongdoing and result in the wrongdoer being readmitted to the 'moral community' – but (*pace* Bennett) atonement will not (and cannot) undo the wrong itself or unpick the past.[32]

---

[28] The response of Zacchaeus to Jesus (Luke 19:1–10) illustrates Swinburne's point.

[29] See Sussman 2005 for an exploration of forgiveness in Kantian thought. Sussman argues that Kantian thought does accommodate the idea of 'a truly redemptive forgiveness' (p. 86).

[30] Cf. Lévinas (1969: 283) whose view is that forgiveness undoes the past and gives the wrongdoer another chance.

[31] The predicament of irreversibility is undoubtedly true but does not take into account that actions may have a range of consequences and within that range there may be – and often are – some consequences that are positive in their outcome. For example, it is not possible to integrate within the predicament of irreversibility the fact that change for good took place within Nagase as a result of his inhumanity to Lomax (and others). (I am grateful to Dr Melanie Bash for this observation.) This does not mean that one should deliberately act immorally in the hope that good consequences will arise (as Paul says in Romans 6:1f.), or that one holds to the view of the Catholic Latin Mass, formerly used on 'Holy Saturday', the day between Good Friday and Easter Sunday, in which is the line, *O felix culpa quae talem et tantum meruit habere redemptorem* ('O blessed sin [literally, happy fault] which has as its reward so great and so good a redeemer').

[32] Compare Swinburne (1989: 87f.) who argues that a victim cannot prevent a wrongdoer's guilt from being lifted provided that the wrongdoer has disowned the wrongdoing, offered sufficient atonement and sincerely sought forgiveness.

In Christian theology, atonement – in the sense of an efficacious way to undo and reverse the 'predicament of irreversibility' – is only through the cross. In contrast, atonement by a wrongdoer is a form of reparation or a course of action that expresses an apology, remorse and penitence for previous wrongdoing. An example of such a course of action might be if a former armed robber sets up an organisation to help victims of violent crime. Murphy (2003: 81) is right to say that such actions can 'earn . . . the forgiveness and love of the person victimized', though I would want to add that the forgiveness and love are not a *quid pro quo* but an expression of grace, inspiring and precipitating a change of heart in the victim.

The actions of Nagase described in Lomax 1996 are slightly different. Nagase did repent of his actions and spent much of the rest of his life demonstrating his repentance (of that and other wrongdoing in which he participated) by charitable and benevolent works in memory of those who built the Burma–Siam railway line. These actions convinced Lomax that Nagase's repentance was indeed authentic repentance; they helped to generate the 'forgiveness and love' of which Murphy wrote (see above). But Nagase's actions were also more than expressions of repentance and contrition: in them there was also an element of seeking atonement for guilt. This was in part a response to Buddhist theology, which was explained to Lomax as being 'whatever you do you get back in this life and if what you have done is tainted with evil and you have not made atonement for it, evil is returned to you in the next life with interest' (Lomax 1996: 269 and see note 27, above). The dread of hell for the evil he had done during the Second World War and the desire to atone for that evil in part drove Nagase's actions. Lomax's forgiveness helped 'release' Nagase from the burden of his guilt and shame and (according to Nagase's viewpoint) from evil in the next life.[33]

Acts that amount to repentance may, however, greatly help the wrongdoer. We can see this in the epiphanous experience of 'pardon' (*sic*) that Nagase experienced in 1963 (Lomax 1996: 251–3), eighteen years before Lomax met and subsequently forgave Nagase. Nagase wrote in his autobiography of an experience at the war cemetery at Kanchanaburi in 1963 after eighteen years of repentance and atoning works: 'The moment I joined my hands in prayer . . . I felt my body emitting yellow beams of light in every direction and turning transparent. At that moment I thought, "This is it.

---

[33] This raises the question whether Nagase's repentance was as authentic as Lomax thought, for it was, in part, apparently impelled by self-interest and not necessarily by genuine remorse for his wrongdoing.

You have been pardoned." I believed this feeling plainly.'[34] Even so, this was not enough for Nagase who clearly felt the need for Lomax's forgiveness (and not just because this would have added to his stock of merit for the life to come).

Even though atonement does not (and cannot) undo the past, it may make forgiving a wrongdoer a morally responsible act. Victims will not be compromising the fact that the wrongdoing was wrong; they will not be making light of what happened to them; and they will not be ignoring the fact that the wrongdoer violated them and the moral order. By atoning for wrong, wrongdoers demonstrate that they acknowledge that they did wrong and will seek to put right what they can. Though the moral consequences of the wrong are irreversible, the relational consequences are not, and there is no necessary reason why victims should not forgive if they are able to do this. Kolnai (1973–4: 101) says that in such a case the act of forgiveness will 'eliminate the offence from the texture of [the] relationship', thereby ensuring that the creative and transformative effects of forgiveness can take place. Even so, as Garrard (2003: 237) rightly argues in relation to some particularly horrific actions, repentance does not provide a reason for forgiveness. She writes, 'Some evildoing is so great that later repentance just seems irrelevant – there are some moral journeys from which there is no returning down the repentance route.'

How can one tell if the wrongdoer's repentance is genuine? Moule (1998: 23) makes an interesting suggestion and links the Parable of the Prodigal Son in Luke 15:11–32 with other sayings of Jesus on the subject of forgiveness (e.g., Matthew 18:21–35).[35] Moule observes that the concerns of the wrongdoer should not only be directed to the person offended (this is self-evident) but also extend in forgiving compassion towards other people. He says: '[The prodigal] will not really have repented, he will not have accepted his parent's forgiveness . . . until he is able to treat those who wrong him with as much generosity as he has received from the forgiver.' Thus, it is how the prodigal reacts to the older brother that will determine whether he has truly repented and so received forgiveness, for '[i]f he has accepted forgiveness from his father, he will himself be forgiving towards his brother'. Repentance involves a thoroughgoing inner moral transformation such that the wrongdoer, when forgiven, will behave differently in encounters with others and will, for example, be able to practise and

---

[34] See p. 73, note 27, above, on the Buddhist notion of good works cancelling the negative effects of sins and demerits.

[35] See also the account of Zacchaeus in Luke 19:1–10 where the genuineness of Zacchaeus' repentance was demonstrated by reparation and penance.

model the forgiveness that the wrongdoer has personally experienced. This accords with the teaching of Jesus on forgiveness set out at pp. 93–7 below and points to the fact that forgiveness when offered and received can reorder and restore relationships.

Is it appropriate for a wrongdoer, who is contrite and repentant, to ask the person wronged for forgiveness? The request may be covertly expressed in the form of an apology. If the spirit of the wrongdoer is to barter or if the wrongdoer is, in effect, seeking to manipulate or goad the person wronged into forgiving them, then the answer is 'no', for the repentance then will not be being freely offered but offered in the hope of personal benefit.[36] If the request for forgiveness is genuinely a request, with the contrition and repentance unaffected by the response (whatever it may be) of the person wronged, then the wrongdoer may ask for forgiveness. The issue is *why* the wrongdoer seeks forgiveness. If it is so that the wrongdoer will feel better, it is sought for morally suspect reasons; if it is for the sake of the victim out of regret and contrition, then the wrongdoer's request is probably morally appropriate.

### FORGIVENESS AS A MORAL IDEAL

Notwithstanding that the idea of unconditional forgiveness is difficult to defend from a pragmatic, practical and philosophical point of view, most people still believe that to forgive unconditionally is a moral good and sometimes represents what is noble and virtuous in human beings. We consider this further in chapter 6. First, and in order to address the question more fully in chapter 6, we consider the New Testament on the subject of forgiveness.

---

[36] See p. 73, note 27 and p. 76 above, in which I suggest that Nagase's repentance was at least in part impelled by hope of gain through Lomax's forgiveness.

# CHAPTER 5

# Forgiveness and the New Testament

Most people would agree that a defining characteristic of Christian faith is to forgive. If we were also to ask the same people if Christians are to forgive the unrepentant, the answer would again be 'yes'. Most people can quote the cry of Jesus on the cross 'Father, forgive them, for they know not what they do' (Luke 23:34)[1] and the words in the Lord's Prayer in their traditional form, 'forgive us our trespasses as we forgive them that trespass against us' (based on Matthew 6:12 and Luke 11:4).[2] It is fair to say that the idea that forgiveness is integral to, and a moral imperative of, Christianity is part of the unconscious narrative of many people.

Jones (1995: 133, 216, 219–20) describes forgiveness as being 'embedded' in the meta-narrative of the Bible. To forgive is an attribute of God – part of the essential being of God – and human beings, whom God made in the image of God, are to be forgiving. By this, Jones means that human beings are to practise the self-giving love that characterises God. The corollary of this is that people are not to be unforgiving.

Given these things, the astonishing fact is that there is relatively little about forgiveness in the New Testament.

Paul the apostle mentions forgiveness only rarely – and that, despite the fact that in popular understanding forgiveness is a significant category of Pauline thought. Of the synoptic writers, Luke writes the most about forgiveness (though even that is relatively little) and Matthew and Mark

---

[1] It is widely doubted that these words are part of the original Lucan text, although the manuscript evidence is finely balanced. Even if the words are authentic, it should be noted that *Jesus* did not forgive the sins of those who were crucifying him but that he prayed that *God* would. What his words do model is the dominical command to love one's enemies, even in the face of appalling abuse and violation.

[2] Which is forgiven: sins or sinners? On the one hand, in the Lord's Prayer, God is entreated to forgive trespasses, not trespassers (Matthew 6:12/Luke 11:4 – and see also Matthew 6:14; Mark 2:7, 11:25; 1 John 1:9, for example) – but in the same prayer, the supplicant forgives other trespassers, not trespasses. Elsewhere in the New Testament, such as Colossians 3:13, sinners forgive other sinners, not sins.

barely at all.[3] John in his Gospel says nothing explicitly about forgiveness.[4] Yet it is undeniable that forgiveness is central to Christian faith and *praxis*. Any statement of the Christian gospel that does not have forgiveness as one of its foci is a misstatement of the gospel.

Forgiveness in the New Testament, though presented as straightforward, is the subject of considerable scholarly debate and discussion, and it is to this that we now turn.

## REPENTANCE, JOHN'S BAPTISM AND FORGIVENESS

In recent years, an important question that has been implicit in discussion about John's baptism is whether John's baptism, a 'baptism of repentance for the forgiveness of sins' (Mark 1:4 and Luke 3:3), together with repentance, brought about forgiveness (see Webb 1991, Taylor 1997 and Klawans 2000). Webb (1991: 190–4), for example, says that baptism was a rite that mediated forgiveness, that it was the channel through which God forgave sins and that John was the mediator of that forgiveness. At issue is whether baptism and repentance *ex opere operato* bring about forgiveness. If they do, to forgive would be a divine duty and God would be morally obliged to forgive when certain preconditions (baptism and repentance) were met.

### Repentance and forgiveness

Certainly, repentance lay at the heart of John's message.[5] In essence, repentance means a change of attitude and action by 'the disobedient' towards 'the Lord their God'. It results in restored relationships (such as between parents and their children) and a return to 'the wisdom of the just' by those who had deviated from that wisdom (Luke 1:16–18). Examples of John's insistence on repentance and its ethical outworking are in Luke 3:7–14 (addressed to the crowds, tax collectors and soldiers) and Matthew 3:7–10 (addressed to the Pharisees and Sadducees).

In the phrase 'baptism of repentance' in Mark's Gospel (Mark 1:4) and in Luke's Gospel (Luke 3:3),[6] the word 'of repentance' in Greek is either a subjective genitive (repentant people were baptised) or possibly epexegetic

---

[3] Bash and Bash 2004: 29.   [4] Cf. John 20:23.

[5] Luke 1:16, 3:3; see also Josephus, *Ant.* 18.117 (in Thackeray *et al.* 1926–65), *The Gospel of the Ebionites* 3 ('John . . . baptised with the baptism of repentance in the river Jordan' in Ehrman 2003a) and *The Gospel of the Nazareans* 2 ('John the Baptist baptises for the remission of sins' in Ehrman 2003a).

[6] 'Repentance' (*metanoia*) in the phrase 'baptism of repentance' is a noun: much more typical would be for the idea to be expressed by a participle, namely, a baptism for people who were repenting (or who had repented). This is the sense of the text.

(the baptism involved repentance or repentant people) (Turner 1963: 211, 214). It is also possible that the genitive could be a genitive of purpose, indicating that the people were baptised in order to show that they were repentant. Whichever it is does not make a great deal of difference because all three indicate that the baptism was associated with repentance, that repentant people were baptised and that the baptism was an indication or expression of their repentance.

Matthew's version of John's baptism (Matthew 3:1–6) omits the phrase 'a baptism of repentance for the forgiveness of sins', though Matthew also emphasises that repentance and confession of sin were at the heart of John's baptism. Matthew refers to the water of John's baptism as being 'for repentance' (3:11), meaning that the people were baptised because they had repented.[7] The order of events remains the same: John calls the people to repent (3:2) and baptism with confession of (previously repented) sins follows (3:6). There was no baptism without repentance: in Matthew 3:8 John upbraided the Pharisees and Sadducees who came for baptism because they had not already repented.

Matthew probably omits the phrase 'a baptism of repentance for the forgiveness of sins' because he emphasises that it is through Jesus' death that sins are forgiven (see, for example, Matthew 1:21, 26:28) and he wants to prevent his readers and hearers from thinking that forgiveness came through baptism. He also wants to ensure that his readers and hearers understand that the focus of baptism is the coming Lord. Forgiveness of sins is mentioned in 26:28 where Matthew makes it clear that it is the 'poured out' blood of Jesus that effects forgiveness.

In the synoptic Gospels, repentance is not a moral virtue in itself and its end is not baptism, though baptism was its sign. Its end was to ensure that people were ready and prepared 'for the Lord' when he came,[8] for he was the one – and not baptism and repentance – that brought forgiveness. In all three synoptic Gospels, those who received the 'baptism of repentance' were signifying, through the public expression of their repentance, that they were ready for the one of whom John spoke. Luke specifically alludes to God's future salvation – and this includes forgiveness by implication – that would come with the coming of the Lord (Luke 3:6).

John did not tell those who repented to go to the priests to offer sacrifices to atone for their sins (e.g., Luke 3:10–14).[9] This might suggest that

---

[7] *Eis metanoian* (for repentance) in Matthew 3:11 is causative.

[8] Mark 1:3; Luke 1:16f., 76; Matthew 3:3, 11f.

[9] Josephus implies in *Ant.* 18.117 (in Thackeray *et al.* 1926–65) that the people did not also make offerings in the Temple for their sins. This inference can be drawn because, since the sins of the people were excused, there was no need for them also to make offerings.

forgiveness had already come about through repentance. So, for example, Dunn suggests that John did not do so because he 'offered his own ritual as an alternative to the Temple ritual', and that 'baptism took the place of the sin-offering' without a priest. '[M]ore likely', says Dunn, the repentance expressed by the baptisand is 'the effective agent in achieving the forgiveness or excusing the sins confessed' (Dunn 2003: 360). John's role was a priestly role (Dunn 2003: 359) and the baptism John offered was a ritual effecting atonement (Klawans 2000: 139, 143; Thyen 1971: 132, 135 and 167). If this is right, there may perhaps be some connection with 1QS 3:6–9 (in Vermes 1987) where a 'humble submission . . . to all the precepts of God' will result in a person's sins being atoned (but cf. Webb (1991: 146–51) who suggests that immersion in the Qumran community cleansed a person not only from ritual defilement but also from sin).

There is a much more straightforward explanation as to why the people did not offer sacrifices for their sins. It is because John and the people expected atonement and forgiveness to come through the coming kingdom of heaven (Matthew 3:2), the salvation of God (Luke: 3:6) and the baptism with the Holy Spirit (Matthew 3:11, Mark 1:8, Luke 3:16). To have said otherwise would have been to divert people from seeing the true source and place of their eschatological hope and to have distracted the people from looking forward to the coming of Jesus who, as we shall see, was to bring *aphesis* (freedom, liberty, forgiveness).

We see perhaps most clearly in Matthew's Gospel (in the account of the death of Judas Iscariot) that repentance does not automatically bring about forgiveness of sins. Judas deliberately betrayed Jesus in exchange for money (Matthew 26:14–16)[10] and after the arrest of Jesus realised he had done wrong and deeply regretted his actions. It would be right to say that he repented, because he appears to have recognised that his actions were, before God, *morally* wrong. The Greek words almost invariably used in the New Testament to express the idea of repentance are either a verb, *metanoeo*, or the verb's cognate noun, *metanoia*.[11] Of Judas a different verb is used, *metamelomai* – a verb deliberately used by Matthew perhaps to point the reader to the fact that Judas' repentance did not lead to forgiveness.[12] Even though Judas realised he had sinned (Matthew 27:4), it seems that he despaired about what he had done and did not believe that he could

---

[10] Cf. Luke 22:3–6 and Mark 14:10f. where the money was to be paid after the betrayal.

[11] Cf. Matthew 21:32, but here the meaning is that the chief priests and elders did not change their minds and believe John's message, *not* that the chief priests and elders did not repent of sins.

[12] The same verb also occurs in Matthew 21:29, 32; 2 Corinthians 7:8 (twice); and Hebrews 7:21. See also Psalm 109:4 (LXX).

or would be forgiven.[13] The chief priests and elders to whom he sought to return the money were indifferent; they refused to take it back, and by implication did not offer Judas absolution for what he had done, presumably to avoid acknowledging their own complicity. Matthew 27:5 says that shortly afterwards Judas committed suicide,[14] an action sometimes characteristic of people who feel hopeless, helpless and trapped, and think that there is no way out of the situation they face.

### Baptism and forgiveness

Did baptism result in a repentant person's sins being forgiven? The phrase 'baptism of repentance for the forgiveness of sins' could be interpreted that way.[15] Baptism was a rite that already existed in the Jewish cult, and we now consider whether contemporary Jewish baptismal practices help to interpret John's baptism and to answer the question whether baptism brought about forgiveness of sins.

Jewish immersions were in a bath called a *miqveh* and were for the removal of ritual impurity (e.g., Numbers 19:10–13, Leviticus 13, 14:8f. and 15) and (probably only from the second century AD) for proselytes. In contrast, under the Jewish sacrificial system, only a priest atoned for sin. It is important, therefore, to distinguish between ritual impurity under the Jewish cult and sin (Sanders 1985: 182f. and Taylor 1997: 94). John's baptism was different from these immersions as it was not for the removal of ritual impurity but an expression of repentance from sin.

John's baptism is also different from the water purification practised in the Qumran community: there, in keeping with other Jewish traditions, water purification was for the removal of ritual impurity, not sin.[16] There may be a point of connection: at Qumran, following instruction in the

---

[13] Matthew 26:24 supports this interpretation, as it implies that Jesus' betrayer would face damnation.

[14] Cf. Acts 1:18f. which says that Judas kept the money he was paid and died either from illness or from an accident (according to what *prenes genomenos* in verse 18 means). There is also an account in Papias (in Ehrman 2003b) that Judas died when he was run over by a wagon. Given that the sources we have are so diverse, we cannot be sure about what really happened.

[15] There is a widespread view that through John people experienced forgiveness. Nolland's solution (1989: 142f.) is to suggest that John offers forgiveness 'ahead of time' and that it takes on 'distinctly the quality of readiness for the arrival of the Lord'.

[16] Cf. Klawans (2000: 90): 'At Qumran, sin was considered to be ritually defiling, and sinners had to purify themselves.' Webb (1991) denies that the Jews of the period distinguished between 'soul' and 'body'. Consequently, he argues (e.g., p. 195) that John's baptism was a bodily washing that cleansed the whole being of sin. He also suggests that immersion in the Qumran community cleansed a person not only from ritual defilement but also from sin. In 1QS 3:6–9 (in Vermes 1987) the distinction between sin and ritual impurity is obscured. The following references to Qumran literature may be found in Vermes 1987.

ways of the community, an initial immersion took place to rid the body of ritual impurity that had occurred outside the community (1QS 3:9). Earlier immersions that had taken place outside the community – immersions that would have taken place before the baptisand had accepted the teaching of the community and repented of not following the ways of the community – would not have purified and the person would have remained unclean (1QS 3:3–6). In this sense, both John's baptism and immersions at Qumran were initiatory in that they both indicated a turning from unrighteousness to righteousness, but neither was a rite of initiation into a new community. The connection is that 'immersion is pointless without prior cleansing of the heart (the inner self) through repentance and the practice of righteousness' (Taylor 1997: 81). This connection may be no more than coincidental and does little to elucidate the essential point of John's baptism, which was certainly not about ritual impurity.

Josephus also comments on John's baptism (*Ant.* 18.116–19) and does appear to suggest that his baptism brought about forgiveness.[17] He links baptism with ritual purification, says that John's baptism was for the 'purification of the body' and – inconsistently with Jewish tradition – adds that the bodily purification was because 'the soul had been cleansed already by righteousness' (*Ant.* 18.117). Josephus also links John's baptism to the 'excusing' of the sins (*epi tinon hamartadon paraitesei*)[18] of those who were baptised (*Ant.* 18.117).[19]

Is there syntactical and theological support for Josephus' view that baptism and turning to righteousness remitted sins?

Syntactically, the answer turns on the meaning of the word *eis* in the phrase 'for [*eis*] the forgiveness of sins'.[20] *Eis* can be interpreted purposively (meaning that people were repentant with this purpose or end in mind, namely, that their sins should be forgiven) or causatively (meaning that people were repentant because their sins would be forgiven). Turner (1963: 266) thinks that *eis* in this context is purposive, encapsulating the idea 'with a view to', and distinguishes it from Acts 2:38 where the forgiveness on the Day of Pentecost was 'on the basis of' the forgiveness of sins

---

[17] The references from Josephus are taken from Thackeray *et al.* 1926–65.

[18] *Pareitesis* can also mean 'request' (e.g., for pardon). When the word occurs with other words from the *hamart-* word group in other phrases in Josephus, it generally carries with it the idea of 'excuse'. In *Ant.* 3.238, 241 *pareitesis* means 'expiation'. See also *Ant.* 3.221, 246, 247; 11.137, 233 (in Thackeray *et al.* 1926–65).

[19] See Taylor 1997: 96–100. Taylor's view is that 'John's immersion was wholly in keeping with other Jewish immersions of the time in having to do with ridding the body of uncleanness, but it also entailed the different idea that previous immersions and ablutions were ineffective for Jews without the practice of true righteousness' (pp. 99f.).

[20] The same phrase is in Luke 24:47.

(causal), though (if preferred on theological grounds) 'with a view to' is also possible.

A purposive interpretation of *eis* means that we can interpret John's baptism in the eschatological setting of his preaching. The 'excusing' of sins – forgiveness – was through the one of whom John spoke, and came in the future, after John's death. This meaning of *eis* points not to forgiveness as a result of repentance and baptism but as a result of the coming and ministry of Jesus. Even if the meaning of *eis* is causal (indicating that John's baptism was 'because of' the forgiveness of sins), the phrase is still consistent with the broader picture in Luke-Acts. The baptism indicated repentance from sin and that the people were ready to receive the gift of forgiveness. What *eis* points to is something that was to come, not something that the people had already received or experienced.

The broader social and theological setting of John's baptism lends support to this conclusion. First, despite what Josephus seems to imply in *Ant.* 18.117 (in Thackeray *et al.* 1926–65), in the Jewish milieu in which John lived it was understood that righteousness came about though sacrifice in the Temple and not through turning to righteousness. Second, since 'it is highly unlikely that the early Christians would willingly attribute forgiveness to any means other than faith in Jesus Christ',[21] one cannot imagine the synoptic writers taking over the phrase so uncritically if it contradicted the idea of forgiveness through faith in Christ.[22] Matthew has clearly wanted to avoid any ambiguity on the point by omitting the phrase 'for the forgiveness of sins' in Matthew 3:1–6. Third, Luke is particularly clear that John's baptism did not bring about forgiveness of sins. In Luke-Acts, the heart of John's message is that salvation was at hand – John's task was to inform ('give knowledge' to) the people of that – and that that salvation was to come about 'in' (through, by means of or (perhaps even) as a result of) the forgiveness of sins (Luke 1:77).[23] Salvation was from the coming universal judgment and depended on repentance (evidenced in John's baptism) and a future baptism in the Holy Spirit (Luke 3:16f., Mark 1:8 and Matthew 3:11). That John's baptism did not itself bring about forgiveness of sins is

---

[21] Webb 1991: 172.

[22] Cf. Webb (1991: 171) who notes that Luke is careful to distinguish between John's use of the phrase 'repentance for the forgiveness of sins' and later Christian usage (such as in Luke 24:27; Acts 2:38 and 10:43, where people are forgiven on account of their faith in Christ) and says that the Christian reinterpretation is 'a fundamental shift from the significance of John's baptism'.

[23] This Semitic usage reflects the meaning of the inseparable preposition *beth* (in = *en* in Greek) in an instrumental sense. I am grateful to Professor P. J. Rhodes in personal correspondence for informing me that *en* may properly have an instrumental meaning here (and see Turner 1963: 252f. but without citing this verse). Professor Rhodes believes that Luke used *en* rather than *dia* at this point for variety to avoid repeating *dia* which is in verse 78.

evident from Acts 13:24 and 19:4 where the baptism is described as being 'a baptism of repentance', the implication being (as Acts 2:38 makes clear) that the forgiveness of sins came through Jesus Christ. For Luke, the water of John's baptism signified not cleansing from sin or from ritual impurity but repentance. John was the forerunner of another, and his ministry was not to forgive but to point others to and prepare them for that person. That person, not John, would establish 'the way of peace', that is, reconciliation between humanity and God, and between people in conflict (Luke 1:79).

The most likely explanation of John's baptism, therefore, is that the baptism was an outward sign of inner repentance. It expressed that the people were ready to receive the person of whom John was the forerunner. The people believed that that person was the long-awaited saviour of Israel who would bring, among other things, forgiveness of sins. Baptism indicated that the people were ready to receive the saviour and the forgiveness of sins he would bring. According to the synoptic Gospels, baptism did not automatically produce the forgiveness of sins.

This conclusion has an important implication for our discussion. It is that forgiveness was the gift of God to those who received the salvation that 'the coming one' brought and, on syntactical and theological grounds, that forgiveness was not necessarily given in response to baptism and repentance. With God, just as with human beings, forgiveness is a gift and to forgive is not a duty. Receiving God's forgiveness is part of receiving God's gift of the saviour.

This still leaves open the question, why did John baptise? Why did John choose a rite that was open to a degree of misinterpretation if it did not cleanse and bring about forgiveness of sins?

The answer is straightforward and the synoptic Gospels point to it. It is that the synoptic writers interpreted John's ministry as looking forward to the one who was coming and whose baptism would be not in water but with the Holy Spirit and fire (Luke 3:16, Matthew 3:11; cf. Mark 1:8). The baptism of the Holy Spirit – symbolised in and prefigured by water baptism – demonstrates that God has forgiven a person's sins. Water baptism envelops a person and washes away dirt. Luke emphasised that the baptism of the Spirit also enveloped (and even indwelt) people (Acts 2:1–4) and had a cleansing effect because the baptism was like fire (that purged) and wind (that blew away dirt).[24] According to this interpretation, neither John's water baptism nor the baptism with the Spirit brought about forgiveness of sins: rather, they point to what forgiveness of sins means.

---

[24] John in his Gospel also links the idea of receiving the Spirit with the forgiveness of sins (John 20:22f.).

JESUS, REPENTANCE AND FORGIVENESS

The synoptic Gospels indicate that forgiveness is God's gift, given out of grace to those who seek God's mercy. In Luke 18:9–14, the Pharisee who in prayer rehearsed his self-righteousness – and by implication his supposed entitlement to what Luke terms 'being justified' – assumed that God had nothing to forgive him for; in contrast, the tax collector who in prayer could cry out only 'God, be merciful to me, a sinner' *was* justified and (by implication) forgiven.

## Jesus and repentance

Jesus, like John, preached that people should repent. In Jesus' teaching, repentance and faith go together (e.g., Mark 1:15); repentance and faith are evidenced by changed lives and forgiveness is the result (Luke 24:47). People demonstrated that they were repentant by the way they responded to Jesus. Jones (1995: 121) observes that within Christianity there is an assumption that repentance is 'an indispensable component of the habit of forgiveness'. He also says that God '*requires*... the conversion of [wrongdoers] through a turning to their particular victims to seek forgiveness and reconciliation' (1995: 127).

Repentance was integral to Jesus' message and that of his disciples (*pace* Sanders, and see, for example, Mark 1:15, 6:12; Matthew 4:17), but Jesus' notion of repentance was not always as the law prescribed and recognised. Repentance remained a response to God's gracious call (as it had always been in Judaism) but restitution, Temple sacrifice and obedience to the law were not always necessary to demonstrate it. Some did voluntarily accede to the demands of the law without prompting from Jesus: Zacchaeus the tax collector in Luke 19:1–10 is a case in point. Sometimes Jesus said that people should make an offering according to the law, though it is possible these are later glosses: see for example, Mark 1:44.

Jesus permitted most people to demonstrate repentance according to the ethic of the kingdom of God, 'contextualised within the announcement of God's inbreaking Kingdom' (Jones 1995: 110). For example, the sinful woman in Luke 7:36–50 demonstrated her repentance by anointing Jesus: her humility and evident brokenness also confirm that she was repentant. In response to criticism that his followers were not repentant but remained 'sinners', Jesus told parables about 'joy in heaven' (Luke 15:7) and 'joy before the angels of God' (Luke 15:10) over each one who repents. Immediately following is the Parable of the Prodigal Son that celebrates the father's joy over his repentant son (Luke 15:11–32).

Sanders (1985: 108, 322) says that there 'is very little evidence which connects Jesus directly with the motif of collective, national repentance in view of the eschaton' although he does affirm that Jesus did not repudiate the idea of repentance (Sanders 1985: 112). Such material as there is has been added, according to Sanders, by the evangelists. Jesus did not preach about repentance 'because he understood that John had taken care of that part of the overall task' of preparing people for the kingdom.

As to personal repentance, Sanders (1985: 206–8, 323) offers a 'speculative' suggestion that the 'offence' Jesus caused in Mark 2:7 (paralleled in Luke 5:21) was that Jesus offered sinners inclusion in the kingdom while they were still sinners and without requiring them to repent. The condition was that sinners accept him and his message that promised them a share in the kingdom as they were.[25] The result is that 'he could have been accused of being a friend to people who indefinitely *remained* sinners'. In other words, Jesus welcomed and included those who heeded him (because he was convinced of the imminent *eschaton*) and did not require repentance as the law prescribed but offered it in a more informal way. In contrast, John the Baptist, also convinced of the imminent *eschaton*, preached repentance and righteousness (but not sacrifice in the Temple). Sanders concludes: 'Jesus offered companionship to the wicked of Israel as a sign that God would save them, and he did not make his association dependent on their conversion to the law.' That Jesus did not require sinners to convert to the law and to repent was 'the most distinctive aspect of Jesus' own message'. Sanders suggests that in the period of the early church this was changed. Luke, for example, reintroduced the idea of repentance in his Gospel and in Acts; and the material in the Sermon on the Mount on the law and repentance is later material, attributable to Matthew or to a pre-Matthaean author or editor.

Sanders' view that Jesus did not call for national repentance has been challenged on two grounds: first, that the distinction between national and personal repentance is unsustainable; and, second, that Jesus *did* call for national repentance (e.g., Wright 1996: 256). In addition, to dismiss repentance as a central (albeit often implicit) motif in Jesus' teaching is to take Jesus out of his Jewish milieu and to ignore the moral changes that took place in the lives of many who responded to Jesus. Such changes are expressions of repentance, often expressed outside the typical pattern of the law, and the result of encountering Jesus. With Jesus, forgiveness is not contingent on the presence of particular forms of repentance or the fulfilment of stipulated criteria, though both may properly occur. With Jesus, forgiveness is a

---

[25] Alternatively, the objection of the scribes may be not because Jesus had pronounced forgiveness (see pp. 90–2, below) but because Jesus did not require the paralytic to offer a sacrifice after being healed.

gift, given out of love and given sometimes in unexpected ways. As with the man who wanted to 'inherit eternal life' (Mark 10:17–22, Matthew 19:16–22, Luke 18:18–23), it is not a case of fulfilling laws and of assuming that by rights one is entitled to – and that God is duty-bound to give – what one expects. Forgiveness is not earned; neither is it deserved. It is the gift of the forgiver, given in response to the ideal that it is morally virtuous to forgive.

One may interpret Jesus' approach to repentance under the law in one of two ways. One is to say that Jesus rebalanced the law's requirement to repent with other requirements of the law, such as to show love and mercy. In effect, Jesus implicitly questioned the accepted view of the hierarchy of requirements and, in particular, questioned whether the result of that hierarchy was to undermine the intent and purpose of the law. Matthew 23:23 illustrates this point, for example: Jesus condemned the scribes and Pharisees for obscuring the requirement to show justice, mercy and faithfulness by what he regarded as an excessively formal approach to tithing. Jesus forgave (for example, those outside the covenant community because of their sin) without *in some cases* also insisting on the usual expressions of repentance: this is a legitimate, albeit different and untypical, expression of the law's requirements when properly balanced in the situation to which they were being applied.

The other approach is to suppose that Jesus recognised that the law's demands sometimes posed a threat to what the law purposed. To adhere to the requirements of the law could produce, in some circumstances, an undesirable result that contradicted the moral good that the law intended. For example, it was accepted that to leave an animal trapped in a ditch on the Sabbath was wrong, even though to rescue the animal meant to work, in breach of the fourth of the Ten Commandments (Matthew 12:11f.). Always to insist on repentance may be another example of undoing the good the law intended, especially if the person concerned was outside the covenant community because of sin. Jesus relaxed the rigour of the moral requirements so as to achieve an outcome that accorded with the end that the law sought to achieve. Jesus therefore forgave outside the law's requirements and did not insist on the typical signs of repentance prescribed by the law (for example, restitution and sacrifice), while at the same time upholding and affirming the moral claims of the law. Philosophers would say that forgiveness in such a context is a supererogatory virtue, that is, it is given in 'adherence to the claims of impersonal morality prior to their modification to accommodate the normal limitations of human nature'. The result is that 'some of the starker conflicts' between 'morality and the good life' are 'softened by . . . reductions of moral demands due to tolerance' (Nagel 1986: 204).

*Jesus, forgiveness and the kingdom of God*

For Luke, forgiveness is at the heart of the message of the kingdom of God. The word that is most commonly used for forgiveness in Greek (*aphesis*) occurs at two programmatic points in Luke's Gospel, the ministry and message of John the Baptist and Jesus' so-called 'Manifesto at Nazareth'. *Aphesis* is much more than simply about forgiveness: it also denotes release and freedom from what constrains people – whether from sin and its effects, from physical oppression or captivity, or from the consequences of not having 'the salvation of God' (Luke 3:6) and 'the Lord's favour' (Luke 4:19).

The first of the two programmatic points is Luke 3:3–6, when John called the people to repentance and baptism with a view to the forgiveness that was to come with the arrival of the Lord and his salvation. The second is at the start of Jesus' ministry when, in a Galilee synagogue, Jesus quoted Isaiah 61:1f. and set out his future ministry (Luke 4:16–21). The good news of the gospel was that 'release' or 'liberty' (*aphesis*) was promised to those who were 'captives' with the coming of the kingdom of God. The kingdom was a new order that God would introduce: it would, for a time, coexist with the material world of the present.

Forgiveness is the gift of God at the *eschaton* when the kingdom of God is consummated. Luke's point is that God's forgiveness is for the age to come: it is part of the *aphesis* of the kingdom of God. We also know from elsewhere in Luke that forgiveness (as well as the healing and salvation that came with the kingdom) could be experienced in the present. Such experiences anticipated and were foretastes of future blessing – they were proleptic, because the kingdom, though inaugurated, had yet to be fully established. Until the kingdom will be established, forgiveness is to be practised and its future forms demonstrated in the present among Jesus' disciples. In other words, forgiveness is an ideal of human conduct, modelled on the eschatological forgiveness of God.

*Did Jesus forgive sins?*

Jesus forgave sins (if that is what he did) on only two occasions (a paralytic in Luke 5:20, 23 and a sinful woman in Luke 7:48),[26] not with words of absolution but with a verb in the perfect passive (literally, 'your sins have been forgiven') without specifying by whom, how or when. This use of the verb in Mark 2:5, 9 (corresponding to Luke 5:20, 23 and Luke 7:48) points,

---

[26] The healing of the paralytic in Luke 5:17–26 is also in Mark 2:1–12 and Matthew 9:2–8. The story of the sinful woman is only in Luke 7:36–50.

according to Jeremias (1971: 11), to divine action (i.e. Jesus was speaking for God). Sanders, in considering Mark 2:5, 9, says that Jesus is not making a claim to divine status as one who himself forgave sins (Sanders 1985: 273). Both Jeremias and Sanders are right: Jesus here was not arrogating to himself divine power to forgive but was confirming and affirming the eschatological fact that God in mercy had forgiven the paralytic and the sinful woman. Indeed, he would not have arrogated such power to himself, as it would have been blasphemy to do so.

In the story of the healing of the paralytic (Luke 5:17–26), some friends of a paralysed man let him down through a roof so that Jesus could heal him. Jesus said to the man that his sins had been forgiven. Onlookers interpreted this statement as blasphemous. In response Jesus healed the man to demonstrate 'that the son of man has authority on earth to forgive sins' (verse 24).

Leaving aside for the time being the question whether Jesus did in fact claim to forgive sins, why might the onlookers have taken offence? There are two reasons. First, in the Jewish mind, there was a connection between physical illness and sin.[27] When Jesus healed the man (Luke 5:24), he demonstrated (according to the way of thought of the time) that the man's sin had been forgiven. Second, as Dunn rightly suggests, offence arose because Jesus had pronounced forgiveness (and, I would add, healed the man) 'both *outside* the cult and *without reference* (even by implication) to the cult' (Dunn 2003: 788, echoing Sanders 1985: 301). This constituted blasphemy because it appeared to offer another route to forgiveness that was independent of the cult.

However, these are not the reasons that Luke gives for the offence. The reason Luke gives is in Luke 5:21. It is that the onlookers understood Jesus to be claiming that he himself *did* forgive sins. Jesus himself appears to have confirmed that view with the words '. . . that you may know that the son of man on earth has authority to forgive sins' in verse 24. What we have, therefore, are two strands in the story, one in which Jesus pointed to God as the one who forgave and another in which he pointed to himself as one who also could forgive.

There is undoubtedly a conflict in the two strands of the story. The most likely resolution is to say that the earlier strand records Jesus affirming that God forgave the paralytic and healing him in demonstration of that forgiveness.[28] The other strand is from a later period and suggests that the

---

[27] See John 9:2f. for an example of this way of thought.
[28] Hooker (1991: 84) suggests that the original story may have been Mark 2:1–5a, 11f., omitting even the phrase '"My son, your sins are forgiven"'.

story has been developed to address Christological issues in the early church or, according to Hooker (1991: 84), to justify the claim of the early church to forgive sins in the name of Jesus.

The same development can be seen in another Lucan story, Luke 7:36–50. In this story, Luke recounts how a prostitute lavishly and effusively anointed Jesus, to the embarrassment of Simon, a bystander, who thought that Jesus should not have been touched by such a person. The point of the story is that the woman's actions reflected her gratitude for having been forgiven her many sins. Jesus affirms that her sins had been forgiven (verse 48): his words cannot be words of absolution because the woman knew – and her actions demonstrated this – that her sins have *already* been forgiven.[29] The only way to take the words is, as Jeremias (1971: 11) suggested, as pointing to divine action (i.e. Jesus was speaking for God). In the light of this, the reaction of the onlookers in verse 49 ('"Who is this that even forgives sins?"') is incongruous, and suggests that here, as in Luke 5:21, the idea of Jesus forgiving sins is a Lucan addition to the story.

## *Jesus, the forgiving victim*

Jesus exemplifies what it means to forgive. What marks out Jesus is, for example, his capacity not to respond to lies, violence, hatred, wrongdoing and the other forms of human evil directed against him – and that he did not respond in kind. In 1 Peter 2:24, it is said of Jesus that he 'bore' humanity's sins on the cross. In this context, the sins that are being referred to are the varieties of human wrong actions that were directed personally against Jesus. More than that may also be meant: implicit may also be the idea that what Jesus suffered symbolised or represented the range and extent of all other forms of human sinfulness too. By bearing humanity's sins, Jesus brought about 'healing' of humanity's condition (1 Peter 2:24) and left an example to follow (1 Peter 2:21).

Jesus modelled what it means to be abused and to be powerless and voluntarily to remain that way. Jesus eschewed summoning more than twelve legions of angels (Matthew 26:53) in order to master those who were to destroy him. On the cross Jesus prayed that the Father might forgive his executioners their sins (Luke 23:34).[30] His own personal forgiveness – given

---

[29] Verse 47a also confirms this: Jesus says that the woman's sins 'have been forgiven' – a verb in the perfect passive tense.

[30] Judaism made provision for the forgiveness of unintentional sin (Leviticus 4:22–31 and Numbers 15:27–9), which is why Jesus affirmed that 'they know not what they do'. The ignorance was not in the soldiers's crucifixion of Jesus (this was clearly their deliberate purpose) but in their lack of understanding of the true horror of their actions in relation both to Jesus' innocence and to Jesus' role as sin-bearer of all human wrongdoing. See also note 1, above.

to unrepentant people as a gift that was not asked for, expected or even sought – is implicit in these words, but his words did not *absolve* the killers, that is, by the words he did not purport to remove the wrongdoing from the divine record, thereby obviating the need for the Father's forgiveness.[31] What is evident at this point in Luke's account is the humanity of Christ, and what Luke is emphasising is that Jesus, in the context of brutal and unjust suffering, modelled the ideal of forgiveness, without at the same time being vengeful, angry or defiant. He thereby set an example of what later could be called 'the Christian ideal of forgiveness'.

The approach of Jesus – non-retaliatory and not vindictive – is in contrast to those who are unforgiving and seek revenge. The difference between being forgiving and being unforgiving has to do with power. Being unforgiving may express a wish to exercise power – power over the offender – in order to exact retribution and to redress the sense of powerlessness that the wronged person may feel. It is also a way to restore the imbalance in the power relation between wrongdoer and victim: the wrongdoer abused the victim, and so the victim, to 'get even', exacts revenge or retribution. Though the wrongdoer has been repaid in kind, both are now victims. In contrast, Jesus chose to remain powerless and to surrender to the evil against him. Paul takes up this theme, particularly in 2 Corinthians, and argues that voluntary powerlessness is the means by which divine power can be demonstrated and is the conduit of the power of God (2 Corinthians 1:8–10, 2:14f., 3:5, 4:7–12, 12:9).

### DIVINE AND HUMAN FORGIVENESS[32]

In the Parable of the Unforgiving Servant (Matthew 18:23–35) we see how divine grace shapes human relations and, in particular, how people should forgive one another. This parable, though central to the idea of forgiveness in the New Testament, is only found in Matthew's Gospel. It is worth exploring the parable to see the point that it makes.

A man owed a king ten thousand talents. This sum is almost unimaginably enormous. According to Josephus (*Ant.* 17.320 in Thackeray *et al.* 1926–65), the total tax on Judaea for one year amounted to six hundred talents. The sum remitted in the parable is more than sixteen times this amount. The king remitted the whole debt when the man entreated him.

---

[31] Many early manuscripts omit the prayer and its authenticity is frequently questioned.

[32] In this section, I have not commented on the 'unforgivable sin' of blasphemy against the Holy Spirit (Luke 12:10, Matthew 12:31–7 and Mark 3:28–30). I believe that blasphemy against the Holy Spirit is to deny that Jesus is empowered by the Holy Spirit to save people from their sins. See further the discussion of the passages in Bash and Bash 2004: 36f.

An important element in the story is the fact that waiving debt and forgiving are related ideas in the New Testament. (Letting someone off a debt is not the same thing as forgiving someone, since owing money is not a sin. Even so, the two ideas are connected: Bash and Bash 2004: 34f.) After leaving the king, the man refused to remit a debt that a fellow servant owed him. The debt was one hundred *denarii*, the equivalent of about three months' wages of a day labourer.[33] On hearing of the man's hard-heartedness, the king rebuked the man for his lack of mercy after the man himself had received mercy (verse 33). The king required the man to repay his former debt and imprisoned him until he should do so.

The point of the parable is that forgiveness is a gift to the undeserving, often of unimaginable generosity. In the New Testament, the experience of such a gift is regenerative, transformative and paradigmatic.[34] Thus, forgiveness should lead to change, and the change should affect other relationships: in particular, a person who has experienced the gift of God's forgiveness should strive to forgive others. The failure of the man whose debt of ten thousand talents had been remitted was not that he failed to forgive but that he failed to *want* to forgive and that he failed to *try* to forgive.

This last point is expressed rather more strongly in the parable in verses 33 and 35. These verses apparently say that those who receive mercy *must* show mercy to others and those who are forgiven *must* forgive others. The implication is that if they do not do these things (rather than simply wanting and trying to do them), they will forfeit God's mercy and forgiveness.

This language is certainly hyperbolic, for no one can be merciful in the way God is merciful, and no one can be forgiving in the way God is forgiving. Human beings are not duty-bound to forgive precisely as God does. At best, people can act imitatively – but deficiently –, aspiring to practise the divine pattern of forgiveness but never attaining it. What verses 33 and 35 mean is that human beings should strive to practise the ideal of forgiveness that God models. Human beings will inevitably fail adequately to do what God can do. There is a clear link between receiving God's forgiveness and seeking to forgive others – and a clear link between God's *continuing* forgiveness and forgiving others. Human beings have been given a moral virtue to practise and an ideal to follow, but, because of the human condition, they can never fully attain it.

The same issue is evident in the Lord's Prayer. What does the word 'as' (*hos* in Greek) in the phrase 'forgive us our sins, as we have forgiven

---

[33] See Matthew 20:2 on payment for a day's labour.
[34] The same idea is in Matthew 7:2 (on judgment) and Matthew 7:12 (on behaviour towards others).

those who sin against us' (Matthew 6:12; Luke 11:4) mean? Does it mean that if – and only if – I forgive others God will, in some sort of *quid pro quo* arrangement, forgive me?[35] If that is the right view, the bestowal of divine grace is dependent on human beings being forgiving. This is clearly impossible because God's love and forgiveness are not, and cannot be, earned. Another interpretation of the phrase is that God will forgive people 'in the same way' or 'in like manner' that they forgive others (Kierkegaard in Hong and Hong 1995: 380).[36] This would be a prayer asking that, when people forgive those who sin against them, in like manner God would continue to forgive the forgiver. Divine forgiveness is given, according to this view, on a 'like for like' basis. Even this is not a satisfactory explanation, because the capacity to forgive principally arises from God having first forgiven. It also means that human forgiveness limits the extent of divine forgiveness and makes it no more than a correlate, on a reciprocal basis, of human forgiveness. A better interpretation is that the word *hos* in this context means 'since', meaning that, since people have forgiven others (and so demonstrated what it means to be transformed by God's forgiveness), God may continue to forgive the forgivers, unlike the unjust steward who forfeited forgiveness through being unforgiving.

Mark 11:25f. also has to be seen within the broader picture of the transformative power of God's forgiveness. According to Jesus in the passage, whenever people pray, they are to forgive anyone towards whom they have been unforgiving 'so that' – indicating a result of having been forgiving – God would forgive them their sins. The verse that follows is not in all manuscripts ('but if you do not forgive, neither will your father who is in heaven forgive you your trespasses'), but reinforces the point. Matthew's version of the saying (6:14f.) is even more explicit: 'if people forgive others, then God will forgive the forgivers – and God will not forgive those who do not forgive others. Luke 6:37 ('. . . forgive, and you will be forgiven') makes the same point (though here it is not clear whether human or divine forgiveness is the result of forgiving others).

## INTERPERSONAL FORGIVENESS

How and when are people to forgive others? Is the ideal that victims should forgive only if the wrongdoers repent or is the ideal that forgiveness should

---

[35] This is the view of Pokrifka-Joe (2001: 166f.).

[36] See also Mark 11:25b where *hina* meaning 'so that' (indicating result) is used. Verse 26 (not in all MSS) makes the same point.

always be practised regardless of the attitude, reaction or response of the wrongdoer?

Certainly, the ideal is that victims should forgive repentant wrongdoers, even if the wrongdoers repeatedly do wrong. Some of the rabbis had suggested (Davies and Allison 1991: 793) that a person should forgive another three times. In Luke 17:3f. Jesus says human beings 'must' forgive – and go on forgiving – seven times a day. The number seven indicates completion or perfection, and what Jesus means is that, no matter how many the wrongs are and no matter how frequently they recur, a victim must go on forgiving a repentant wrongdoer.

By an argument from silence, the ideal is also that a victim should always strive to forgive even an unrepentant wrongdoer, no matter how many times the wrongdoer does wrong. In Matthew 18:21f., Peter asks Jesus how many times he is to forgive another. Peter suggests it might be as many as seven times. Jesus' answer is that forgiveness is to be offered many more times than that – four hundred and ninety times in all.[37] Peter's question does not distinguish between repentant and unrepentant wrongdoers and the answer, by implication, is that both repentant and unrepentant wrongdoers are to be treated identically.

What Jesus' answer points to is that forgiveness, in all circumstances, is to be not only lavish but also impossibly generous – 'impossibly' generous because, if the number seven expresses the idea of completeness or perfection, a greater number suggests an impossible (and illogical) increment. The same idea of lavish abundance is in Mark: when people pray, they are to forgive if they have 'anything' against another – and, presumably, to forgive without the repentance of that other (Mark 11:25).

The story of the woman who anointed Jesus (Luke 7:36–50) illustrates and refines these principles, and introduces a difficulty. The passage refers to a prostitute who lavishly anointed Jesus. A Pharisee named Simon observed the woman's actions and was critical that Jesus allowed such a person to touch him. In response, Jesus told a parable about a creditor who forgave two debtors: one debtor was forgiven 50 *denarii* and the other ten times that sum. In response to a question, Simon agreed that the more grateful debtor would be the one remitted (i.e. forgiven) the larger sum. Jesus then applied the principles of the parable to Simon (the sum of whose sins was not much) and to the prostitute (the sum of whose sins was great).

---

[37] There is debate as to whether the number Jesus stipulated is seventy-seven times (seventy plus seven) or 490 times (seventy multiplied by seven). See Davies and Allison 1991: 793. Whichever is right makes little difference, for the point is that forgiveness is not to be limited.

Jesus makes the point that there is a correlation between the extent to which people are forgiven and the extent to which they are changed as a result. Those who are 'forgiven little' – because they have done little wrong – will, he says, love little in response (verse 47b). One would have expected Jesus also to say that those who have been 'forgiven much' because of their many wrongs would love much in response. This would also be the expected inference from the preceding parable about debt that Jesus gave (Luke 7:41–3). The woman's lavish treatment of Jesus would then have been explicable as an expression of her heartfelt gratitude for being forgiven so much.

Jesus does not say what we expect to read about those who have sinned much. Jesus says of the woman that she was forgiven because (the Greek is *hoti*, indicating causation) she loved much, implying that her love for Jesus preceded forgiveness, and not that she loved much because she had been forgiven. The verse is doubly confusing because the verb used in the verse to express the fact that the woman was forgiven is a perfect passive – implying that forgiveness had *already* taken place – and yet in verse 48f. the bystanders interpret Jesus' words 'Your sins have been forgiven' (in verse 48) as absolving the woman of her sins.

There is no obvious way out of this confusion except to say that, as with the story of the healing of the paralytic in Luke 5:17–26, Luke has inelegantly developed the story to make a point about forgiveness and Christology in the early church that conflicts with the material he was editing. Verse 47a should surely read, 'Therefore I tell you, she loves much because her many sins have been forgiven . . .'. This is consistent with the parable Jesus tells Simon in verses 41–3 and with the affirmation of God's forgiveness in verse 48 (if this verse is originally part of the story). It is perhaps also worth noting that it is only Luke who includes forgiveness in the story (cf. Matthew 26:6–13, Mark 14:3–9, John 12:1–8), adding further weight to the view that Luke has adapted the story to make a different point.

## PAUL

As for Paul, many who read the New Testament assume he has the most to say about forgiveness. The truth is that, among New Testament writers, he says very little on the subject, though the idea is implicit in his writings, especially on justification.[38]

Justification is a juridical concept and does not specifically imply forgiveness, but (in the context in which Paul uses it) refers to God's act of deliverance through the death and resurrection of Christ whereby persons

---

[38] For an exploration of Paul's thought on forgiveness, see Bash and Bash 2004: 37–9.

are set or declared to be in right relation to God (e.g., Romans 4:25) and made full participants in the community of God's people.[39]

Paul uses the verb *charizomai* (and not the synoptic *aphesis* and *aphiemi*) to express the idea of forgiveness (in 2 Corinthians 2:7, 10; 12:13).[40] This is in contrast to the idea of release and liberation implicit in the idea of forgiveness in the synoptic Gospels. *Charizomai* is used of God's forgiveness in Christ for humanity in Colossians 2:13 and of both human and divine forgiveness in Colossians 3:13 and Ephesians 4:32. This verb is sometimes used to refer to the cancellation of a money debt (e.g., Luke 7:42f.) and etymologically carries with it the idea of grace. In using this word, Paul is emphasising that forgiveness is a gift, freely and generously given, presumably (though Paul does not formally make this connection) as a consequence of our having been made full participants in the community of God's people through justification.

Certainly, in Paul's writings the idea of forgiveness is an axiom of Christian living. Implicit is the idea that to forgive is to embody what it means to be a Christian. God in Christ has forgiven human sin and Christians are to live imitatively of the God who has forgiven them (Philippians 2:5–11, especially verse 5).

How are Christians to do this? Paul does not explicitly answer this question but the answer can be inferred from the axioms of Paul's thought. Most probably, the answer that Paul might give is that the power (or capacity) to forgive as God forgives comes from God. Taking the death and resurrection of Christ as his paradigm, Paul observes that Christ was not resurrected by his own self-effort or by virtue of his own intrinsic capacity: rather, in his lifelessness after the crucifixion, he was raised (in Greek, always a verb in the passive voice), indicating that the action occurred to the subject, Christ, by God's power alone. In the same way, Christians can cease to rely on the power and capacity that they may have as human beings (always deficient to do what God wants) and instead yield to God in such a way that God's power – the same power that raised Christ from the dead – shapes, strengthens and enables Christians to live God's way and so to forgive (e.g., 2 Corinthians 1:5, 8–10). God's gift of forgiveness can be received and, when received, can change people so that they themselves become forgivers in the same way that God forgives. It is impossible, argues

---

[39] Some have suggested that the noun *paresis* in Romans 3:25 is a synonym for *aphesis* but this is now widely doubted (e.g., Barrett 1991: 75, Dunn 1988: 181 and Fitzmyer 1993: 351f.).

[40] The exceptions are the verb *aphiemi* in Romans 4:7, quoting from Psalm 31:1 LXX (= Psalm 32:1 MT) and the noun *aphesis* in the related passages of Ephesians 1:7 and Colossians 1:14. Paul is widely doubted to be the author of Ephesians and some doubt that he authored Colossians.

Paul, to live God's way without God's power. It follows, as a corollary, that to forgive God's way is also impossible without God's power. Living God's way demonstrates that Christians have experienced God's resurrection power. They can then forgive in the way that God requires and be confident in the future resurrection of the physical body.

### CONCLUDING REFLECTIONS

In the New Testament, as in the popular mind, there is undoubtedly a degree of confusion about forgiveness.

To forgive is to practise a moral virtue, modelled on God's essential being. To forgive is to follow an ideal and a way of life practised by Jesus. Those who wrote about Jesus and his teaching in the New Testament affirm that way of life. Despite what appear to be statements to the contrary (e.g., Ephesians 4:32 and Colossians 3:13), to forgive is not to carry out a moral duty: it cannot be, because to forgive may sometimes be impossible.

Forgiveness is a characteristic ethic of the kingdom of God. Those who practise the ethics of the kingdom of God (and these include love and mercy) will demonstrate the presence of the kingdom of God – its irruption into human society and the evidence of its reality – in the here and now.

As for absolution and forgiveness, despite Lucan suggestions to the contrary, Jesus did not absolve sins, though, as Jones (1995) properly says, he did 'embody' forgiveness and in his being was forgiving. True absolution – release from sin – will take place when the kingdom of God is established. In addition, neither baptism nor repentance in the period of the New Testament brought about absolution and forgiveness: forgiveness – then, as now – comes through responding to a person, Jesus Christ, and it is a gift of God. Forgiveness may be experienced proleptically, in the present, but in its essential form forgiveness is a gift for, and will be fully experienced in, the kingdom of God.

Forgiving others does not earn or merit God's forgiveness. Certain sayings may appear to say the contrary (for example, Matthew 6:12, 14f.; Mark 11:25f.; Luke 6:37, 7:47a) but, in the broader context of the New Testament, this is not their true meaning. The Gospel writers have not always set these sayings in their broader context, perhaps because they regarded that context as self-evident or perhaps because the sayings did not come to them in that context. In particular, Luke seems to have made editorial revisions that have had the inadvertent effect of contradicting the purpose and intention of some of Jesus' sayings on forgiveness.

The capacity to forgive interpersonally is a correlate of having experienced divine forgiveness because (proleptic divine) forgiveness is regenerative, enabling the recipient to become a forgiving person. Despite Lucan editorial revisions to the contrary, divine forgiveness is not a correlate of first loving God. Those who experience God's forgiveness and who become forgiving people will continue to experience divine forgiveness. Jesus' parables warn that those who have experienced forgiveness but who do not forgive others (or whose forgiveness is grudging, reluctant or insubstantial) will receive from God no greater forgiveness than they give others. These words are warnings to those who have received God's forgiveness to seek to excel in being regenerated and transformed by it; otherwise, their experience of divine forgiveness will be deficient.

This has important implications for human behaviour. On pragmatic grounds, one can infer that those who experience forgiveness will often be better able to forgive others; one can also say that forgiveness multiplies forgiveness. When forgiveness is not a moral ideal of human behaviour, revenge, retaliation, anger and bitterness are the principal alternatives, together with the destructive personal and social consequences that they bring.

At the heart of the idea that unforgiving people will not be forgiven is a contradiction. For if divine forgiveness is an unimaginably lavish gift to the undeserving, how can it be made contingent on the degree to which one person forgives another? Perhaps the contradiction can be resolved this way: if people strive to forgive as best they can, responding fully to their own experience of God's forgiveness, then God will forgive those people with all the lavishness that God offers. If they take what God gives and resist its transformative power, then God will limit their experience of divine forgiveness. To forgive is to strive to practise a moral ideal: the sin is not to fail to *attain* the ideal (who can say they have attained it?) but to fail to *strive to practise* that ideal.

In addition, the Parable of the Prodigal Son illustrates that forgiveness remains, to some extent, inchoate and incomplete until it has been expressed to and accepted by the wrongdoer. When forgiveness is expressed and received in this way, reconciliation results.

Now that we have completed our survey of the New Testament on forgiveness, we can explore further the ideal of forgiveness.

CHAPTER 6

# *The ideal of forgiveness*

Philosophers distinguish between moral duties and moral virtues.

Moral duties *must* be performed and not to perform them is wrong. Since moral duties must be performed, they must be *capable* of being performed. In contrast, there is no obligation to do virtuous acts, even though the need to do them may be compelling.[1] For example, if one were a non-swimmer, to seek to rescue a child drowning in deep, shark-infested waters at great personal risk would be to do a virtuous act but not to perform a moral duty, and philosophers generally hold that it would not be wrong not to attempt the rescue. On the other hand, to fail to rescue a child (at no personal risk to oneself) who was drowning in shallow water is probably not to perform a moral duty.[2] What matters are the circumstances of each case – in this particular example, the circumstances concern the risk to the rescuer and whether the rescuer was likely to do the act successfully.[3]

There are three reasons why to forgive is not a moral duty.[4] The first is that it is not always morally right to forgive, and it cannot be a moral

---

[1] But compare Lévinas who argues that our responsibility to the 'other' is 'indeclinable', that is, not to be declined or refused.

[2] Adopting the language of the Parable of the Good Samaritan in Luke 10:30–7, Thomson (1971: 62f.) would say this is not being even a 'Minimally Decent Samaritan'. (This is in contrast to being a 'Splendid Samaritan', that is, someone who is prepared even to face death for the sake of the good of another.)

[3] This principle has recently been discussed when Mark Inglis, a mountaineer with two prosthetic legs, successfully reached the peak of Mount Everest on 15 May 2006. Inglis and his fellow mountaineers on the upper slopes of Everest did not go to the aid of David Sharpe, who had run out of oxygen and was dying. It was reported that to have stayed would have exposed Inglis and his colleagues to great personal risk. Inglis and his party have been criticised for abandoning Sharpe but it is hard to see on what moral grounds the criticism can be legitimately made. However, even though it is open to question whether it was a moral duty to seek to rescue Sharpe or even to stay with him until he died, it would certainly have been a virtuous act to have sought to do so. See www.abc.net.au/7.30/content/2006/s1647727.htm, http://news.bbc.co.uk/1/hi/magazine/5016536.stm and www.abc.net.au/cgi-bin/common/printfriendly.pl? www.abc.net.au/pm/content/2006/s1645748.htm (all accessed 28 May 2006).

[4] Cf. Kant whose view in *Metaphysics of Morals* (1797), in Gregor 1999 06: 460s is that forgiveness is a duty.

duty to do something that is wrong. The second is that sometimes it is not possible to forgive, and it cannot be a moral duty to do the impossible. The third is that it is not a moral duty to give a gift (such as the gift of forgiveness), because a gift, by definition, is a voluntary act that one does not necessarily have to do.[5]

When it is a moral virtue to forgive depends on what is right in the circumstances.[6] At pp. 11–13 above, I referred to certain types of wrong that may be unforgivable. To try to forgive such acts is not a moral virtue. At p. 43 above, I referred to occasions when a person, for psychological reasons, may find it impossible to forgive. On such occasions, one cannot be blamed for failing to do what one finds impossible.

Richards (1988: 80, 82) rightly states that both to forgive and not to forgive may, in certain instances, 'enact flaws of character'. For example, people may forgive because they are weak, effete, compliant or uncritically supine. They may forgive in order to avoid confronting painful issues or injustice. Even to urge forgiveness as an ethical ideal to practise can inadvertently be to promote a tool of oppression: for example, in many cases women who forgive men who have abused them are colluding with oppression and laying themselves open to further abuse. The 'forgiveness' the victim offers in these examples is morally suspect because the motives of the victim are suspect. Richards summarises it this way: '[I]t is sometimes wrong to forgive, sometimes wrong not to forgive, and sometimes admirable to forgive, but acceptable not to do so.' He concludes: (i) it is wrong not to forgive if one's refusal arises from a flaw in one's character; (ii) it is wrong to forgive where to do so would amount to a flaw in one's character; and (iii) it is neither right nor wrong to forgive if to do so would not amount to a flaw of character.

In general, philosophers agree that there is not a duty to forgive. Novitz (1998: 313) thinks '. . . there can be no duty to forgive; this simply because it is not directly within one's power to do so' (and see also Downie 1965: 133 – 'to forgive is a virtue and unwillingness to try to forgive is a vice' – but cf. Lang 1994 and Haber 1991: 101–3). Richards (1988: 88, 90) does not think that there is a 'mandate' to forgive a repentant wrongdoer: to forgive

---

[5] Cf. Thomas (2003: 221f.) who suggests that profound repentance may render a person worthy of – but not entitled to – forgiveness.

[6] This idea in relation to moral actions generally is explored by Porter (1995) who argues that moral reasoning is analogical, not deontological or consequentialist. Thus, to forgive is to carry out a rational moral act, though such an act cannot always be understood in terms of apodictic rules that determine a correct solution to every moral conundrum. On this, see further pp. 183–4 below.

'is admirable to do but not wrong to omit'.[7] Kolnai (1973–4) recognises that forgiveness is a 'noble and generous . . . attitude'. It 'may' be argued, he says, that a 'genuine change of heart, and it alone, tends to make forgiveness a "duty"' but in his view it is not a 'strict obligation' but rather a quasi-obligation, which has its origin in virtue and which reveals virtue, so that the more virtuous a person, the more disposed they are to forgive and the more they reveal their virtue. The balance of opinion, therefore, is that to forgive is to act virtuously, not to perform a duty, and so it is supererogatory.[8]

It follows that even where a wrongdoer deserves to be forgiven because of some intrinsic merit or worth (for example, where continued resentment is unwarranted or inappropriate or where the wrongdoer has repented, made restitution or been punished – see Calhoun 1992: 78–80), there is no necessary reason why a victim *has to* forgive in such a situation. It is a victim's privilege to withhold forgiveness, even though it may be regarded as churlish and a defect of character not to forgive.[9]

One implication of forgiveness being a moral virtue, not a duty, is that a wrongdoer has no right to be forgiven. Forgiveness cannot be earned, even by acts of atonement.[10] Richards (1988: 90–2) says that it is *not* heartless to withhold forgiveness from 'anyone who is genuinely repentant'. If forgiveness could be earned, then, as Kolnai (1973–4) has pointed out, forgiveness would be otiose because there would be nothing left to forgive. People cannot demand to be forgiven even if they are repentant and they cannot berate others for not forgiving them. One can appeal for forgiveness, beg for it and urge it; one can appeal to another to be morally virtuous and forgive – but there remains no moral obligation to forgive. Forgiveness is a gift that may or may not be given by a person who has been wronged. To choose not to forgive may show moral defects of character, such as hardness of heart, callous indifference to another or a failure to engage with our common humanity.[11] Not forgiving may inflict perhaps even greater

---

[7] But in Richards 2002: 77 in critical dialogue with Enright *et al*. 1998: 47, Richards writes: '. . . although it is very often true that there is no obligation to forgive, then there are also times when there is an obligation to do so. The other way is to say that although forgiveness is always a gift, it is sometimes a gift one would be wrong not to give.'

[8] This view is reinforced by recent research that shows that people may have an inbuilt psychological predisposition towards forgiveness or unforgiveness. For a summary of research and measures to assess the disposition to forgive, see McCullough and Worthington 1999; McCullough and Witvliet 2001: 448–50; Exline *et al*. 2004; Mullet *et al*. 2005. See also Roberts 1995.

[9] McGary (1989: 350) denies that forgiveness is even a gift.

[10] Cf. Swinburne (1989: 87f.): if a wrongdoer has sincerely done all the wrongdoer can do to repudiate the wrong and made sufficient 'atonement' (being penitent, apologising, repairing the damage and doing penance) the burden of guilt will be lifted even if the victim refuses to forgive.

[11] See Garrard 2003: 242f.

suffering and harm on the (now repentant) wrongdoer than the unforgiven wrong inflicted on the victim. Even so, there remains no obligation to forgive and an unforgiven wrongdoer cannot insist that the victim of the wrong be morally virtuous.

IS THERE A CHRISTIAN MORAL DUTY TO FORGIVE?

According to Meirlys Lewis (1980: 244), Christian forgiveness is predicated on the unconditionality of God's love: just as God loves all people, so God's forgiveness extends to all people. Christians are also to love all people, and their forgiveness is to extend to all people. Lewis recognises that 'unconditional forgiveness is virtually impossible' but that is not to say that 'the forgiveness of God cannot and does not function as an ideal in the life of the believer'.

On balance, and as I have indicated in chapter 5, the New Testament documents do not insist that there is a Christian moral duty to forgive.[12] To forgive is presented as a moral virtue, desirable to do but not mandatory, an ideal to which one should strive. In two passages, the New Testament does apparently present a moral duty to forgive (Ephesians 4:32 and Colossians 3:13) but these passages must be set against the broader canvas both of New Testament teaching and of philosophical insight.[13] Forgiveness is a demonstration of divine grace and imitative of the love and grace of God towards humanity. It is a gift – one that Christians are urged to give – but, as I argued in chapter 5, it is not a duty or obligation – and, indeed, cannot be because it may sometimes be impossible to forgive, or even immoral to attempt it.

There is a relationship between those who experience God's forgiveness and their capacity and willingness to forgive others, as I also showed at pp. 93f., 96f. above, when I discussed Matthew 18:23–35 and Luke 7:36–50. The effect of receiving and experiencing God's forgiveness is to transform a person so that they develop a predisposition to forgive others. Forgiven people will, because they have been forgiven, strive to practise the moral virtue of forgiveness towards others, whether or not those others have repented. As a result, they will less often demonstrate 'flaws of character'

---

[12] Swinburne's argument (1989: 88) that Christians have a duty to forgive because they have received and accepted God's forgiveness on condition that they will forgive others is, as I showed in chapter 5, based on an exegetical misinterpretation.

[13] They may also represent a later development of the thought and teaching of Jesus in the post-Pauline period: see Bash and Bash 2004: 39f.

(Richards 1988: 80, 82) and so fail less often to forgive when it would be morally virtuous to do so.

One can express this more unequivocally. Although, almost certainly, there is not a moral duty to forgive in the New Testament, there is, I suggest, a moral duty to do all that one can so that one is able to forgive if it is possible – and this includes even the unrepentant. It is not enough to say 'I cannot forgive this wrongdoing because it is difficult and because the wrongdoer does not acknowledge the wrong.' One must do all that one can so that one forgives if one is able. The moral duty is to strive to forgive and God will respond, not according to whether one has forgiven, but according to whether one has sought to forgive as best one could. ⟶

## DIVINE FORGIVENESS

Is God morally obliged to forgive? If God is not, is forgiveness a moral virtue practised by God – a virtue that God may practise, but one that God is not bound to practise if God should choose otherwise? The questions are not strictly germane to the issues explored in this book but only incidental to them. For the sake of completeness, we consider the questions briefly.

Forgiveness is part of the essential being of God. God is, in God's own being, forgiving and God cannot be unforgiving. God's forgiveness is one aspect only of God's moral being: God is also, for example, just and even vengeful.[14] This means that though God is forgiving, God does not *always* forgive; God may respond in other ways to human beings and to the human condition.

It is also clear that, though God is forgiving, human beings do not always necessarily *experience* that forgiveness. This is perhaps clearly illustrated in the Parable of the Prodigal Son (Luke 15:11–32). The father in the parable had clearly forgiven the son *before* the son had decided to return home. When the son did return, the father's expression of forgiveness was swift, immediate and unconditional, and did not depend on the son's apology and repentance. Reconciliation was the result. The parable implies that the father longed to express his forgiveness to the son – he watched in hope that the son would return so that he could tell the son he was forgiven. The son could not experience the father's forgiveness until he had returned

---

[14] Deuteronomy 32:35, quoted in Romans 12:19 and Hebrews 10:30. See also Psalm 94:1 and 1 Thessalonians 4:6. Romans 11:22 refers to the 'severity' of God.

home and received the father's mercy. Neither could the son be reconciled to the father until he had experienced that forgiveness.

To answer the questions posed at the start of this section, God always practises the moral virtue of being forgiving because God, unlike human beings, is, in God's being and identity, forgiving. God's 'forgivingness' is different from human 'forgivingness' because God is forgiving in God's being. God stands in a forgiving relationship with humanity, but, for humanity · to experience that forgiveness, human beings must seek that forgiveness and respond to God's grace. In other words, they must seek the gift in the way that God will give it. As with the son in the Parable of the Prodigal Son, until human beings put themselves in the place or situation where they can experience God's grace of forgiveness, they will not be forgiven. Baptism and repentance are ways of putting oneself in the place or situation to receive and experience that forgiveness, but they are not the only ways. In the Gospels, there are examples of people who were forgiven without baptism (e.g., one of the thieves crucified with Jesus – Luke 23:40–3) or apparently even without repentance (Mark 2:1–12). But human beings have no right to experience the gift of divine forgiveness; they may do so – will do so – if they seek it appropriately.

These observations address the difficult observation made by Lévinas (1990: 20), who has objected that God 'cannot support or pardon the crime that man commits against man'. The reasons Lévinas gives are, first, that God forgives faults that pertain to God only and not faults that pertain to human beings ('[t]he personal responsibility of man with regard to man is such that God cannot annul it') and, second, that '[n]o-one, not even God, can substitute himself with the victim'. We might also say that otherwise it would be that divine forgiveness dishonours the suffering of the person wronged and apparently offers an easy let-out for the wrongdoer. Clearly, it is the case that only the person wronged can forgive the wrongdoer and it is repulsive to suppose that God offers a route to forgiveness that spares the wrongdoer from engaging with the person wronged. There is an obligation on the wrongdoer to seek forgiveness from the person wronged (Matthew 5:23f.). If the wrongdoer will not do this, there will not be divine forgiveness for the wrongdoer, as shown in the discussion on the Parable of the Unforgiving Servant (Matthew 18:23–35) at pp. 93f. above.[15]

---

[15] What if one does all one can to repent and to seek forgiveness but the victim refuses to forgive? Lévinas appears to have no hope for the repentant wrongdoer – who is now a victim – even though for God to forgive in such a situation neither dishonours the (former) victim nor offers an easy let-out for the (former) wrongdoer now become victim.

## A PRAGMATIC APPROACH TO FORGIVENESS

Even though forgiveness is an ideal that people should strive to practise for morally virtuous reasons, one can make out a case for urging people to forgive on pragmatic grounds.

To forgive is to act expediently. Not forgiving can perpetuate the suffering and distress of the victim and may reinforce the sense the victim has of being a victim (that is, someone who has been unjustly wronged). With unforgiveness comes an emotional cost that in the long term sometimes produces physical consequences.[16] Forgiveness militates against the corrosive effects of anger, fear, self-pity and bitterness that often arise when someone will not (or cannot) forgive another.

In contrast, to seek revenge can be personally and communally destructive and does not ameliorate the underlying fact of being and feeling unforgiven. Revenge may seem pleasant at the time; it may feel just and it may seem to restore the balance between wrongdoer and victim,[17] but, in the words of a popular aphorism, 'two wrongs don't make a right'. Lomax (1996: 276) expressed it this way: 'Sometime, the hating has to stop.'[18] From the wrongdoer's point of view, Kierkegaard (Hong and Hong 1995: 296–7) observes that not forgiving is unloving and highlights the fact of the sin and can even sustain it.

Archbishop Desmond Tutu has powerfully made out a case for forgiveness even where there have been gross violations of human rights, communal and government-inspired violence, political oppression and racial discrimination.[19] In such situations, there is, he warns, 'no future without forgiveness' (as the title of Tutu 1999 declares, and see also his contribution to the Symposium in Wiesenthal 1998: 268). By forgiving, he writes, the victim may succeed in 'opening the door for the other person to begin again' (Tutu in Enright and North 1998: xiii) and may well also enable the wrongdoer to put closure on the psychological effects of the wrongdoing.

The Truth and Reconciliation Commission in South Africa demonstrates both the value of taking a pragmatic approach to forgiveness and also the drawbacks.

It is undoubtedly the case that the Commission's work has done much to help South Africa put away some of the social and psychological scarring of

---

[16] Enright and Coyle 1998: 139.

[17] Reiss and Havercamp (1998) postulate that vengeance (which they define in Table 4 of the article as 'the desire to retaliate when offended') is one of fifteen fundamental human motivations.

[18] On Lomax, see pp. 73–4 above.

[19] See Cherry 2004 for a critical appraisal of forgiveness and reconciliation in South Africa as a result of the Truth and Reconciliation Commission.

the era of *apartheid.* Tutu began with the view that if victims forgave wrong-doers unconditionally 'healing will happen, and so contribute to national unity and reconciliation' (Tutu 1999: 91). Seven years later, Tutu's own view of the work of the Commission (which he chaired) was that it 'failed to engage the white community enough, those who had been privileged in the apartheid system, or to get beyond the foot-soldiers. We really didn't get the big fish, [and] the kind of acknowledgement and accountability from those who gave the orders.' The result is that though 'amnesty was given to so many . . . there is little to show for it in a reciprocal way'.[20] In other words, a pragmatic approach to forgiveness meant that many of the per-petrators of the *apartheid* system escaped accountability. It also meant that many of those who benefited from and enjoyed the privileges of *apartheid* without actively promoting or sustaining the regime (the people Tutu refers to as 'the white community') did not have to acknowledge that they were collaborators who had tacitly colluded with an iniquitous system.

Others would say that, though the Commission *did* help to promote national reconciliation through enabling people to tell their stories and discover the truth about their oppressors, it did not also help to achieve rec-onciliation by addressing the educational, social and economic inequalities that remained from the period of *apartheid.* In other words, the Commis-sion did not address many of the inequalities of the *apartheid* system but only limited aspects of the wrong that had been done, such as the physical brutality people had suffered. Unaddressed were some of the wider struc-tural wrongs, the effects of which many black South Africans continue to experience and about which there remain bitterness and anger.

Three further observations about the Commission may be made. First, though the Commission could make recommendations to the South African government about payment of reparations to those who had suf-fered violations of their human rights (and the Commission did make fifty-two recommendations), the government made payments only to vic-tims (and not their survivors) and the payments were regarded as too late and too little. Among those who received reparations – and among many who did not – there is the view that neither the government nor the per-petrators of the wrongs have properly acknowledged the suffering that so many experienced.

Second, undoubtedly there was pressure to forgive during the hear-ings of the Commission, fuelled in part by Archbishop Tutu's belief that

[20] Reported by C. Chivers in *Church Times* 17 February 2006, p. 20.

unforgiveness was personally and psychologically damaging and put the future of a new and peaceful South Africa at risk. This had two results. The first was that some apparently 'forgave' before they had properly engaged with their own feelings of abuse, degradation and resentment.[21] Where there was 'forgiveness', it was more in the nature of a pardon if the victim did not come face-to-face with the wrongdoer or if the wrongdoer did not repent. The second result was that some wrongdoers, though 'forgiven', did not repent or show remorse. This undermines the moral element of forgiveness (the wrongdoers did not acknowledge that they had done wrong) and the relational element of forgiveness (there was no restoration). What was promoted was 'premature closure for a still hurting individual or community' (Cherry 2004: 168).

Lastly, the very name of the Commission, 'The Truth and Reconciliation Commission', caused a degree of confusion because in some of the local languages there is one word both for 'reconciliation' and for 'forgiveness'.[22] Tutu emphasised the element of forgiveness in the work of the Commission but many people who 'forgave' were not also reconciled to those who had wronged them because the wrongdoers showed neither remorse nor repentance. Some of what the Commission said was forgiveness is more in the nature of a pardon, and Tutu's own working definition of forgiveness (waiving one's right to revenge) is questionable, for to waive a right to revenge does not necessarily mean that one demonstrates the moral virtue of forgiveness or that one has let go of unforgiving feelings and thoughts. There may well be 'no future without forgiveness' but, more likely, there is 'no future without forgiveness *and* reconciliation'.

The Commission has, nevertheless, been of enormous value in helping some South Africans to put behind them a shameful and traumatic period of their history. Tutu cites many examples of people who have 'forgiven' their former oppressors, usually after an apology; as a result, they are (in Tutu's words) no longer 'locked into victimhood' and have discovered peace, freedom and restoration. Even though the Commission may well have been in part the result of the political pragmatism of the new South African government, the Christian commitment of the Chairman (Archbishop Tutu) and the Vice Chairman of the Commission (Alex Boraine), led the Commission to promote forms of forgiveness that had the transition to a more just society as their goal. History will judge the experiment,

---

[21] For an example of someone who would not do this, see p. 116 below.
[22] Derrida alludes to the difficulties in Kearney 2001: 55f., and see Cherry 2004: 164f.

but the best early evaluation is that much bloodshed has been avoided and oppression and abuse revealed by the pioneering application of Christian ethics.[23]

We consider next the application of the ethics of forgiveness not to individuals but to groups and communities.

---

[23] I am grateful to Dr Stephen Cherry for advice in connection with this paragraph.

# CHAPTER 7

# Forgiveness and structural wrongdoing

This chapter explores whether wrongs that groups do can be forgiven and, if they can, who can forgive them. After some introductory remarks and a brief discussion of apologies, we look in particular at three interlocking questions. The first is this: Can groups forgive or be forgiven? We ask this question because some say that, just as there cannot be peace and reconciliation between individuals if they pass over and ignore wrongdoing, so there cannot be peace and reconciliation between groups if they pass over and ignore wrongdoing. The second question, which is related, is: Can individuals forgive groups? In other words, are groups 'forgivable' (that is, able-to-be-forgiven) by individuals? The third question is: To what extent are individuals personally responsible for the actions they do on behalf of groups? For even if groups cannot forgive and be forgiven, are the individuals who acted for the groups personally responsible for what they do for the group?

In the following discussion, I usually refer to collections of people – whether corporations, nations or other social organisms – that have a distinct identity beyond that of the constituent members as 'groups'. I refer to the wrongdoing that the groups do as 'structural' or 'systemic' wrongdoing or simply as 'wrong' or 'wrongdoing'.

Individuals within groups may wrong other individuals on behalf of groups in relatively minor ways. For example, people may be unjustly passed over for promotion because of their gender; a doctor in a hospital may treat a patient incompetently and the hospital deny the wrongdoing; or due process may not be followed in a court of law. It is also the case that some forms of wrongdoing by individuals on behalf of groups can be almost unimaginable in their horror, brutality and effectiveness. This is evil 'inflicted deliberately . . . in a manner no reason sets limits to, in the exasperation of a reason become political and detached from all ethics',[1] and

---

[1] Lévinas 1998: 97.

not only pollutes individuals but also introduces evil into communities and becomes part of the matrix of societal norms. In this chapter, we consider, therefore, a wide range of types of structural wrongdoing.

Towards the end of the twentieth century and in the early part of the twenty-first century, there were unusually large numbers of public apologies by politicians for past wrongdoing by former (usually now dead) members of the groups that the politicians represented. In part, this was probably because the groups were seeking to find a language to say that the groups had moved on from the historical legacy and collective memory of their past wrongdoing, that the groups were now new communities with new values and that the groups desired to dissociate themselves from the wrongdoing of the past. The historical significance of the end of the millennium also played a part in the wish to leave the memory of the wrongdoing in the past and to start afresh in the third millennium.

Of course, not all political leaders apologised for the former misdemeanours of their groups. For example, despite public pressure, the Turks denied (and so would not apologise) that 1.5 million Armenians were either deported or killed between 1915 and 1923 by the Ottoman Turks. The French also did not apologise for the deaths of 200,000 Algerians killed in the war of independence between 1954 and 1962. But apart from exceptions such as these – there are also many others – we can point to other cases when political leaders publicly apologised for former national wrongdoing with a view to seeking restored relations and reconciliation. For example, Britain's Prime Minister Tony Blair apologised for English indifference during the Irish Potato Famine of the 1840s (1997). President Clinton apologised for leaving syphilis untreated in men in Tuskegee, Alabama, in a federal experiment beginning in the 1930s until its exposé in 1972 (1997). President Kwasniewski of Poland apologised for the part played by Poles in a massacre of Jews in 1941 at Jedwabre (2001). In 2002, the Prime Minster of New Zealand, Helen Clark, apologised that the government of New Zealand had failed to quarantine an influenza-carrying ship in 1919 and for the subsequent influenza epidemic in Western Samoa. She also apologised that New Zealand soldiers shot dead leaders of the non-violent Mau movement during a procession in 1926. On 13 June 2005, the US Senate formally apologised for having rejected for many years pleas to make lynching a federal crime. This was partly in response to research conducted at the University of Tuskegee that showed that between 1882 and 1968 4,743 people were lynched and that, although nearly 200 anti-lynching bills were introduced in Congress, only three were passed.

There have also been apologies by people of faith for group wrongdoing, particularly by leaders of the Roman Catholic Church. In 1997, French Roman Catholic bishops apologised to the Jewish people for the silence of their predecessors in the 1940s about the oppression of the Jews. The Roman Catholic Church offered many apologies following the publication of a document in 1999 entitled *Memory and Reconciliation: The Church and the Faults of the Past.*[2] As a result, the Roman Catholic Church sought to focus on repentance and renewal in its jubilee celebrations of 2000. That year, Pope John Paul II sought God's forgiveness for seven categories of sins by the Roman Catholic Church in the past[3] and, later in 2000, on a visit to Israel, he apologised to the Jewish people for their suffering at the hands of Christians. In 2001, he apologised to Orthodox Christians for the wrongs perpetrated by the Roman Catholic Church against eastern Christianity.[4] In 2001, the Polish Bishops apologised and offered penitential prayers for the fact that Poles had wronged Jews.

It is, of course, not wrong to revisit the actions of previous generations, to come to a different conclusion from one's forbears, to express that different conclusion and to acknowledge the hurt or harm that has been caused.[5] That is not the same as *apologising* for their actions. Even so, it is, I suggest, difficult to support the idea of apologies for the actions of one's forbears, for the following reasons. First, those who apologise sometimes assume that *their* understanding of the moral issues their antecedents faced is necessarily better: their understanding may be different and they may have new perspectives, but that does not mean that what the previous generation did was, with the understanding and insights that that generation had *at the time*, wrong. A soldier who refuses to fight may today be regarded as suffering from 'post-traumatic stress disorder' (rather than from what formerly was called 'cowardice') and that disorder may now be regarded as more

---

[2] *Memory and Reconciliation* refers to and reflects the theology of the Bull of Indiction of the Great Jubilee of the Year 2000, *Incarnationis mysterium* (29 November 1998).
[3] General sins; sins in the service of truth, sins against Christian unity, against Jews, against respect for love, peace and cultures, against the dignity of women and minorities and against human rights.
[4] See other examples in Biggar 2001: 211.
[5] Despite the rhetoric, this seems to have happened in Australia's 'National Sorry Day' that was held annually between 1998 and 2004 to give people the opportunity to acknowledge the impact of the practice of removing Aboriginal children from their families so as to integrate them into western culture. In 2005 the day was renamed 'National Day of Healing for all Australians'. See www.forachange.co.uk/index.php?stoid=143 (accessed 28 August 2006).

complex than what was formerly called 'shell shock'.[6] Even so, we cannot blame those in earlier generations who did not know about post-traumatic stress disorder, and it is an anachronism to do so. Second, to apologise for the actions of members of a group in the past censures their actions but without giving them opportunity to respond. Apologising creates a different set of victims who, because they are dead, cannot defend themselves. Third, some apologies are offered without reparation. The apology apparently costs little or nothing, requires no practical action and often is of little measurable benefit to the group that receives the apology. When a politician makes the apology, the cynical may sometimes wonder whether expediency, popularity and political ends at least in part motivated the apology.

CAN GROUPS FORGIVE AND BE FORGIVEN?

Those who reflect on forgiveness typically assume that forgiveness concerns relations between individuals. Although modern thought is individualistic, some regard groups as having identities distinct from the individuals who comprise them. They believe that groups can (and sometimes should) repent, forgive or be forgiven. They also think that forgiveness, when it pertains to groups, may be an instrument of public policy, whether within nations domestically or between nations internationally. Shriver (1995: 9) describes forgiveness in a socio-political context as 'a collective turning from the past' and says that it is 'an act that joins moral truth, forbearance, empathy, and commitment to repair a fractured human relation'. Forgiveness in this context is part of a wider social process that takes groups of people away from revenge and corporate self-interest towards forbearance and, eventually, reconciliation.

'Liberation' theologians suggest that not only individuals but also social organisms can be 'forgiven' for wrongdoing. In practical terms, for social organisms this means that the structural sin must be unmasked, confronted and eradicated and individuals who are affected by it 'liberated' from its effects. In the place of what was evil and corrupt, there should be just, new structures that safeguard freedom from systemic oppression.

In contrast, the New Testament refers to repentance and forgiveness only in personal terms (though judgment is understood both individually and corporately). This is odd, since in the period of the New Testament identity

---

[6] On 16 August 2006, the British government announced that it was granting posthumous pardons to 306 British soldiers who in the First World War were executed for cowardice or desertion.

and personality were understood in collective terms (Malina 2001: 58–80). It is perhaps significant for our discussion below that the New Testament appears to assume that groups *cannot* forgive or be forgiven, even though it was written in an era when identity was understood so strongly in collective terms.

From a legal point of view, groups such as sovereign states, institutions and organisations, though comprising a collection of individuals, often have a legal identity of their own that is distinct from the individuals who comprise such groups. This means the groups may be sued and sue, be prosecuted, enter into contracts and so on, in a similar way to an individual. For example, in English law (and in many other common law countries), a company or corporation is a legal person, distinct from those who are members at any given point. As a legal person, it has rights and responsibilities, many of which can be enforced in the courts.

Legal liability for criminal acts usually requires both *mens rea* (criminal intent) and *actus reus* (a criminal act). To establish a company's *actus reus* is no different from establishing an individual's: much more difficult is to establish *mens rea*. *Mens rea* is established in one of two ways. By the 'identification theory', *mens rea* can be inferred in circumstances where the 'knowledge and intention of the [company's] agent must be imported to the body corporate'.[7] By the 'attribution theory', a person's knowledge and intention (such as *mens rea*) can be attributed to and count as the knowledge and intention of the company.

Despite certain groups having a legal identity distinct from their members, such groups do not share all the legal attributes that individual identity normally carries. Although statutes and common law sometimes impose on both groups and individuals the same legal liability for certain actions (such as for negligence and personal injury), the law also imposes some responsibilities that are unique to groups (for example, 'corporate manslaughter', and in relation to issues of health and safety).

As for group identity outside the ambit of the law, groups do not exist with the same attributes and markers of personal identity as human beings. They do not have a moral 'self' in an organic sense. One cannot therefore speak of groups 'forgiving' or 'being 'forgiven'[8] because integral to forgiveness are ideas to do with personal moral agency and responsibility, such as 'intentional action', 'acknowledgment of responsibility', 'repentance' and so on. To borrow the language of Martin (1997: 145) from a different

---

[7] McNaghten J. in DPP *v*. Kent and Sussex Contractors Ltd [1944] KB 146 at p. 156.
[8] Haber 1991, Martin 1997; but cf. Arendt 1958: 236–43; Shriver 1995: 71; Govier 2002: 85–99.

(but related) context, to speak of forgiveness here (or, we might add, of apologies) involves 'an illegitimate transfer of the moral criteria which may properly govern face-to-face relations between an identifiable malefactor and an identifiable victim'.[9]

One can put this another way. Since a group exists only metaphorically, it is a metaphorical entity, and so inanimate. Just as we do not apologise to or forgive rocks, buildings or other inanimate entities, so we cannot apologise to or forgive groups. Neither do these inanimate entities apologise to or forgive human beings. Even though groups comprise people, groups *qua* groups are inanimate. Groups cannot therefore forgive or be forgiven.[10] A woman powerfully made this point to Archbishop Tutu during the hearings of the Truth and Reconciliation Commission.[11] She said, 'First, no government can forgive, no commission can forgive, only I could forgive and I am not ready to forgive.'[12]

There are two further reasons why groups cannot forgive or be forgiven.

The first reason is that a group cannot speak or act on its own but only through a mouthpiece as representative of the group – and for all the members of the group. So if one member of the group disagrees, the representative cannot speak for the entire group. A group cannot confess, repent, forgive or be forgiven unless *all* of its members do so – in which case, there is no difference between the actions of the group as a whole and the actions of its constituent members.

The second is that, though it is true that in law a group's legal liability will continue even after a change of members (e.g., for liability in contract),[13] it is hard to envisage outside the law how a current member of a group can be morally liable for the actions of a former member. This introduces the idea of 'transferred moral liability' that philosophers rightly eschew.

The effect of these arguments is that current members of a group cannot properly express or receive remorse or contrition about the acts of the group carried out by former or current members except as a matter of goodwill for the sake of better relations. Martin (1997: 149, 151) says that there is no 'retrospective responsibility or contrition' by current members of a group whose antecedents did wrong and, similarly, those whose antecedents were

---

[9] Martin is referring to collective national guilt.
[10] It may not be possible to identify who the victims are. Löschnig-Gspandl (2003: 153) explores corporate wrongdoing where the victims are 'either an anonymous group of people one cannot exactly define, or even the general public'.
[11] See the earlier discussion on the Truth and Reconciliation Commission, pp. 107–10 above.
[12] Quoted by Derrida in Kearney 2001: 55.
[13] It is also true that occasionally former members of a group do remain personally legally liable for the unlawful actions of the group undertaken while they were members.

wronged but who were not themselves wronged cannot expect contrition or offer forgiveness. Groups can only act or omit to act. To attribute to groups the moral attributes that pertain to individuals is an oxymoron. Martin (1997: 151) adds that 'those who did not perpetrate a wrong cannot express contrition to those who have suffered no wrong'. It is a confusion of mind to assume that since groups comprise individuals, groups share the same attributes as their individual members. If ideas such as 'forgiveness', 'repentance', 'victim' and 'wrongdoer' are to be applied to groups, they can only be applied by *analogy* as bearing a 'family likeness' (see p. 170 below) to the more analytically coherent forms that these words have in relation to individuals.

Despite the logical difficulties, there are benefits in groups seeking to forgive or to be forgiven and I have already incidentally alluded to these. The example of Andrew Hawkins, a descendant of England's first slave trader, Admiral John Hawkins (1532–95), illustrates the point clearly. (The example concerns an individual, as an individual, seeking the forgiveness of a group; by analogy the point still holds good for a group seeking the forgiveness of another group.)

In June 2006, Andrew Hawkins and about twenty others knelt in front of a crowd of about 25,000 native Africans. Andrew Hawkins wore chains of the type formerly used to imprison slaves. He asked for forgiveness for John Hawkins' former actions as a slave trader. His request for forgiveness was accepted by the Vice President of The Gambia, Isaton Njie Said, who came forward and removed the chains from Hawkins as a symbolic expression of that forgiveness.[14]

From a moral point of view, Andrew Hawkins was not in a position to ask for forgiveness. It was John Hawkins, not Andrew Hawkins, who did the wrong – more than four hundred years ago. Andrew Hawkins was not morally responsible for the wrongdoing of John Hawkins and John Hawkins' guilt cannot be attributed to him. Nevertheless, what Andrew Hawkins' actions did communicate, apparently very powerfully, was his own sense of shame and revulsion about Britain's former trade in slaves and the fact that many others in Britain today think the same way as he. His actions symbolised not only Britain's changed views about slave trading but also the active determination of some to demonstrate those changed views.[15] (One can also add that Isaton Njie Said did not in any

---

[14] On the other hand, at another point in Hawkins' visit to The Gambia, Hawkins' 'reconciliation walk' through the village of Juffreh was met with bewilderment.

[15] See www.timesonline.co.uk/article/0,,3-2236871.html – accessed 22 June 2006; http://news.bbc.co.uk/1/hi/uk/5105328.stm – accessed 23 June 2006.

true sense represent the 25,000 native Africans present, and one wonders on what basis – except out of courtesy to Hawkins – she thought she was empowered symbolically to express forgiveness.)

There is a sense in which groups do carry a measure of guilt and responsibility for the actions of current and former members, especially where there is a measure of continuity between the current outlook of the group and the outlook of the group in the past. Tutu (1999: 223) agrees that it does 'feel' wrong not to address in the present the former wrongdoing of a group. He wrote that '. . . it would be an oddly atomistic view of the nature of a community not to accept that there is a very real continuity between the past and the present and that the former members would share in the guilt and the shame as in the absolution and glory of the present'. So how can we acknowledge these points without compromising the logic of the views set out above?

The approach of Shriver (1995) is to identify forgiveness in a political context as a 'multidimensional process' comprising a number of 'strands' (moral truth, forbearance from revenge, empathy and commitment to repair fractured relations) that will result in reconciliation. What he has identified is something approximating to the 'pure' forgiveness that individuals may practise but different from it because it does not (and cannot) contain all the elements that one would expect to see where individuals are concerned. The result is a process that can lead to reconciliation.[16] De Gruchy (2002: 173) develops the idea of 'political forgiveness', which he defines as 'a risk taken on the basis of mature insight and political acumen and one that displays moral courage'. This is a pragmatic approach to structural wrongdoing. The result may be renewed and restored relations and eventually reconciliation.

An important theological attempt to address the issues has been made by the Roman Catholic Church. In both the Bull of Indiction of the Great Jubilee of the Year 2000, *Incarnationis mysterium*, and in *Memory and Reconciliation* (see above, p. 113) the Church sought to address in a theological way the question of groups forgiving and being forgiven and set out the basis of Pope John Paul II's subsequent public apologies and repentance. (As will be apparent, at many points the distinctions between pardon and forgiveness and between repentance and apology are blurred, but this does not affect the validity of the comments I make below. This is partly because an apology is often a covert expression of repentance with an implicit request for forgiveness.)

---

[16] Reconciliation does not only come from forgiveness.

While acknowledging that people are personally responsible for their own actions, the Bull acknowledges that because of 'the bond which unites us to one another in the Mystical Body [of Christ], all of us . . . bear the burden of the errors and faults of those who have gone before us'. In *Memory and Reconciliation*, the idea of bearing the errors and faults of others is said to come from the 'corporate personality' of the church (section 36) through 'incorporation into Christ and the work of the Holy Spirit' (section 56) that is 'absolutely unique in human affairs, able to take on the gifts, the merits, and the faults of her children of yesterday and today' (section 45). The document also refers to the 'intergenerational solidarity in sin' (section 38) and 'an objective common responsibility' (section 69) of the members of the church. On this basis, the church through its pontiff is able to acknowledge and confess those past sins of its members in which the church shares objective – and therefore corporate – moral responsibility.

Implicit in the theological basis of the document is that the 'communion of saints' (that is, the spiritual union that all people – living and dead – share with one another and with Christ if they are Christians) imparts to the church a shared burden of moral responsibility for the sins of others. It is for this reason that the church can apologise for others' wrongdoing.

This is a morally dubious concept. One might say by analogy that members of a family also have, to some extent, a common identity, sharing as they do a common pool of genes. It is not appropriate to speak of one member of a family sharing moral liability for and so seeking forgiveness of the wrongdoing of another member of the family. *A fortiori*, one cannot seek forgiveness for the actions of a member of the family in a former generation. In the same way, the common identity that Christians share, being both 'in Christ' and (according to Roman Catholic theology) members of the church of Christ, does not qualify one generation to apologise for the misdeeds of former generations. There may well be a link – confessional and spiritual – but that does not involve transferred moral liability (even if it is expressed as a shared 'burden' of responsibility, as it is in *Memory and Reconciliation*).

The document speaks of being liberated from the 'weight of . . . responsibility' for the sins of the past 'through imploring God's forgiveness for the wrongs of the past' (thus addressing the question not of reconciliation between *people* but of reconciliation between the wrongdoer and *God*), and then, in the present, presents a twofold approach. First, echoing the words of *Incarnationis mysterium*, it refers to 'purification of memory' in the present for the sins of the past. Thus the document at this point seems tacitly to acknowledge that there can be no forgiveness for the sins of the past where there are no victims to receive the apology – but the fact of the apology can help heal the hurt and memories of past sins. There can be a form of reconciliation as a result: confidence about future relations, mutual understanding about the past, and a shared ethic of communion. Acts of reparation may accompany expressions of repentance and contrition (section 96).

Second, the document refers to 'mutual pardoning of sins and offences in the present'. (Compare Tutu (1999: 223) who implies that not only may the sins of the dead be forgiven but also that the dead may 'share in the absolution . . . of the present'.) At best, the pardoning *today* of sins and offences of the *past* may help restore relations between those still suffering from the effects of the sins and offences of the past (the victims) and the institution in whose name they were carried out (the wrongdoer); it cannot effect forgiveness between those who were wronged in the past and those who at the time wronged them. This approach perhaps offers a way forward out of the prison of historically conditioned and historically based unforgiveness, such as we see in Northern Ireland. It also offers a way forward for modern communities to address and forgive the sins of the past *insofar as those sins continue to affect their experience of the present*. In this sense, there is a degree of reconciliation.

In *Memory and Reconciliation* (1999), the Roman Catholic Church, in reflecting on its own past mistakes, distinguished between 'objective responsibility' and 'subjective responsibility' for the acts of individuals in its name. Acts for which there is 'objective responsibility' are 'imputable', that is, they are acts attributable to the church as a whole and carried out representatively for the church; for these the church as a body is responsible. Acts for which there is 'subjective responsibility' are the personal acts of an individual. The acts may be morally good or morally bad, and the moral culpability of the individual for the act will depend on the nature of the act (section 69).

The concept is bedevilled with difficulties. For example, the church has not set out guidelines on how to distinguish whether an act is one for which there is subjective or objective responsibility. All that we are told is that there is a distinction. To use an example, the use of force in the service of truth is an act for which the church has accepted objective responsibility (section 5.3). Thus, the church accepts objective responsibility for the Inquisition. But what of the man who, in good faith, turned the screw on the rack? Could he argue, like Eichmann, that he was 'carrying out orders', that the church had told him he was doing an upright deed in extracting confessions from heretics in this way, and that therefore his actions (based on the orders and rhetoric of the church) are the responsibility of the church? The answer will depend on whether we regard the man as morally culpable for what we now see as his misguided actions encouraged by the misguided teaching of the church.

What, then, is the value of apologies for the misdeeds of the past, whether offered by politicians or the church? At best, 'repentance' about past actions is an expression that the group dissociates itself from its former actions and repudiates them as morally reprehensible. Such 'repentance' is more in the nature of an apology; it is an expression of regret and is usually politically, not personally, driven. Apologies can be taken, in the sense that Shriver (1995) suggests, to be part of a process that has as its goal the intention to repair fractured relationships and the result could well be a measure of restoration of relations and even reconciliation. Scarre (2004: 73) puts it this way: the best that can happen is that modern leaders 'express their regrets for the mistakes of their predecessors; they can explain how the . . . present stance differs from [the] former stance and ask for the organisation and its members to be given a fresh chance; but they are neither individually nor collectively guilty of the offences themselves' – and so are in no position to ask forgiveness of them. The elected representatives of a group may receive the apology, acknowledge that it has been given in integrity and choose to disregard the wrongdoing in future dealings with the group that did wrong.

Sometimes public apologies are the result of previous constructive communication between members of different groups, often initiated by organisations that promote friendship between estranged groups. The idea of 'international friendship groups' is well known: these groups aim to foster friendship, respect and communication between different nations. Another type of organisation is BridgeBuilders (www.bridge-builders.org), which according to its website believes it is 'time to look beyond the paralysis of politics as usual and cultivate a new **Common Ground** that allow[s] people to forge broad-based agreements that don't minimize their differences, but treat them fairly. This is . . . where statesmen and stateswomen rise above self-interest and reassert a common ground that encourages diverse groups to work co-operatively **without compromising their deepest convictions**.'[17]

Bole *et al.* (2004) drew on the earlier work of the Woodstock Theological Center (see pp. 34f. above) and of Shriver 1995,[18] Johnston and Sampson 1995, Gopin 2000, and Appleby 2000, and case studies in Bosnia, Northern

---

[17] Accessed 6 April 2006. Bold type in the text.
[18] Shriver (1995: 9) identifies forgiveness in the political sphere as a multifaceted phenomenon: see p. 114 above.

Ireland and South Africa. They explored forgiveness as part of a wider strategy for conflict prevention, conflict resolution and reconciliation where there has been structural wrongdoing.[19] They identify that what is required is for representatives of a community to express corporate repentance and for corporate agents to express the community's forgiveness. What is typically accepted and acceptable is an apology, and what then often follows is 'a commitment to repairing fractured relationships between communities' (Bole *et al.* 2004: 70). Primarily needed are expressions of forbearance from revenge, forgiveness and reconciliation by individuals to other individuals (Bole *et al.* 2004: 75–81). Together these help promote a measure of peace and reconciliation in communities. It is also worth noting that the process is often slow and sometimes cannot be shown to work: Appleby (2000: 191) observes that 'Skeptics will note that while Northern Ireland boasted more peacemakers per capita and per square mile than any other site of conflict in the world, sectarian violence persisted. To date the strongest argument in favor of this concentrated and persistent peace work is virtually impossible to demonstrate empirically . . .'

Finally, we turn to the question whether groups can forgive individuals. Benn (1996) has made an important contribution to the question.

Benn acknowledges that a victim alone may forgive an offender. He recognises that others also will have been affected by the wrongdoing. For example, in the case of the murder of a child, the child's parents and siblings will have been affected, as well also as the wider community of the child, such as the child's school and neighbourhood. The former group, Benn suggests, are 'secondary victims', the latter 'tertiary victims'. The question Benn poses is this: since the wrongdoers can never be forgiven, must they remain for ever the objects of moral opprobrium and so excluded from the possibility of reconciliation and reintegration into society? (One is reminded here of Cain who murdered Abel, his brother: see Genesis 4:8–16.) Benn's solution (see page 8, above) is to introduce the concept of 'quasi-forgiveness'.[20] If a wrongdoer repents (and so implicitly reaffirms the moral integrity of the victim), the wrongdoer may be readmitted as a member of the moral community.

The notion of 'quasi-forgiveness' is clearly important not only in the case of wrongdoing by one individual towards another but also in the

---

[19] Volf (1996) also explores reconciliation in the context of what he calls 'embrace', welcoming others by making space for them non-judgmentally. Forgiveness has a crucial part if there are difficulties with making such an 'embrace'.

[20] This idea is echoed by Horsbrugh (1974: 274), Haber (1991: 45) and (without reference to Benn) Biggar (2001: 209). The idea is also expressed by Hollis in Wiesenthal 1998 (and earlier editions).

case of conflicts and wrongdoing between groups of people, such as there have been in recent years in South Africa, Rwanda and Bosnia, and in the less recent past as a result of the Second World War. It establishes a moral framework for reconciliation where there are no longer victims who survive to forgive. The key is repentance by the wrongdoer as the basis of reconciliation, though, as I have said, it is difficult meaningfully to speak of groups 'forgiving'.

### CAN INDIVIDUALS FORGIVE GROUPS?

People experience distress because of wrongs perpetrated on behalf of groups just as they do because of wrongs by individuals. To take one out of many examples, protests continue by surviving 'comfort women' from Korea, Taiwan and the Philippines who had been taken in the period 1932–45 to 'comfort stations' for the sexual gratification of soldiers in the Japanese army. Even though the Japanese government set up the Asian Women's Fund to collect private donations for the surviving women, the surviving women continue to protest that the government has failed to reveal the full extent of what happened, acknowledge responsibility, apologise or punish those responsible.[21]

Individuals cannot forgive groups for the same reasons that groups cannot forgive or be forgiven by other groups (see above). Even if individuals could forgive groups, it would be very difficult to do so because within a group there are so many different degrees of responsibility and accountability. For example, with the system of *apartheid* in South Africa, there were at least three categories of people (not necessarily exclusive) who could be regarded as wrongdoers. First, there were those who actively supported, promoted and upheld the structures of *apartheid*. These people were the architects of the oppressive system who managed and sustained its oppressive effects. Second, there were individuals who personally committed acts of violence and abuse. Third, there were those who benefited from *apartheid* without actively engaging in its overtly violent expressions and who, because they were tacit participants, also share in responsibility for the system: either they did not oppose the system (but enjoyed its benefits) or, by their inaction, they appeared to condone the system.

One could imagine with a model of unconditional forgiveness such as that of Enright and the HDSG that one could 'forgive' a group, because

---

[21] See www.bbc.co.uk/go/pr/fr/-/hi/world/asia-pacific/4749467.stm, accessed on 9 August 2005, www.ipsnews.net/news.asp?idnews=29789, accessed on 10 August 2005 and www.amnestyusa.org/news/document.do?id= 80256DD400782B84802570590039A155, accessed on 10 August 2005.

Enright's model does not involve the victim engaging with the wrongdoer except as a mental construct in the victim's mind. But even if an individual could forgive a group, the amount, extent and variety of what would need to be forgiven beggars belief and is probably more than most people could do. For it is not only those who perpetrate specific acts of wrongdoing who would need to be forgiven but also those who sustained the oppressive system and those who put that system in place.

When it comes to individuals forgiving groups, it is very significant – and this in part accounts for the outcome of the Truth and Reconciliation Commission in South Africa – that Archbishop Tutu fused the Christian (individualistic) idea of forgiveness in the New Testament with the African (corporate) idea of *ubuntu*.

*Ubuntu* (so far as it can be expressed in non-African thought according to Tutu 1999: 34f.) means 'humanness' or 'humanity to others' and it implies that corporate and social needs take priority over what is personal and individualistic. Life is most fully experienced, according to the concept of *ubuntu*, in a corporate setting in which actions are judged according to whether they are socially responsible, and individuals are interdependent parts of the corporate whole. A person's awareness that he or she belongs to a 'greater whole' means that 'he or she . . . is diminished when others are tortured or oppressed, or treated as if they were less than who they are'. The goal of *ubuntu* is social harmony. To have *ubuntu* means that one is compassionate, generous, loving and forgiving. *Ubuntu* 'speaks of the very essence of being human' and '[a]nger, resentment, lust for revenge . . . are corrosive of this good. To forgive is not just to be altruistic. It is the best form of self-interest.'

The idea of *ubuntu* drove Tutu's belief that there was no future for the nation and for the individuals within it without a corporate focus to forgiveness. It was on the corporate dimension of forgiveness – making a better society for South Africa – that Tutu focused and, given that corporate focus, not on the traditional (individualistic) elements of repentance and remorse. According to Cherry (2004: 170), people forgave in part in response to pressure 'to testify that the oppressed . . . adhered to a world-view or theology which was the complete antithesis of apartheid'. Forgiveness demonstrated that 'a new sense of common humanity was emerging' in South Africa, a 'tragically and violently divided country'.

The chairman of the Commission, Archbishop Tutu, believed that it was right for victims to forgive wrongdoing unconditionally, even when the wrongdoing was by unknown individuals acting for state organisations. From the comments of the victims who gave evidence to the Commission, it is clear that many were not able to forgive those who did not or would not identify themselves as perpetrators of wrongdoing. This is not surprising since, for most people, a group will seem too nebulous to forgive. As I have said, forgiveness is personal, relational and moral and has to do with justice. For most people, if there is to be any possibility of forgiveness, what will be needed are personal acknowledgments of wrongdoing by identifiable individuals. Even then, forgiveness can be difficult. For example, during a series of television programmes with Archbishop Tutu aimed at promoting peace and reconciliation in Northern Ireland, a Belfast woman came face-to-face with the soldier who killed her brother. The soldier described the circumstances of the fatal shooting and then apologised. The woman said, 'I haven't got the power to forgive anyone . . . but I thank you for telling the truth.'[22]

Given that it is difficult – if not impossible – for victims to forgive structural wrongdoing, a mechanism has been devised that sometimes enables individual wrongdoers from a group to be identified and for the individual wrongdoers to express repentance and contrition for their part in the wrongdoing. The mechanism is to set up a commission called a 'Truth and Reconciliation Commission' or something similar. Since the early 1980s, Commissions have been set up in Latin America (Argentina, Peru, Bolivia, Chile, Guatemala, Uruguay, El Salvador), in Asia (East Timor), in Africa (Uganda, Ghana and South Africa) and in Europe (Serbia).[23] Such commissions usually have three roles: to gather facts about violations of human rights, to investigate the causes of the violations (for example, whether social, economic or political) and to compile a public report containing a detailed account of the findings, often with recommendations. The aims have been to avoid vengeance, retaliation and victimisation and to promote in their place understanding, reparation and reconciliation. In the course of the work of the Commissions, individual victims sometimes meet those who have wronged them.

The Truth and Reconciliation Commission in Serbia (set up in 2001) has not been successful. Its limited aims were to establish facts that had led to civil war, to disseminate the results of its findings and to co-operate with similar commissions and bodies in other countries. The Commission has been strongly criticised in Serbia and many consider that it was set up too hastily and without public support (Nikolić-Ristanović 2003).

---

[22] Reported in www.timesonline.co.uk/article/0,,6-2074741.html. Accessed on 17 March 2006.
[23] Only the Commissions in South Africa and Chile were called 'Truth and Reconciliation Commission'.

In contrast, probably the most successful and the best-known example of a Truth and Reconciliation Commission is the one set up by the South African government in 1996 under the Promotion of National Unity and Reconciliation Act (1995). Those who framed the Act recognised that there were human rights abuses in every section of society. The aim of the Act was to seek to address and heal the scars of *apartheid* in South Africa through the work of the Commission.

The word 'forgiveness' does not appear in the Act, though words such as 'restoration' and 'reconciliation' do. The Act (according to its preamble) seeks to establish the truth about the country's troubled past and, in the pursuit of national unity 'in a spirit of understanding which transcends the conflicts and divisions of the past' (§ 3(1)), aims to promote national unity, reconciliation and social reconstruction.

The Act set up bodies to establish the facts about the violations of human rights in the country between 1960 and 1994. Paragraph 11(g) permitted the use of 'informal mechanisms for the resolution of disputes, including mediation, arbitration or any procedure provided for by customary law'. The hope was that those brought before the Commission would acknowledge the wrong that they had done under the *apartheid* system and express contrition, and that a measure of relief and then reconciliation would ensue.

The Commission had a number of powers that Commissions in other countries did not typically have. For example, provision was made for those who had committed violations of human rights to apply for an amnesty. Public hearings to consider the applications could be held (§ 29(1)(c)); so long as full disclosure of all relevant facts was made and if need be compensation paid to the victims, an amnesty could be granted. A body was set up, the Committee on Reparation and Rehabilitation, which was empowered to make recommendations 'in an endeavour to restore the human and civil dignity' of the victims of wrongdoing (§ 26(3)). There was also a fund, the President's Fund, out of which payments to victims for 'reparation' (§ 42(2)) could be made. The Commission also had power to recommend criminal prosecution instead of an amnesty, to subpoena witnesses and to 'search and seize' in pursuit of its investigations.

Laudable though the aims of the Commission were, it soon became clear that it was unable to secure justice or redress for many who had suffered (for some anecdotal examples, see Cose 2004: 103–7). The hope of the Commission and those who set it up was that victims would accept the work of the Commission as a means to promote national unity and peace in the future. Some wrongdoers did acknowledge their wrongdoing; others refused, denied their involvement or disputed the version of events. Cose (2004: 15) wrote of one victim, a woman called Thandi, who 'came [to the Truth and Reconciliation Commission and gave her evidence in public] expecting some sort of closure but instead ran into a wall of denial . . . Thus the scars of the so-called reconciliation process were added to the scars apartheid had left . . .'

Sometimes, evidence of wrongdoing was destroyed by wrongdoers before the Commission could investigate; many victims waited a long time for compensation – and when they did receive compensation, they did not regard it as adequate recompense for their suffering. Those who acknowledged their wrongdoing did so knowing they would almost certainly benefit from an amnesty and would not face criminal penalties for their actions. The Commission did not have power to set or enforce penalties for wrongdoing as part of the process of restoration, and for this reason some who wanted retribution were deeply dissatisfied with the Act and its aims. It was also very difficult for some to come to terms with the amnesties that those who had committed gross crimes were given on the basis only of their disclosure of facts. The Commission did not seek to promote forgiveness and wrongdoers were not required to demonstrate repentance, remorse or contrition. The Commission was also significantly under-resourced: it was impossible to uncover and document all the facts and often impossible to identify and confront the perpetrators of wrongs. Carmichael (2003: 131) quotes one person who refused to forgive her son's murderer. She said: 'It is easy for Mandela and Tutu to forgive . . . they lead vindicated lives. In my life nothing, not a single thing, has changed since my son was burnt by barbarians . . . Therefore I cannot forgive.' There was no justice for the woman and she was not in a position to forgive.

What the Commission did achieve for some people was to enable them to put emotional closure on some of the issues they faced. They were given the opportunity to face the wrongdoers and to hear a measure of regret and remorse. Emotional healing, if not often forgiveness and true reconciliation, has sometimes been the result, and this has enabled victims and their relatives to let go of much of their anger and hate and to invest in the new future of South Africa. The effect of the work of the Commission has been not only to help to avoid what many feared would be an orgy of revenge, hatred and reprisals in the country but also for some to open 'the door for the other person to begin again' (Tutu in Enright and North 1998: xiii). To this extent, the Commission was a success.

The question whether individuals can forgive groups has also been particularly clearly highlighted with regard to Jewish–German relations – but with a difference. The difference has to do with the extent to which individuals in *later* generations can be attributed with continuing responsibility and accountability for the wrongs of individuals in *former* generations. For example, some continue to hold modern-day Germans responsible for the actions of Germany in the period 1933–45. We discuss the following example to illustrate the issues.

When Rabbi Joseph Polak was a young child, he was imprisoned in the concentration camp at Bergen-Belsen. On 9 April 1945, the Germans began to transfer him and some 2,500 others to gas chambers at Theresienstadt. The journey should have lasted only one day but, because of the chaos in Germany at the time, the train driver could not find a clear route. On 23 April 1945, the train stopped at a destroyed bridge on the river Elster, near Troebitz, and the Russian army rescued the surviving passengers. Fifty years later, in 1995 at a commemoration of the event, the German Minister of Culture reminded his hearers that, of German people alive in 1995, 85 per cent were aged five or under when the train journey took place. Polak wrote in response, 'The deeds of your parents cannot be forgotten, and as long as memory stirs . . . you are bound to be their representative, and your hands will be stained with blood that you yourselves may not have spilled. For as long as people remember history . . . you are destined to take responsibility for this darkness and never, ever to be forgiven for it.'[24]

Polak's view is difficult to justify. Not all Germans in the period 1933–45 supported what their government did, and many born after 1945 have repudiated what the National Socialists stood for. In addition, there is hardly continuity between the republic of 1919–45 and the republic established by a new constitution after 1945. Martin (1997: 145) observed that culpability cannot be 'attributed to every member of a social category' (such as a nation) because it 'blurs the distinction between innocent and culpable so essential to all justice' and because it 'implies the automatic transfer of guilt from one generation to another through membership in the nation'. Scarre (2004: 75) argues that 'guilt is not a heritable commodity . . . Neither the status of wrongdoer nor that of being wronged can be bequeathed.' The same conclusion has been clearly expressed by Elie Wiesel, a former inmate at Auschwitz and Buchenwald concentration camps and subsequent Nobel Prize winner. On 19 April 1985, he said in response to President Reagan who

---

[24] Quoted by Smedes (1984: 349). Additional information from www.ddaymuseum.org/about/news_032204.html, accessed on 4 May 2005. An article by Polak on the subject entitled 'The Lost Transport' appeared in *Commentary* 100 (1995).

had presented him with a Congressional Gold Medal: 'I do not believe in collective guilt, nor in collective responsibility; only the killers were guilty. Their sons and daughters are not.'[25]

It is therefore not appropriate to hold all Germans responsible for the acts of the National Socialists in the period 1933–45, and it is not appropriate to seek to 'forgive' modern Germans for actions they did not do, or with which they do not agree and the morality of which they have repudiated. It is also not possible for a Jew (or anyone else) to forgive a modern-day German for the acts of that person's parents or grandparents in the period of the National Socialists: modern-day Germans, who are from a later generation, do not have moral responsibility for those acts. Guilt – and the resulting responsibility – is personal, not collective; neither is it transmissible through generations.[26]

So why do some hold modern-day Germany genealogically responsible for the misdeeds of the National Socialist era? I suggest that it is fear that the persecution of Jewish people may recur and that modern-day Germany has not repudiated its National Socialist past. It is also because the consequences of German misdeeds continue to last, both in their effects and in the memories of survivors. The call for today's Jews to forgive is, in effect, a call for today's Jews to engage with Germany's express repudiation of the past. One generation cannot forgive the wrongs of a previous generation; but that generation can accept that successor generations have repudiated the sins of the past.

### INDIVIDUAL WRONGDOERS IN GROUPS

We turn now to the third question posed at the start of this chapter: To what extent are individuals personally responsible for the actions they do on behalf of groups? Can individuals hide behind the mask of corporate identity, arguing that what they did represented not their own actions but the actions of the group? Can they thereby protect themselves from personal responsibility for the wrong they did and from accountability to the people they have wronged?

Quite simply, it is repulsive to deny that individuals remain morally accountable for their own wrongdoing, whether carried out on behalf of

---

[25] www.pbs.org/eliewiesel/resources/reagan.html, accessed on 4 May 2005. Wiesenthal (1998: 93) wrote of Germans sharing the 'shame' of what the Nazis did: what is not clear is whether Wiesenthal is referring to Germans who were contemporaries of the Nazis or those of subsequent generations. On the subject, see also Pettigrove 2003.

[26] See the example of Andrew Hawkins, referred to at pp. 117–18 above.

a group or on their own behalf. In the case of wrongdoing carried out on behalf of a group, though a group may be *legally* accountable for some of the actions of individual members (see below on this), the group cannot be *morally* responsible for the actions of its individual members. If individuals do not remain morally responsible for their own actions, there would be a genus of individual behaviour that was outside the purview of personal moral accountability.

This point has been illustrated by the actions of William J. Kimbro, a US Navy dog handler who worked in the Abu Ghraib detention centre in Iraq. At the court martial of another dog handler, it was said that unmuzzled dogs were being used to frighten and intimidate Iraqi detainees. Kimbro described how he had refused to do this and had walked away with his dog from an interrogation of a prisoner. In his evidence at the court martial on 15 March 2006, Kimbro said, referring to this practice, 'To me, it's a wrong thing to do. It's my morals. It's my morals and it's my professional opinion.'[27]

It is not always straightforward to establish personal moral responsibility for wrongdoing by an individual who is part of a group. Martin (1997: 154–61) explores the difficulty cogently. There is, he says, sometimes 'an extended chain between major decisions and minute implementations' that results in 'a dispersal of moral responsibility' that makes it 'difficult to arrive at some [personal] moral accountancy' (pp. 155f.). Put simply, were those who lit the pyre that consumed Cranmer guilty of wrongdoing – and if not they, then who?

Since the Second World War, individual legal liability for wrongs carried out on behalf of groups has been refined through the concept of 'crimes against humanity' and 'human rights'. The root of these ideas is a certain 'sacredness' about human beings, a sacredness that means that people should be treated with dignity and respect and that people, by virtue of their common humanity, share certain rights and obligations towards one another. According to Derrida (2001a: 30), secular thinking has borrowed what he calls 'Abrahamic' ideas about forgiveness (by which he means the thinking about forgiveness of the three great monotheistic faiths) and, as a result of notions such as 'crimes against humanity' and 'human rights', gives a secular legitimation for these ideas and sets the context for discourse on them.

---

[27] Reported in www.foxnews.com/story/0,2933,188008,00.html. A summary of Kimbro's evidence is in www.publicintegrity.org/docs/AbuGhraib/Abu21.pdf and the Taguba Report that commended Kimbro's action can be found at http://news.findlaw.com/hdocs/iraq/tagubarpt.html (all accessed on 13 August 2006). Kimbro's actions are discussed further at pp. 137–8 below.

In relation to nations, the doctrine of 'act of state' at one time protected state agents who acted in their official capacity on behalf of the state from personal legal liability for international criminal acts: only the state could be called to account. This was known in customary international law as 'functional immunity'. After the Second World War, functional immunity was regarded as no longer applicable to senior state officials accused of war crimes, of crimes against peace or crimes against humanity. More recently, the immunity also no longer applied to those who committed torture (see Cassese 2003: 267, n. 8). This lifting of immunity is now regarded as a rule of customary international law (Cassese 2003: 268) and was enunciated in *obiter dicta* by Lord Millet and Lord Phillips of Worth Matravers in an appeal case by the Judicial Committee of the House of Lords.[28]

A customary rule of international law has now also evolved whereby it is no longer a defence to argue that an international crime committed by a subordinate (whether military or civilian) may be excused because the subordinate was acting on 'superior orders'. The changed view came about as a result of the International Military Tribunal in Nuremberg (1945–9) and the International Military Tribunal for the Far East (1946–8), which tried what were termed 'crimes against peace', 'war crimes' and 'crimes against humanity'.

International war crimes have recently been successfully prosecuted by *ad hoc* International Criminal Tribunals set up by the Security Council for the former Yugoslavia (Resolution 827 of 25 May 1993 and www.un.org/icty) and for Rwanda (Resolution 955 of 8 November 1994 and www.ictr.org).[29] In 2002, the International Criminal Court was set up under the Rome Statute of the International Criminal Court (1998): this is a permanent court that has jurisdiction to try war crimes and serious violations of human rights committed after 1 July 2002. The creation of the Court has been described as 'perhaps the most innovative and exciting development in international law since the creation of the United Nations' (Schabas 2004: 25). The Court is currently investigating war crimes committed in the Democratic Republic of Congo and in the Darfur region of western Sudan; it is also

---

[28] R. *v.* Bow Street Metropolitan Stipendiary Magistrate, and others, *ex parte* Pinochet Ugarte (Amnesty International and others intervening) (no. 3); judgment on 24 March 1999 in [1999] 2 All ER 97–192. *Obiter dicta* at 171–9 and 186–90.

[29] By March 2005, there had been twenty convictions, including the former prime minister and four government ministers. The tribunal has regarded rape and other sexual crime as constituting genocide in the same way as any other serious bodily or mental harm, so long as the acts were committed with the intent to destroy a particular group targeted as such.

considering whether to investigate war crimes in northern Uganda (see www.icc-cpi.int).[30]

The trial of Adolf Eichmann (1961) illustrates the legal changes that have been taking place. Eichmann was head of the Department for Jewish Affairs (1941–5) in Germany. Part of his responsibilities was to oversee the deportation of Jews to extermination camps. About three million Jews were deported and most died.

One of the grounds of Eichmann's defence at his trial[31] was that, because he had obeyed orders, he was not responsible for his actions and so not personally culpable. In effect, he was arguing that there was no moral connection between himself and his acts, that his acts were the acts of his military superiors and that therefore he was not legally or morally responsible for those actions.

In the court of first instance, there were several lines to Eichmann's defence at this point. The first (paragraph 232) was that only those who gave orders were fully responsible for their actions; those who received orders were supposed only to obey them and carried no burden of moral responsibility for them. Even if that were right, the judge found that Eichmann himself gave orders and (paragraph 235) that he was 'energetic, full of initiative and active to the extreme in his efforts to carry out the Final Solution'. In other words, he was not an automaton mindlessly obeying superior orders.

The second line of defence was, in the words of the judgment (paragraph 228), that Eichmann was 'an insignificant official, with no opinion of his own in all matters with which he had to deal, and as lacking all initiative in his work'.[32] The judge's finding was that this was not true: Eichmann had carried out his tasks 'wholeheartedly and willingly . . . and also because of an inner conviction . . . that he was thereby fulfilling an important national mission' (paragraphs 228, 231). It was not that 'his mind [had] . . . ceased to function, or that it functioned only out of blind obedience . . . He acted within the general framework of the orders that were given to him. Within this framework, he went to every extreme to bring about the speedy and complete extermination of all Jews' (paragraph 241).

---

[30] See also www.sc-sl.org/, on the Special Court for Sierra Leone for the trial of Charles Taylor on war crimes, crimes against humanity, and other serious violations of international humanitarian law, (including sexual slavery and mutilations allegedly committed in Sierra Leone).

[31] Attorney-General of Israel *v.* Adolf Eichmann: District Court of Jerusalem (ET of the judgment of 12 December 1961 in 36 *ILR* 5–276); appealed in the Supreme Court, sitting as a Court of Criminal Appeal, with judgment (ET of the judgment of 29 May 1962 in 36 *ILR* 277–341).

[32] On this, see p. 10 above.

Notwithstanding Eichmann's defence, the judge made it clear that an act of such moral turpitude as the Final Solution could never be regarded as a 'political act' or 'act of state' for which there would be no personal criminal responsibility (paragraph 216). State agents, acting in their official capacity, remained personally responsible for international criminal acts, even if they were carried out in obedience to the orders of the state (paragraphs 28 and 216, and paragraph 14 of the appeal).

What happens when an individual participates in an act that could be regarded as part of a pattern of wrongdoing initiated, promoted and carried out by individuals on behalf of the group? If the individual comes to regret the action, can the individual be forgiven and, if so, by whom? These questions have been disturbingly highlighted in Simon Wiesenthal's book, *The Sunflower* (1998). The particular issue in the book is whether an individual, who recognised that he was a wrongdoer and who spoke about his personal remorse for the wrongdoing, could be forgiven not by the victims (they had been killed by the wrongdoing) but by someone whom the wrongdoer regarded as a representative of the victims.

Wiesenthal writes about when he was a prisoner in the Lemberg concentration camp and was asked to hear the 'confession' of a young German *Schutzstaffel* (SS) soldier, named Karl, who lay dying in hospital. The soldier spoke of how he had shot dead three members of a family, including a child, who had jumped from a burning house in Dnepropetrovsk that he and other soldiers had set alight. The house had been crammed with hundreds of Jews, mainly women, children and the infirm. Wiesenthal says: 'Here was a dying man – a murderer who did not want to be a murderer but who had been made into a murderer by a murderous ideology. He was confessing his crime to a man who perhaps tomorrow must die at the hands of those same murderers. In his confession there was true repentance' (Wiesenthal 1998: 53). When the man asked for forgiveness, Wiesenthal was silent and left the room. The question Wiesenthal poses is whether his silence at the bedside of the dying man was right or wrong. He also asks his readers what they would have done in that situation. The book was first published in 1969. The most recent edition of the book (1998) contains an inter-faith symposium with contributions from fifty-three people exploring the dilemmas Wiesenthal faced.

Wiesenthal's book raises very complex questions. They have to do not only with guilt, repentance and forgiveness when it comes to personal acts of wrongdoing but also with personal guilt arising from being part of an oppressive system. They also have to do with the degree to which individuals within such a system can be held responsible for their wrongful actions – and, very significantly, the degree to which they can repent. Also implicit is the question discussed by Scarre (2004: 4ff.): whether it is necessary to distinguish between wrongs that amount to an 'atrocity' (such as the Holocaust, the bombing of Dresden, the massacres at My Lai, and so on) and 'more common-or-garden' wrongdoing that is not so severe and extensive in its effects. In the following discussion, I am less concerned with distinctions between different kinds of evil than with the existential impact that wrongdoing has on the person who suffers.

Turning first to the questions concerning personal guilt, repentance and forgiveness, the answer is easy to give. It is regarded as axiomatic that only victims can forgive wrongs against them. This is the widely held view among writers on the subject (e.g., Holmgreen 1993: 341; but cf. Neblett 1974: 270). Karl cannot therefore be forgiven by someone who is regarded as a representative of the victims: in asking Wiesenthal for forgiveness, he was asking the wrong person. Forgiveness is the gift of the person who has been wronged, and not of any other person. Wiesenthal therefore *could* not forgive the soldier, even if he had wanted to. Wiesenthal's friend in the concentration camp, Josek, said the same to Wiesenthal:

I feared at first that you had forgiven him. You would have had no right to do this in the name of people who had not authorized you to do so. What people have done to you yourself, you can, if you like, forgive and forget. That is your own affair. But it would have been a terrible sin to burden your conscience with other people's sufferings. (Wiesenthal 1998: 65).

This also seems to be Wiesenthal's own conclusion (pp. 97f.). There was no possibility of *any* human being expressing forgiveness to the soldier, for there were no human beings still alive whom the German soldier had wronged.

Wiesenthal could not forgive on behalf of the murdered Jews. This is because the Jews had not authorised or asked him to forgive and he was not their representative. Karl *regarded* Wiesenthal as a representative (Wiesenthal 1998: 66, 81) but Wiesenthal was not. Josek said that he believed in life after death and that Wiesenthal would meet the Jews whom Karl had killed. He then asked, '"How would it seem then if you had forgiven [Karl]? Would not the dead people from Dnepropetrovsk come to you and ask: 'Who gave you the right to forgive our murderer?'"' (p. 66). And in regarding Wiesenthal as representing Jews in general and the Jews whom Karl murdered, is there not an element in Karl's thinking that Jews were different from other human beings, that they could be treated as having a collective, not individual, identity and that an apology to any one Jew was therefore good enough to serve as an apology to other Jews? In this connection, see Asch (1946) who demonstrated that the way a person was given personal information about others could colour the entire impression. Thus, the hostile description of the Jews – and travellers, disabled people and homosexuals – by the Nazis would have coloured what little good the soldier already knew.

The request to forgive is, in my view, a request that reinforces the abuse that Wiesenthal was suffering. Agents of the Nazi 'system' had incarcerated Wiesenthal and treated him as being in a subhuman category of existence. But another agent of that system, Karl, was asking of Wiesenthal an act of selfless humanity that would have contradicted the system's designation of Wiesenthal – at the same time that Wiesenthal's inhumane treatment was continuing and was not repudiated by Karl. Wiesenthal in part noticed the abuse and the absurdity of the request, for Karl 'was confessing his crime to a man who perhaps tomorrow must die at the hands of those same murderers' (Wiesenthal 1998: 53).

We turn next to questions to do with personal guilt arising from being part of an oppressive system. It is clear that the soldier had repented of his wrongdoing to do with the murder of the Jews in Dnepropetrovsk. What is not clear is whether the soldier had repented of his participation in the oppressive system set up by the Nazis.[33] *If* Wiesenthal had been able to forgive the soldier for the murders, the question 'What should Wiesenthal have done when asked to forgive?' is best illustrated hypothetically as follows.

Suppose that Wiesenthal had been one of the victims of the atrocity that the soldier had helped to carry out and that Wiesenthal had survived to face the dying soldier. Should he have been morally virtuous and forgiven the soldier? Justice and moral integrity point away from any compelling reason why forgiveness was morally desirable. Wiesenthal remained oppressed (as a prisoner in a concentration camp) by the *same* abusive system that had promoted the murder of the Jews by the soldier. It is not just the act of killing that was wrong; also wrong is the fact of belonging to and participating in the oppressive system. The soldier remained part of that system. In his confession to Wiesenthal, it was only the act of murder of which he repented. He did not repent of his membership of the SS, or of participating

---

[33] Benn's notion of quasi-forgiveness (1996) is not relevant here because, though the soldier had repented of his actions at Dnepropetrovsk, he remained unrepentant about the system of which he remained part that oppressed people such as the citizens of Dnepropetrovsk and prisoners such as Wiesenthal.

in and colluding with the ideology of the Third Reich that overtly promoted racism and genocide.

Two reasons may militate against the answer I suggest to Wiesenthal's hypothetical dilemma. The first arises because some people may live in a culture where to speak of personal, moral responsibility for their actions is not appropriate. So, for example, one of the respondents in Wiesenthal's book, Harry Wu (who was imprisoned by the Chinese Communist government for nineteen years in Laogai for 'anti-rightist tendencies') wrote this: 'In China, there was no understanding that what the Communists did to their own people was in any way morally wrong. People . . . had no regard for an individual's well-being. There was no value put on a human's life because, quite simply, the leaders of the country placed no value on human life' (Wiesenthal 1998: 274). So when he met the woman who had engineered his imprisonment, Comrade Ma, Wu realised he had nothing to say to her and that she saw no reason to apologise or seek forgiveness. She said, '"It's over. It's over . . . All that happened is in the past. The whole country has suffered, our Party has suffered. There have been terrible mistakes. I'm very happy you have come back. We can do something together in the future"' (p. 273).

Second, Dith Pran, a victim of the Khmer Rouge under Pol Pot (and whose biography was the basis of the film *The Killing Fields*) distinguished between the leaders of atrocities (Pol Pot and the other principal leaders of the Khmer Rouge) and others, that is, uneducated people, many young, who were 'brainwashed' into carrying out the killings. People who are 'brainwashed' are not responsible for their actions in the same way as people who freely act. Wiesenthal raises this point as a supposition on p. 66 where he says to Josek, '"Obviously he was not born a murderer nor did he want to be a murderer. It was the Nazis who made him kill defenceless people."'

Scarre (2005) has explored how much excuse people may have if they sincerely adhere to a perverted ideology that leads them to commit immoral acts. Scarre (2005: 469) concludes that though some may be 'decent and misguided souls, many are not' and that in the cases of some ideologies we are not dealing with 'gigantic intellectual errors, with moral blame attaching only in so far as there was carelessness in checking the facts'. According to Scarre (2005: 462), '[n]ot all careless believing is morally blameworthy': but carelessness is blameworthy if 'both avoidable and likely to have harmful consequences' and if those who could exercise a critical stance fail to do so. What must be reckoned with as well are 'the cruelty, the sadism, the vicious hatred and the self-seeking' (Scarre 2005: 469) that characterise the actions of many who gladly upheld, promoted and practised those ideologies.[34]

The seminal work of Asch (1951) may also help explain why the soldier repented only of the murders. In a series of experiments, social psychologists in the United States invited students to join groups to participate in a 'vision test'. In each group, all except one of the participants were associates of the social psychologists. Members of the group were invited to state which one of three lines of different lengths shown on a card was identical with a line shown on another card. They were also asked to say of the remaining two lines which was the shorter and which the longer. The associates all gave demonstrably incorrect answers. The aim of the experiment was to study the conditions that induced individuals to resist or to yield to group pressure to conform and modify their interpretation based on the opinion of the majority.

About one third of those who were not associates of the social psychologists conformed to the view of the erroneous majority. They did so for one of three reasons:

(i)  they believed their own perception to be wrong; or
(ii)  they believed the majority perception to be correct; or
(iii)  they wanted to avoid being different and so conformed to the majority, even though they believed the majority to be wrong.

Is the soldier in Wiesenthal's example someone who supported Nazi oppression because of misplaced conformity? There is no evidence that he conformed because he thought his own perception to be wrong or because he did not want to be different. Although he was deeply troubled about the acts of brutality he had committed, it appears that he believed the majority to be correct. He is morally blameworthy for failing to exercise a critical stance – especially after his conscience had become troubled about his actions – and for unthinkingly participating in an evil ideology.

I referred above (p. 130) to the refusal of William J. Kimbro to use unmuzzled dogs to assist in the interrogation of Iraqi prisoners in the Abu Ghraib detention camp. Kimbro gave two reasons for his refusal: the first was that it was immoral ('To me, it's a wrong thing to do. It's my morals. It's my morals and it's my professional opinion') and the second (perhaps

---

[34]  See also Scarre 2003: 104 on distinguishing between 'the wrong character of the deed and the guiltiness of the doer'. Thus, (mistaken) belief about the moral propriety of an action may explain why it was done, and error, ignorance and cultural conditioning may diminish the extent of the culpability of the wrongdoer without denying or diminishing the fact that the deed is wrong.

already anticipated in the phrase 'it's my professional opinion') was 'It's wrong to use your dog in any way that the dog is not trained to do.'[35]

The first reason clearly shows evidence of a critical (moral) stance but the second is far more pragmatic, reflecting Kimbro's concerns that the dogs were not trained to participate in the interrogation of prisoners and that it was unprofessional (rather than immoral) to use them in that way. In giving the second reason, Kimbro offers an unnecessary additional explanation of his otherwise principled moral stand. He is, perhaps, afraid of himself being court martialled for refusing to participate in what was apparently a widespread practice. It is as if, in his mind, moral reasons alone were not sufficient to justify his refusal to participate in immoral practices. It is at this point that we see how hard it can be for a relatively junior combatant to refuse to carry out what the combatant suspects are immoral orders. We also see how the distinction between orders and operating procedures can become blurred – especially in the heat of the moment – making it difficult to refuse to carry out the latter out of fear of inadvertently refusing the former.

Why also might Karl have participated in brutal and horrific acts? A famous experiment carried out by Milgram (1963) may help to explain. The purpose of Milgram's research was to understand why apparently normal people might engage in horrific acts of barbarity towards other people. Milgram's early work on the question took place around the time of Eichmann's trial for war crimes. In an experiment on the role of punishment in learning, participants were asked by a 'scientist' to give what the participants believed were increasingly severe electric shocks to a 'learner' every time the learner made a mistake. The participant thought the 'learner' was another co-participant; in fact the 'learner' was an actor. The astonishing finding was that 65 per cent of the participants continued to comply with the request of the 'scientist' to administer electric shocks to the learner up to the supposed maximum of 450 volts, and this was despite the screams and pleas for mercy of the 'learner' and even though the participants believed they were causing serious harm to the 'learner'. In *every* case, participants in the experiments supposedly administered a minimum of 300 volts.

Several reasons have been put forward to explain the disquieting results. First, the participants may have felt obligated to continue with the experiment having first committed themselves to take part in it. Second, the participants may have lost sight of the implications of their actions as they became absorbed in the procedures and technical aspects of the experiment.

[35] See www.foxnews.com/story/0,2933,188008,00.html, accessed on 13 August 2006.

This is borne out by the fact (clinically demonstrated) that the closer the 'scientist' was to the participants, the more the participants complied; the further away the 'scientist' and the nearer the 'learner', the less inclined participants were to administer the shocks. In other words, when the participants were more able to engage with the suffering of the 'learner' and less under the apparently authoritative influence of the 'scientist', the more the participants were able to make a principled response to the 'scientist's' requests. Third, the 'scientist' insisted that the scientist, not the participant, was fully responsible for any harmful effects resulting from the electric shocks.

What the results point to is that people tend to abrogate moral responsibility for their actions where they perceive that another has the power, role and authority to request a particular course of action and that other takes responsibility for the actions, especially when they are slightly detached from the victims of the wrongdoing. The findings help explain how authority figures can compel willing subjects to commit harmful acts which in other circumstances they would not countenance doing. The keys to this are the power and role expectations of the person in authority and the recognition of that power and role on the part of the other. The result can be that the person in authority may be able to control others and make them comply with his or her requests.

In the case of the soldier, the brutal acts that he committed may be attributable in part to the moral responsibility that others appeared to take for such actions. Nevertheless, the soldier remains morally responsible for his actions, as his conscience subsequently indicated, probably because it was not just that relatively faceless people were (for example) shot dead in battle, but that individuals – women and children – were heard and seen to suffer as they burned, jumped out of a building and were shot dead. Whatever the reason, the soldier's moral liability remains the same: not only did he do wrong in murdering these people, he also did wrong in adhering to a perverted and sordid ideology that seemed to him to legitimate such actions.

## CONCLUSION

As we have seen, the idea of corporate forgiveness – whether this refers to an individual forgiving a group or to one group forgiving another group – does not stand up to analytical scrutiny. The categories of thought that pertain to repentance and forgiveness concern only individuals and are not transferable to groups. Forgiveness is an interpersonal matter that has to do with the restoration of relations between individuals. Groups can, however, engage in forms of behaviour that are *akin* to repentance and forgiveness. For example, a group through its representatives may seek to restore relations either with individuals whom the group has wronged or with other groups that the group has wronged. If a group seeks restoration in this way, the result may be that people who were formerly estranged are reconciled. Though we cannot say that the group has repented or sought forgiveness, we can say that it has engaged in forms of behaviour that are imitative of what individuals may do.

Victims who have been wronged by individuals within groups will some-times have to accept that they will not be able to identify the individuals who have wronged them. They may also have to accept that many groups do not have mechanisms for establishing that wrongs have been done or who has done the wrongs. Sometimes an act may be so diffused in its incep-tion and execution that it is not realistic to attribute *moral* responsibility to any individual. Groups can also be self-serving and self-seeking and their representatives may do all they can to avoid and evade acknowledging that others within the group have done wrong.

Some victims will, therefore, be unable to seek redress against known individuals within groups who have wronged them. Others will not be able even to find out who within a group has wronged them. Such people may be left disillusioned and even broken or brutalised by the experience.

Is it harder to forgive unidentified individuals within a group for wrong-doing than to forgive a known wrongdoer within a group? I am unaware of research specifically on the question but popular wisdom would indi-cate that the former is the case. If forgiveness concerns the restoration of relations between individuals, it is hard to see how there can be *any* for-giveness if one of the individuals – the wrongdoer – cannot be identified. If this is right, there is a genus of wrongdoing – wrongdoing carried out by individuals within groups and which the victim cannot attribute to specific individuals – that is not simply hard to forgive but is, strictly speaking, impossible to forgive.

CHAPTER 8

# *Forgiveness, punishment and justice*

## RESTORATIVE JUSTICE

An important area of discussion in legal jurisprudence is a recent development called 'restorative justice'.[1] Though forgiveness is not explicitly discussed very often as part of the process of restorative justice, much about restorative justice implies forgiveness (or something closely related to forgiveness). One of the concerns of restorative justice is to reshape and redirect the retributivism that is implicit in the criminal law and for which some victims long. Restorative justice involves an expression of 'atonement' and can result in what may be termed a form of 'secular forgiveness' for wrong done. It is germane to the subject of this book because it focuses on disordered relationships where there has been wrongdoing. The intended outcome of restorative justice includes restoration and reconciliation, hopes that are similar to forgiveness.

Though most frequently discussed in the context of criminal behaviour, the theory of restorative justice is not another theory of criminal law (concerning itself with matters such as definitions of crimes, the nature and purpose of criminal legislation, punishment and personal responsibility).[2] Neither is it an adaptation of existing theories. Rather, as some have argued, it amounts to a new theory of justice (Gavrielides 2005: 93) for, unlike existing theories of criminal law, it is not based on the idea of punishment consequent upon the violation of a criminal law.

So, then, what is restorative justice? It is a process that seeks solutions to ruptured relationships. In one handbook, it is described as involving 'a meeting between victim and offender resulting in an agreed outcome requiring the offender to undertake some form of reparation in order to

---

[1] On restorative justice, see Zehr 1990, Zehr and Mika 2003, McLaughlin *et al.* 2003 and Gavrielides 2005. See also the extensive bibliographies at www.restorativejustice.org, www.iirp.org and www.pficjr.org

[2] Roberts 1998: 289, 302; Moore 1998, chapter 1; Lacey 1998: 13.

repair the harm that they have caused' (Campbell *et al.* 2006: 5). Restorative justice primarily aims to promote reconciliation, repair and restoration for all the parties concerned, that is, the healing of violated relationships (Zehr 1990: 181), often through the work of a mediator, and is not concerned with retribution. In the words of one popular definition, 'Restorative Justice is a process whereby all the parties with a stake in a particular offence come together to resolve collectively how to deal with the aftermath of the offence and its implications for the future' (Marshall 1999: 5). Unlike in the criminal law, restorative justice does not ask the question, 'Is such and such action a crime and should the wrongdoer be punished?' but asks the question, 'Is there a relationship between victim and offender or between offenders and their communities that needs to be restored?'[3]

Underpinning restorative justice is what Gavrielides (2005: 98) calls 'a "social liaison" that bonds individuals in a relationship of respect for others' rights and freedoms'[4] and that creates an obligation to restore what has been ruptured. The liaison is hypothesised as being 'innate' (Gavrielides 2005: 98) or 'spiritual' (Sullivan *et al.* 1998: 16) in origin and results in 'connections' between and interdependence of people and 'a collective ethos and collective responsibility' (Morris and Young 2000: 14). Criminal acts are therefore treated not so much as offences against the state but as actions that disrupt the mutuality of society or communities; and the way to deal with such acts is to seek to restore those disrupted by the crime.

In patterns of restorative justice, does the wrongdoer escape punishment? It remains a matter of debate whether punishment is (or can be) part of a system of restorative justice (see Duff 2001; Wright 2003; Willemsens 2003; Bennett 2003; Gavrielides 2005). It is important not to confuse restoration with mercy: mercy pleads for punishment to be waived: punishment may be integral to the process of restoration. Some speak of 'restorative punishment', that is, punishment that 'aims to restore, create, construct, repair and reintegrate' and that 'promotes a moral education, possibly creating a moral order in society'.[5] In restorative justice, punishment, if applicable

---

[3] On the restoration of relationships as part of the criminal justice system, see www.relationshipsfoundation.org, *The Relational Justice Bulletin* (started in 1998) and Burnside and Baker 1994. On forgiveness seen principally in relational terms, see the 'prosocial model' of forgiveness in Scobie and Scobie 1998.

[4] A similar idea is in Bennett 2003: 132. He refers to people being part of 'the moral community, . . . [that is,] a social group constituted by the shared commitment of its members to certain values, to a certain way of regarding and treating others, to certain ends' and says that if people do wrong, it 'puts their status as a member of the moral community in doubt'. Surprisingly, Gavrielides (2005) fails to identify the Judaeo-Christian background of restorative justice.

[5] Gavrielides 2005: 93. In this sense, restorative punishment is much like punishment in the utilitarian theory of punishment in that it seeks to promote better behaviour and to serve social cohesion. Most

at all, can be part of a process of restoring the wrongdoer as a responsible moral agent and citizen.[6] It also may serve the incidental purpose of affirming society's moral values, of reinforcing social cohesion and of providing a framework in which the wrongdoer can express contrition and then, significantly, move on. In this sense, it is part of a 'communicative . . . process that aims to persuade offenders to recognize and repent [of] the wrongs they have done, to reform themselves, and so to reconcile themselves with those they have wronged' (Duff 2001: 175). However, such punishment is not in the nature of revenge or retribution.

### RESTORATIVE JUSTICE AND THE NEW TESTAMENT

It has been argued (e.g., Gorringe 1996) that one of the principal interpretations of the atonement, the penal substitution (together with theories to do with satisfaction and the death of Christ as expiatory or propitiatory), has buttressed retributive approaches to justice.

Put simply, this interpretation of the atonement assumes that wrongdoing must be paid for by punishment that is deserved (because of the wrongdoing) and commensurate with the wrongdoing. Humanity has sinned against God and God demands a penalty for humanity's wrongdoing. Christ paid for humanity's wrongdoing as humanity's substitute. The sacrifice 'satisfied' God – and God frees the wrongdoer from the penalty for the wrongdoing. What is important to note is that retribution is at the heart of this model of the atonement, and has 'provided one of the subtlest and most profound justifications . . . for retributive punishment' in the criminal law (Gorringe 1996: 12).

The idea of penal substitution is problematic. Christ's death is not offered *to* God but suffered *by* God. It follows that the idea of propitiation (an offering of a sacrifice to God in order to regain God's favour) is not appropriate. In addition, a sacrifice is typically an offer of something that is one's own to another, but this is clearly not the case with the death of Christ. A model of the atonement that has at its heart retribution by an angry God is a corruption of the gospel that offers love and mercy to sinners.

---

modern theories of punishment seek an outcome that ensures that the wrongdoer is reintegrated into society and acts in the future as an accountable citizen. See also Duff (2001: 106) whose view is that 'criminal punishment . . . [is] a species of secular penance. It is a burden imposed on an offender for his crime, through which, it is hoped, he will come to repent of his crime, to begin to reform himself, and thus reconcile himself with those he has wronged.'

[6] This is consistent with the view of Murphy (2003: 111) that 'punishment is best justified in terms of promotion of the common good and the spiritual reformation of the individual'.

Christ's death is also said to be vicarious (Christ suffered and died in the place of the guilty sinner). The sinner's guilt is taken away and so the sinner, no longer guilty, stands forgiven. However, it is perverse to suppose that an innocent person can be deemed – by a fiction – to bear the punishment for another's wrongdoing and for the wrongdoer to evade personal responsibility. (I Peter 2:24 does not imply that Jesus bore the penalty of the sins of the people: he bore the sins, *not* that he might bear the penalty for them but that people might be *free* from them and so 'die to sin and live to righteousness'.)[7] How can guilt be transferable? Where is the justice if one person takes the responsibility for and the penalty of the wrongdoings of another?

Problematic though it is, the idea of the penal substitution does give an answer – albeit deeply unsatisfactory in other respects – to the question of how to reconcile the idea of divine justice with mercy. For if God is just, why does God not exact the punishment or reparation that justice demands and which God will demand of those who do not receive God's forgiveness through the gospel? If God is just as judge, why does God not give all people *exactly* what their wrongdoing merits – and is it not unjust to spare some but not all? The theory of the penal substitution does provide a solution to these questions – Christ has taken the place of sinners and borne their punishment – but, as I have indicated, this solution raises more problems than it solves.

It is undeniable that some of the ideas in this model of the atonement are present in the New Testament. This is especially true of Paul as he sought to understand the cross and the resurrection in the post-Easter period. Even so, these ideas do not exhaust the range of interpretations and explanations of the atonement. Other explanations, though at least equally prominent, are often less explored. These explanations tend to point away from a retributivist view of the atonement and towards a restorative view. For example, for Sanders, Paul's theology of the atonement is not expiatory, substitutionary or propitiatory – Sanders doubts that these categories of thought were relevant in the first century – but has to do with 'participation'. In other words, salvation comes from being incorporated into Christ, not by expiatory sacrifice. It comes from being 'in Christ' (e.g., 2 Corinthians 5:17) and by suffering and dying 'with him' (e.g., Romans 6:5) (Sanders 1976: 465). For Hooker (1990), atonement comes through 'interchange in Christ', not penal substitution. Another view is that the emphasis of Jesus' preaching

---

[7] In the New Testament, this idea of vicariousness probably means no more than that an offer is made to God that God will accept for the benefit of others (e.g., Moule 1998: 7), the benefit being the atonement and, as part of it, forgiveness.

in the Gospels is not on sacrifice, expiation or atonement for sin (Matthew 9:13, 12:8)[8] but on Jubilee and on the kingdom of God (partially present but with its full realisation yet to come), with an emphasis on love, non-retaliation, reconciliation, forgiveness, social justice and renewed communities and relationships (Stegemann and Stegemann 1999: 204–6). Those who practise the ethics of the kingdom of God confront the structures of a world that holds contrary values and, like Jesus, may as a result be destroyed. The resurrection is God's affirmation that such destruction is not the end – and it is God's call to others to practise the ethics of the kingdom and so to take up their cross. And despite language at times that is clearly sacrificial, Paul also transcends that language and transmutes it into a principle for establishing transformed communities and relationships (Romans 12:1f.) that promote reconciliation, forgiveness, love and justice.

The cross is also the place of gross injustice for a victim, the place of judicial murder on false charges because the political and religious *status quo* was challenged. It exposes those who condemned Jesus – and the lies, the desire to protect power, the moral compromise and the self-interest. The cross – and the events immediately preceding it – are points of betrayal, humiliation, scapegoating, sadism, violence and torture. It is here that God was in human form, identifying with and himself being one of the victims of abuse and sharing in human suffering. As Mary said in the Magnificat (Luke 1:46–55), God looks to and exalts such people. It was at the cross that Jesus absorbed the evil he suffered, without retaliation, anger or hatred. Though he suffered, he prayed that God would forgive those who sinned against him and in Christian tradition God is thought, through the resurrection, to offer forgiveness to all who respond to his love.

How might the New Testament support a restorative, rather than a retributivist, approach to justice?

One important strand in Christian tradition – seen, for example, in Matthew's Gospel – is that retribution and vengeance are not God's way for people (5:38f.). God's way is the way of non-retaliation (5:39–42), of love (5:44f.), forgiveness (6:12) and honest self-appraisal that recognises that one is as much a wrongdoer as anyone else (7:1–5). This teaching is echoed in Paul's writings (see, for example, Romans 12:19) and in 1 Peter 2:22–4 where Jesus' example of innocent suffering without retribution or revenge is taken to be the model for Christians to follow in their interpersonal relationships. To the extent that retribution is acceptable (if it is at all), it is, as Murphy

---

[8]   Mark 10:45 is not about sacrifice and it is mistaken to connect it to Isaiah 53:10 (Hooker 1959: 77). The Last Supper discourses are probably more in the nature of covenant ratification (Gorringe 1996: 65) or a celebration of the New Passover (Davies 1965: 252).

(2003: 101–3) argues, as *loving* retribution and not retribution motivated by hate, callous indifference or some other unworthy motive.

Second, restoration recognises that the aim of justice should be to promote restored relationships. Thus, restorative justice attends to the suffering of the victim and engages with it. It seeks to ensure that where possible the wrongs are put right and that they are not repeated. These are also among the principal concerns of the gospel, for the gospel addresses – and provides a solution to – the disrupted relationship not only between humanity and God but also between human beings. The focus of the gospel is love that means reconciliation (2 Corinthians 5:18–20) and restored human relationships. Jones (1995: 133) expresses this more strongly: he writes of God who lives 'in trinitarian relations of self-giving communion' and who longs to see the restoration of human communion 'with God, with one another, and with the whole creation'.

Third, the particular contribution that the New Testament makes to the practice of restoration is that forgiveness and, where appropriate, restitution (resulting from repentance) are the *sine qua non* of reconciliation. The same idea is in Horsbrugh 1974: 270: forgiveness has, he argues, a restorative function 'intended to heal some breach in a personal relationship that has occurred as a consequence of the injury'. It is not enough for the wrongdoer simply to apologise and to acknowledge wrongdoing, however painful that may be. For reconciliation to be effected, the victim must also seek restoration with the wrongdoer, and that too can be a deeply difficult and painful experience.

It is also worth adding that punishment *can* be restorative if it is an outcome agreed to by the parties and appropriate in the circumstances. It needs to be founded on recognition of guilt by the wrongdoer and the self-attribution of responsibility. In this sense, it is much like 'penance', a concept developed in the period after the completion of the New Testament, namely, an agreed punishment voluntarily undertaken as an outward expression of repentance for wrongdoing and as a means for restoring the wrongdoer to the community. There is a fine dividing line between this and retribution, but there does remain a distinction: the distinction has to do with the fact that the wrongdoer is repentant, accepts responsibility for the wrongdoing and (if appropriate) undertakes a self-imposed penalty as an expression of repentance and responsibility.

Finally, the theory of restorative justice recognises that human beings are interdependent and that the restoration of good relationships is essential for the effective functioning of human society and communities. This idea has long been a part of Christian *praxis* and teaching based in part on the essence of the gospel that sought to create new communities in Christ, and on two additional grounds: first, all people are made in the image of God and so in this sense are genealogically related. They should therefore behave and act in demonstration of that interconnectedness, recognising that violating one another amounts to a denial of the relationship people intrinsically have one to another. The second ground is that Christians, as members of the one body of Christ, are part of a mystical unity and it behoves them to act and behave in demonstration of that unity and of Christ into whose image they are being formed. The neighbour to whom we have obligations (and, to use the language of Gavrielides (2005), 'social liaison') is, from the Parable of the Good Samaritan (Luke 10:30–7), anyone with whom we come into contact and who looks to us as neighbour.

There are, nevertheless, points of divergence between the notion of restorative justice and what is in the New Testament. First, the focus of restorative justice is restoration, not forgiveness, and it is important to note that restorative justice does not necessarily mean that wrongdoer and victim forgive one another. What we are here concerned with is a *secular* mechanism designed to bring about reconciliation between estranged parties; the mechanisms of restorative justice are not predicated on the constituents of forgiveness that we have identified, whether from the New Testament or elsewhere. Some Christian thinkers link justice (whether restorative or retributive) with the idea of forgiveness: for example, Tutu (in Wiesenthal 1998: 268) wrote, 'It is clear that if we look only to retributive justice, then we could just as well close up shop . . . Without forgiveness there is no future.' Second, there is an important difference between the conceptual underpinning of theories of restorative justice and what the New Testament says about justice and restoration: on the whole, secular theories relating to restorative justice confine themselves to being 'theor[ies] of Justice Systems and not . . . theor[ies] of life' and do 'not imply that we need to take steps towards a transformation of our relationships or lives' (Gavrielides 2005: 99).[9] On the other hand, the interconnectedness between people that the Christian gospel postulates *does* call for transformed relationships and lives, and also for transformed communities. The kingdom of God is about more than transformed systems of criminal justice.

PUNISHMENT

To be vindictive is to respond in one kind of way to wrongdoing. It is to have a strong or unreasoning desire to hurt or harm someone in return

---

[9] It is hard to follow the logic of this limitation if human interdependence and interconnectedness arise from something innate or spiritual in the human condition. There is no necessary reason to limit the resulting moral obligations to matters of criminal justice only.

for an injury or wrong suffered (or thought to have been suffered) at that person's hands. Murphy offers 'two cheers' for vindictiveness (see p. 53, above). I argued in chapter 3 that it is hard to see how one can cheer at all for vindictive behaviour. I offer below further reasons why vindictiveness is morally ambivalent and probably even morally flawed.

Vindictiveness can result in different types of punishment: retaliation (repayment in kind, or the return of like for like), retribution (recompense for evil done) and vengeance (an act of retribution or vindictive punishment). These three types of punishment often coalesce in popular thought and practice and can be hard to distinguish.

Even those who say that punishment is defensible do not argue that *all* types of punishment are morally good.[10] Punishment can be directed appropriately or inappropriately. As most parents know, to lash out at another's wrongdoing in temper is different from administering reasonable chastisement. An important element of appropriate punishment is that people are held to account as morally responsible for their actions: the punishment is a penalty for failing to act in a morally responsible way (Falls 1987) or for failing to adhere to the norms of a society of which the offender is part (Murphy 1978a). It is also important that punishment should be both proportionate to the wrong done, and deserved.

Most theories of criminal justice insist that individuals must leave retribution to the judiciary. A state or country reserves to itself the right to impose punishment in the cause of justice for many types of wrong that it defines as 'criminal wrongs'. Beyond the sphere of social sanctions in response to wrongdoing (such as Murphy's refusal to have lunch with a former friend or the delivery of some cutting remarks – Murphy 2003: 24, 33), individuals in western societies are not permitted to take vengeance for wrongs that are defined as 'crimes'. Judicially imposed punishment ensures (theoretically at least) that punishments are just (that is, directed only at the guilty), proportionate to the wrong done and for breaches of law.

Judicially imposed retributive punishment has two obvious limitations. First, the judiciary imposes punishment only in response to violations of the law, not violations of moral principles (though the *degree* of punishment may be determined according to moral principles). This leaves unaddressed the question of punishment for wrongdoing that is not in breach of the law. Second, punishment imposed by the judiciary is not on behalf of an individual but on behalf of the state. Thus in criminal cases in the

[10] Reiff (2005: 120) poses this question: given one's vindictive feelings, when is it morally justified to retaliate and so to punish?

United Kingdom, prosecutions are in the name of the Queen who is Head of State. Although in some countries sentencing does now seek to take into account the views and interests of victims through 'Victim Impact Statements' (for example, in New Zealand and in some states in Australia and Canada), judicially imposed punishment is in society's interests and not the victims'. In this way, the criminal law *institutionalises* the retributive behaviour that people typically have towards wrongdoers and so *regulates* the extent, frequency and severity of retributive punishments – but it leaves some victims dissatisfied that *they* have not carried out the punishment.

What is the moral basis of retributive punishment? Different reasons have been given. Hegel (1770–1831) argued that to fail to punish wrongdoers would be to fail to respect the *wrongdoer* who has chosen the way of violence and pain. The view of Kant (1724–1804) is that wrongdoers ought to be punished because of their rationality. Kant assumes that a wrongdoer has implicitly consented to be punished as provided by the law. As wrongdoers wilfully violate the rights of their victims, to fail to punish them would be to disregard the rights that pertain to *wrongdoers* by virtue of their rational nature. His attitude to forgiveness shows 'a deep ambivalence' (Sussman 2005: 88). In its favour, to forgive helps prevent people from being overly vindictive. On the other hand, Kant assumes that to forgive means to wipe away sins and to forgo punishing the wrongdoer, and this is in conflict with the right of the wrongdoer to be punished for wrongdoing. The modern view is that it is morally right to 'return . . . suffering for evil voluntarily done' (Scarre 2004: 116). Others say that retributive punishment restores the moral equilibrium that wrongdoers disorder. Thus, when one person infringes the rights of another, that person 'gains an unfair advantage . . . The punishment – by imposing a counterbalancing disadvantage on the violator – restores the equilibrium . . .' (Hirsch 1976: 47).

At the heart of retribution is the idea that wrongdoing legitimates and requires wrongdoers to suffer in return – but we do not know *why*. It is hard to see a logical connection between retributive punishment and wrong-doing – the two are often thought about together but they are not necessarily related. For the same reasons, it is also hard to see a logical connection between retributive punishment and justice. Some who want retribution think that it will restore the balance of justice. However, retribution cannot do this – it is not possible to restore the *status quo ante* when it comes to morality – although it can create a new *status quo* that feels (but no more than feels) just to the victim.

There are, in addition, drawbacks to the idea of retributive punishment. First, there is no objective way of determining what makes punishment retributive: it is a matter of opinion about which others may disagree.[11] Second, there is no objective way to determine how we can establish what degree of punishment is proportionate to, and deserved because of, the crime. There are many instances where victim and judge disagree. Well known is the heartache of victims if the punishment is regarded as too lenient; also well known is public revulsion if the penalty is regarded as undeserved or too severe.[12] The idea is to give wrongdoers 'what they deserve' for the wrongdoing – like for like – or to make them 'pay' a notional debt that has arisen because of the wrongdoing. The librettist Arthur Sullivan memorably expressed this principle in the phrase 'let the punishment fit the crime' in Gilbert and Sullivan's comic operetta, *The Mikado* (Act II, Song 17) (1885). Even so, there is enormous variation in what people think is fair and just and there are no objective criteria for establishing it.

Third, though the 'debt to society' may have been paid at the end of a criminal sentence and (if we wish to put it this way) the crime atoned for, what of the victim who may continue to bear the physical or emotional scars of the crime? The wrongdoer is then free – but not the victim. Lord Tebbit has most movingly spoken of this. In an interview, he spoke of those who hid a bomb in the Grand Hotel in Brighton that exploded on 12 October 1984. The bomb left (among others) Tebbit badly injured and his wife, Mary, a quadriplegic. He said:

> Terrorists can be let out of jail none the worse for the loss of liberty for a few years.[13] But for victims, the slate is never wiped. Early release has no relief for the victim, unless it is into the grave from a ruined life or a body broken by the barbarous use of the bodies of the innocent to gain what the terrorist wants . . . For [my wife], pain is the ever present companion, disability the load she never ceases to bear.[14]

---

[11] See Reiff 2005: 117–25 for suggestions on how to assess whether an act of punishment is retributive.

[12] An example that made the national press in the UK in May 2006 is of a woman who threw a 'cheesy Wotsit' (akin to a potato crisp) out of her car window and was fined £75 for unlawfully discarding litter (http://news.bbc.co.uk/1/hi/england/beds/bucks/herts/4968534.stm – accessed on 8 May 2006).

[13] This is perhaps an overstatement. A lengthy jail term often has irreversible consequences for the former prisoner. What Tebbit means is that the consequences that he and his wife suffered are not comparable to the consequences suffered by the freed terrorists.

[14] Reported in *The Times*, 30 July 2005, p. 31. But compare the statement of Beth McGrath when Sean Kelly, one of the people who killed her father and sister by a bomb in 1993, was released from prison early under the Good Friday Agreement: 'I don't allow myself to get angry or emotionally involved about his release because if the authorities decide it's going to happen, it will. I would only be hindering my growth and my healing process, my life and that of my children if I allowed myself to be bitter or enraged. If you go through a trauma, you deal with life afterwards from a different perspective' (http://news.bbc.co.uk/go/pr/fr/-/hi/uk/4726915.stm, accessed on 29 July 2005). The fact that Lady Tebbit survived the attack but as a quadriplegic and continues to suffer as a result of her injuries may in part explain the difference between Lord Tebbit's response of largely unresolved anger and the response of Ms McGrath (acceptance and continuing healing).

Next, if a wrongdoer 'pays the debt to society' through retributive justice, it does not necessarily lead to the moral improvement of the wrongdoer. Society will have exacted a quantitively calculated penalty for the wrong done (e.g., a fine or term of imprisonment); unaddressed is the question of what effect the punishment has had on the offender. The high rate of recidivism may well illustrate that punishment does not necessarily work.[15]

Lastly, if crime upsets the moral equilibrium, it should also be important to consider how best to benefit and restore the victim, rather than only to punish the wrongdoer, in order to restore the disequilibrium the victim experiences. The thirst for retribution that is so evident in society is in fact rather less satisfying than it appears to be. Might it not in the long term be more satisfying for the victim to receive an apology, to be reconciled with the wrongdoer, to be sure that the wrongdoer undertakes acts that express remorse and contrition and that the wrongdoer is directed in such a way as to ensure the wrongdoing is not repeated?

Not all punishment is necessarily retributive. Punishment can be intended to rehabilitate a wrongdoer. In such a case, punishment pre-supposes that the victim may forgive the wrongdoer. Rehabilitation is an important element of the former idea of a 'penitentiary', a place where people might go to reflect on and repent of wrongdoing and be reformed. Retribution, even with all its moral ambiguities, must also remain part of such a punishment. If it does not, the nexus between the penalty for the wrong and the wrong itself will be severed and the punishment will be determined, not according to the severity of the wrong and in accordance with the dictates of justice, but according to the degree of reform and rehabilitation the wrongdoer needs. It will become morally impossible to object to severe penalties for minor crimes – or even no crimes at all – if the effect of the punishment would be to reform and rehabilitate a person.

Murphy (2003: 44) also makes the important point that modern, secular states do not punish wrongdoers in pursuit of the ideal of forming virtuous character. The latter should at most be 'a subordinate goal' that is incidental to matters of *realpolitik*. In the absence of a received religious tradition or of a shared political ideology (typical in many western liberal democracies), there may be widespread disagreement about what constitutes 'virtuous character' and how to bring it about. There is also no necessary reason why punishment alone should produce reform: something else might equally well produce the same result.

---

[15] See, for example, *Out For Good*, published by the Howard League for Penal Reform (Farrant 2006). This report explored rates of recidivism among men aged 18–20.

The pitfalls of punishment for moral improvement are all too disturbingly illustrated if the punishments are degrading and dehumanising (for the end does *not* justify the means) or if people are punished for goals that are morally suspect. These pitfalls can be seen in the work of religious zealots (such as in the Inquisition); and in modern times, under Mao Zedong in China during the Cultural Revolution (1966–9), those deemed to be 'counter-revolutionaries' were sentenced to 'reform through labour' or 're-education through labour'. If the 'counter-revolutionaries' repented, their sentences were reduced.[16]

Some say that punishment is principally justified as a deterrent because it is effective. For the wrongdoer, a deterrent punishment should provide an incentive not to commit wrong again; it should also constitute a threat indicating what will happen if the wrong is committed again. To onlookers, it is a warning of what happens to those who commit wrongs. To both wrongdoer and onlookers, the penalty or suffering is intended to show that 'crime does not pay' and, on a simple cost–benefit analysis, that it is better not to do wrong. Deterrence has to do with outward forms of behaviour and not motives or morality. For this reason, neither forgiveness nor repentance plays a part in the idea of deterrence. Empirically there is considerable doubt that punishment does always deter, though there is some evidence that, in some cases and to some extent, it does. As with rehabilitative punishment, an element of retribution must remain part of such a punishment. If it does not, there is no reason why one should not 'punish' an innocent person if it would serve to deter others.

### FORGIVENESS AND PUNISHMENT

Many people do not wish to forgive because what they want is retribution, that is, for the offender to be punished for the wrong committed. In chapter 1 of Carmichael 2003, Carmichael shows how the treatment meted out to certain notorious modern criminals, such as Myra Hindley and Mary Bell, has been almost entirely retributive and characterised by public calls for revenge. In only one case did Carmichael note that 'the Christian case for redemption and forgiveness' had been presented, and that was by the offender herself, Myra Hindley, in an article in the *Guardian* on 18 December 1995, and also by a few of her supporters (see pp. 16–17 above). Carmichael also observes how the press both reflected and fomented the public mood against Hindley and that there was 'little or no attempt on the

---

[16] I have already referred to the example of Harry Wu (p. 136, above).

part of the State as it is represented in the judiciary or its public servants to 'moderate' the public reaction that called for retribution.

It is open to debate whether forgiveness and retributive punishment are compatible (see, for example, Murphy 2003: 42; cf. North 1987: 501, 503). Both Kant and Hegel regard forgiveness and retribution as being in conflict, and believe that forgiveness subverts the demands of justice. (This is right if retributive punishment is necessarily an expression of justice, but, as I have suggested above, this does not follow.) If the effect of punishment is to expiate the offence, there is nothing left to forgive after punishment (Yandell 1998: 42) and the incompatibility remains. In addition, if forgiveness is voluntarily to forswear resentment and vindictiveness, then forgiveness *cannot* be compatible with punishment, because to forgive involves 'the decision to forgo the personal pursuit of punishment for the perpetrator(s) of a perceived injustice' (Affinito 2005: 95).

Despite the logical difficulties, some victims can forswear resentment and vindictiveness and forgive, but only *after* the wrongdoer has been punished. Given that forgiveness is a range of phenomena (as I shall argue in chapter 9), this is not surprising. Forgiveness after punishment may be a less altruistic and attractive form of forgiveness but in my view it remains a form of forgiveness. Anecdotal evidence confirms this: victims do let go of their unforgiving behaviour in course of time because they believe that the wrongdoer has paid the penalty for the crime, the 'debt to society' has been settled and it is time to move on. Sometimes, this is not the case. For example, those most affected by the murderers Myra Hindley and Ian Brady illustrate the point: some were deeply opposed to parole for Hindley and said that if she were paroled they would seek to kill her.

In the Christian tradition, love and mercy are the bases of God's dealings with humanity. Mercy is 'to exact less from [an offender] in the way of punishment or reparation than is appropriate from the point of view of justice' (Scarre 2004: 87) – and, in the case of God's mercy to humanity through the gospel, it is to exact *no* punishment or reparation from the sinner. Christians are to follow this pattern and are to show love as an expression of a forgiving attitude and are to overcome evil with good (Romans 12:19–21).

I discuss later in this chapter how divine vengeance and retribution fit with this *schema* of human behaviour.

### ABSOLUTION

Connected with forgiveness and punishment is the idea of absolution. Some suggest that, when there is forgiveness, the victim absolves the wrongdoer from guilt for the wrongdoing. Certainly, there are many instances of people *feeling* absolved from guilt because of the victim's forgiveness. Typically, this will occur if the wrongdoer has made amends and offered reparation for the wrongdoing, and the victim has accepted these as sufficient or adequate.

Is this true absolution or principally a psychological event, without moral significance? How can apologies, contrition, repentance and reparations *actually* absolve, remove or remit the guilt that comes from wrongdoing? From the wrongdoer's point of view, they do not atone for human sin: they express remorse and regret, and acknowledge that wrong has occurred. They neither reverse nor undo the past. Since, as Nietzsche said, 'no deed can be annihilated' (Hollingdale 1969: 162), neither can guilt for the deed. I may discover that you have stolen money from me and you may, in repentance, return the money to me – perhaps even with interest – but this does not alter the fact that you stole the money from me.

In speaking of absolution, it may be that people mean no more than that a victim chooses to disregard another's guilt and to forgive wrongdoing, particularly if it is evidenced by 'sufficient humility, shame and remorse' (Thomas 2003: 221). Certainly, forgiveness does not cause, produce or result in absolution from guilt.[17] Though Christian theology (as well as common sense) denies that human beings can absolve other human beings from guilt, there *can*, however, be absolution of a psychosocial nature on a person-to-person basis, if a victim accepts the wrongdoer's contrition, repentance and reparation.

### PUNISHMENT, FORGIVENESS AND JUSTICE

One stream of tradition in Christian teaching, typified in the approach of Augustine, is that divine love and mercy (on the one hand) and divine justice (on the other) are distinct and in conflict. The 'Augustinian' dilemma is at the heart of this book but Augustine's proposed solution (see pp. 61–2, above) is not.

Some argue (for example, see Gunton 1988: 159, 161) that, unless divine justice results in punishment for wrongdoing, divine love (expressed as for-giveness) amounts to no more than indulgence and disparages the severity of evil. Others say divine justice is an expression of divine love and mercy and is not in conflict with them. The gospel concerns justice (*dikaiosune*), in the sense of God's right actions restoring the moral equilibrium that sin

---

[17] Absolution by one human being of another is different from God's absolution in Christian theology: God forgives a human being when God absolves that human being from guilt for misdeeds and removes the wrongdoing from the divine record.

dislodges. God's justice will be evident at the *eschaton*. Precisely how this will be so, we do not know.

It does not follow (*pace* Gunton) that divine justice presupposes retribution for wrongdoers. Divine justice comes about through the cross and *precludes* retribution (at least in the sense that human beings understand and mean the term) because the cross is an outflow of mercy and love. Even so, it is undeniable that in the New Testament there is a belief in retributive punishment at the *eschaton*. It is God who metes out the punishment, not human beings (for example, Romans 1:18, 2:2, 5f., 9; 1 Corinthians 3:17; 2 Thessalonians 1:6, 8f.; 2 Peter 2:4–10a; Jude 5–7, 14f.). There is at this point an 'objective demonstration of justice', demonstrating that the world is not 'a morally indifferent place' (Gunton 1988: 163). Matthew 18:35 makes the point that eschatological retribution awaits those who exact temporal retribution from other human beings. (What is not clear is whether God's retributive justice leads to restoration or to extinction – or whether, as in 2 Thessalonians 1:9, the punishment is eternal. Christians differ in their views and the Bible does not fully address the question. On the principle that punishment should be proportionate to the wrong done, it is hard to think of a human wrong that merits punishment that is of eternal duration.) All that one can say is that divine retribution, if it does exist, is different from human retribution and embodies love, mercy and justice.

The idea of one person atoning for the sins of another also subverts the idea of justice that the atonement is said to uphold. This is because the sinner whose sins are atoned for escapes retributive judgment. The same idea also subverts one of the foundations of the atonement, namely, personal responsibility for sin, because another is deemed to take responsibility and so receives punishment. Swinburne's solution (Swinburne 1989: 152–4) is that an individual should offer to God Christ's 'costly gift . . . as his sacrifice'. This is 'the proper reparation and penance' for wrongdoing which, though not a sufficient reparation, is enough for God to accept and release an individual from punishment. This is not a solution: if the sacrifice is not sufficient reparation, how can it atone – and how can the sacrifice of one person be imputed to another except by way of a fiction?

Scripture implies that the cross is central both to the love and mercy of God *and* to the justice of God. At the *eschaton*, they come together. We do not know how; but we are told that it will be so. This is probably as much as we can say with confidence.

Despite its obvious difficulties, the Christian doctrine of the atonement has existential implications that promote justice. The cross confronts people as wrongdoers: they see in Christ a victim of injustice, someone who has been brutalised and oppressed, and who is the object of human unforgiveness and destruction. Christ there represents all who have been treated in that way and who have been broken by human sin. People each bear a measure of responsibility for human oppression and, as they face the cross, Christ calls them to repent of their unforgiveness and of the sin that oppresses others. The proper response is not only to embrace Christ's forgiveness but also to forgive others and to seek the forgiveness of those who have been wronged, in both cases pursuing reconciliation. According to Jesus, there is no forgiveness of sins without these. Thus, the cross, considered from a 'horizontal' perspective, is a dynamic for transforming human relationships, for justice and for restoration; from a 'vertical' perspective, it is the guarantee of justice at the *eschaton* and in the meantime, together with the resurrection, is both assurance of God's forgiveness for those who have done wrong and hope for the oppressed. There is no 'cheap grace' – described by Jones (1995: 104) as being when 'human beings . . . abdicate responsibility for offenses and crimes that they commit against one another'. God by grace will forgive and both the horizontal and vertical aspects of forgiveness cohere.

It is at this point that one of Nietzsche's telling objections to Christianity can be addressed. For Nietzsche, the universe is an inescapably violent and destructive place. The 'master morality' is rule by the strong over the weak. To forgive is not to use violence to achieve one's end, and so it is to be weak. In one sense, these observations are undoubtedly true: had Jesus but called more than twelve legions of angels (Matthew 26:53 – and note the military language in the word 'legions') he could have used violence and destruction to dominate those who were to destroy him. Instead of praying for angels, he prayed that God would forgive those who were killing him; and, in praying as he did, he did not conform to the ethic of the 'master morality'. As a result, he was expunged.

Nietzsche's 'master morality' only works in a universe without God and in a universe in which there is no vindication by the resurrection. Had Jesus used violence to defeat the strong, there would have been no cross and no resurrection. The 'master morality' would then have truly prevailed. What appears to be weakness in Jesus' surrender to the cross without violence is conformity to God's higher morality and demonstrates that the 'master morality' of violence is neither master nor moral.

### RETRIBUTIVE ESCHATOLOGICAL JUDGMENT

It is difficult to reconcile (on the one hand) the love and mercy of the gospel towards those who respond to Christ and (on the other) the idea of retributive punishment for those who reject that gospel and who disregard its moral strictures. Nevertheless, there remains perhaps an element of justice in the idea of retributive eschatological judgment that may initially escape our understanding. An example may make the issue clearer.

Suppose a wrongdoer grievously and criminally wrongs a victim. Suppose, further, that the wrongdoer is caught, tried and convicted but refuses to acknowledge the wrongdoing or the guilt, and does not show remorse or compassion. The victim may have great difficulty coming to terms with the crime, and may not be able to forgive. The wrongdoer has precluded the possibility of reconciliation and, by the criminal sentence, endures a measure of retributive justice. At the end of the sentence, the wrongdoer has 'paid the debt to society' and walks away free, but unchanged, unrepentant and not reconciled to the victim.

So much for the protection of society and the expression of its revulsion of the crime, but two difficult questions remain. First, how can there *ever* be restoration where the wrongdoer does not acknowledge the wrongdoing? Restoration presupposes the willing and voluntary participation of wrongdoer and victim in a process where the hoped-for result will be mutual reconciliation. It is not possible for there to be restoration where one or both of the parties resist the process to achieve it. In the hypothetical example above, the victim for ever remains the victim, unable to experience reconciliation with the wrongdoer – through no fault of the victim – and so carries a double burden: the fact of the wrongdoing and the impossibility of reconciliation and all that would result from it.

Second, in the example, where is justice for the victim? There has been, in a sense, justice for society – the wrongdoer has been punished and society's detestation of the crime expressed – but not justice for the victim. Is it not possible that where the victim has been denied the opportunity of justice temporally, God will grant that opportunity through eschatological judgment and justice? This could be so not only where the wrongdoer remains unrepentant but also where the wrongdoer escapes detection or identification. This approach to the question is hinted at in 1 Peter 2:24 for Jesus, when he suffered unjustly, 'entrusted himself to [God] who judges justly'. If there is no justice this side of the *eschaton*, then perhaps there will be the other.

Several problems with this view remain. First, how can it be that God, who in the atonement brings about restoration and reconciliation, should also judge and retributively punish those who disobey the gospel? Is this not an inner contradiction of the gospel itself? Second, is it right that God, who sets out an ethic of non-retaliation and forgiveness (not retribution) and whose son so famously modelled that ethic, should act retributively towards those who disregard the gospel of non-retribution? The solution is that either God's justice is not retributive or God's retribution is different from human retribution. Either way, a world in which there is not a God who ultimately vindicates the oppressed through the just judgment of wrongdoers is not a world that makes moral sense. The 'Augustinian' dilemma I referred to earlier – of a conflict between divine love and divine justice – would then remain for ever embedded in the matrix of human existence.

CHAPTER 9

# Varieties of forgiveness

It is easy to be glib about forgiveness.

Our study of forgiveness so far has confirmed that the idea of forgiveness is 'fraught with methodological, analytic, and conceptual difficulties' (Flanigan 1998: 95) and that there is even a degree of 'logical havoc' about forgiveness (Kolnai 1973–4: 99). Without, I hope, being glib, I now want to address the question, what is forgiveness?

Many assume that forgiveness is one identifiable phenomenon, recognisable by certain characteristic markers, and that if some of the markers are absent the phenomenon (whatever else it may be) is not true forgiveness. Even in the scholarly literature on the subject, there is debate, in the words of Scarre (2004: 63, 66), as to whether forgiveness is a 'multiform phenomenon' that cannot be forced 'into a single mould' with not all instances of forgiveness having the same 'contours', or whether it is right to hold to a 'rigorous model of forgiveness' and to insist that forgiveness always has certain identifiable characteristics. Murphy (2003: 15) refers to an instance of what he regards as a 'less morally rich definition of forgiveness', though apparently not with approval.

Within the Christian tradition, many people hold the view that the imperative of the Gospels is that people should forgive, that it is wrong not to forgive and that Jesus modelled and practised forgiveness. They may fail to observe that, for example, according to John, Jesus beat the moneychangers in the Temple (John 2: 15), rather than forgiving them. If asked, those who have reflected on the nature and form of Christian forgiveness might say – though perhaps not with the degree of clarity that follows – that forgiveness is a discrete and recognisable phenomenon that represents one sort of response to wrongdoing. Other responses to wrongdoing include anger, vindictiveness, passivity and so on. Forgiveness is, so people often think, identifiable by certain characteristic features that *must* be present if forgiveness is truly to take place.

Many also assume that reconciliation (in the sense of the *status quo ante* being fully restored) necessarily results from forgiveness. This sometimes happens. For example, Bill may forgive Ben (who has apologised for his actions) and Bill may cease to hold resentful or bitter feelings. Bill and Ben may then enjoy a restored relationship. The result is reconciliation and perhaps even a strengthened relationship.

Such a happy outcome does not always result, even when there is forgiveness. Bill may forgive Ben but their relationship may not be restored: for, though Bill may have ceased to harbour resentful, bitter feelings about Ben, Bill may wish never to see or speak to Ben again. Alternatively, Bill may forgive Ben but, because of what Ben did, seek to maintain a relationship with Ben on a different basis: Bill may be neither resentful nor bitter but not want to risk again the sort of wrong that he suffered at Ben's hands.

In trying to identify what forgiveness is, one may start with a dictionary definition. This was the approach of Minas (1975) who explored some of the definitions in the *Oxford English Dictionary*. She identified four types of forgiveness relevant for discussion. First, forgiveness is the 'retraction or modification of a previous adverse moral judgment about the act in question'; second, it is 'giving up a claim for requital to an offence'; third, forgiveness is about giving up resentment towards a sinner; and, lastly, forgiveness is directed to actions that wrong the forgiver. This approach begs the question, because it starts with what we commonly denote by forgiveness and precludes enquiry into whether these meanings of 'forgiveness' are philosophically, theologically or morally right.

We can also say with a reasonable degree of confidence that forgiveness is 'an elective response to culpable wrongdoing' (Calhoun 1992: 81). Even this, however, is too narrow because forgiveness is a particular kind of elective response, namely, an elective, *moral* response.

Another approach is to say that forgiveness is a process that frees a wrongdoer to live as if the wrongdoing had not occurred (and, according to Lévinas (1969), that gives the wrongdoer another chance) while also holding that it is a fact that the wrongdoer's actions were morally wrong. Forgiveness of this kind may be possible if the wrongdoer has repented of the wrong, for, in this example, both victim and wrongdoer hold the same judgment about the wrongdoing. However, it would be hard to call this 'forgiveness' if the wrongdoer has not repented. In such a case, the 'forgiveness' is more like a pardon.

Most commentators say that forgiveness takes place if the victim has a 'change of heart' and overcomes[1] feelings of resentment[2] about the wrongdoing. The victim puts aside the wrong and disregards it when it comes to how the victim views and responds to the wrongdoer.

Despite the received orthodoxy that forgiveness is the overcoming of resentment, there are four drawbacks to this view.

First, it is problematic to say that one has overcome resentment at the same time as insisting that the wrongdoing is *wrong*. The passing of time may soften one's sense of anger and injustice about a particular act of wrongdoing (perhaps because the memory will have faded) but, if one were to stop and re-imagine the wrong and how one felt, it is likely that one's resentment would return. If it did not, it might be either because one has forgotten or because one condones, excuses or ignores the wrongdoing or because, as is typical in cases of child sexual abuse or domestic violence, one even blames oneself that the wrongdoing happened.

Second, if a wrongdoer repents, the victim may find it easier to overcome the former feelings of resentment – but it is the (now repentant) wrongdoer whom the victim forgives for the (now repudiated) wrong, not the (former unrepentant) wrongdoer for the (not repudiated) wrong. In other words, when the act of forgiveness takes place, both the wrongdoer and the victim will have changed from how they were when the wrong was done (Milbank 2003: 51–5). The forgiveness given and received is from people who have become different: the forgiveness cannot relate to the act of wrongdoing as originally done and as originally experienced. We are faced with a temporal paradox: we forgive people now for offences committed previously by people who, by virtue of the passing of time, have changed.

Next, and this is connected with the previous point, it is naïve to think that, if one forgives, one does not also retain *some* resentment about the wrongdoing. What one needs to overcome is resentment as the *determining* emotion and one that precludes one from forgiving. Forgiveness and a degree of resentment *can* coexist and many victims who forgive acknowledge this. When this happens, forgiveness is little more than a psychological process (albeit morally motivated), that is, a process whereby negative

---

[1] Or 'abandons' such feelings (Enright *et al.* 1998: 46).
[2] Butler (in Gladstone 1995) described forgiveness as forswearing resentment. See also Strawson 1968a: 76. Other emotions that have also been referred to include 'indignation' (Kolnai 1973–4) and 'moral hatred' (Hampton in Murphy and Hampton 1988). Thus, unforgiveness may come from any one or more of a range of emotions: see Richards 1988. Murphy (2003: 16) calls these emotions '*vindictive passions*'.

*feelings* about the wrongdoer and the wrongdoing are addressed in such a way as to enable the victim to make a cognitive and emotional shift.

Lastly, this description really describes the stages preparatory to forgiveness: one may overcome resentment about a wrongdoer and the wrongdoer's actions, and this may result in a 'change of heart' both about the wrongdoing and the wrongdoer – but none of these amounts to forgiveness. Something else is needed if we are to be able to recognise that the victim has forgiven the wrongdoer: most probably, this will be some form of action relative to the wrongdoer.

Derrida takes a different approach to forgiveness, which he has considered under the *topos* of gift.[3] According to Derrida, forgiveness is a gift and should be given out of love freely (that is, given not in response to duty or obligation and given without self-interest) and without reciprocal obligation on the recipient. Derrida's view is that to receive forgiveness and, at the same time, to be indebted to the forgiver for the forgiveness contradict the very idea of gift that forgiveness presupposes. With a true gift, Derrida argues, the recipient does not incur debt or obligation, and the very idea of debt or obligation is inconsistent with the idea of gift.[4] Even to know of the gift or the identity of the giver brings the gift into the realm of economy and exchange. Even for the *giver* to know that the giver is giving perverts the gift because to know destroys the unconditional nature of the gift. It is not that Derrida thinks that gifts can be given without egotism and implicit obligations: it is that gift giving can *never* be given unconditionally and unequivocally dissociated from reciprocity and self-interest. Hence forgiving the forgivable is impossible because it will never be 'aneconomic', that is, unconditional, without encounter and without thought of exchange (Derrida 2001a: 34).

Transposing this idea into the theological realm, Derrida would say that God's gifts are not a means of economy and exchange that incur credits

---

[3] So also Lévinas (1969). He says that in identifying one's obligations as a result of encountering the 'other', our relationship is not reciprocal (*pace* Buber) but asymmetrical. In other words, one is obligated to the other without regarding the other as correspondingly obligated. Thus, the relationship is not contractual or reciprocal. Forgiveness too can be a gift only if it is not symmetrical.

[4] Marion, in contrast and in debate with Derrida, takes the view that debt is integral to the idea and definition of gift, so long as the debt does not arise causatively from the gift (Caputo in Caputo and Scanlon 1999: 212). Milbank (2003: 57) prefers a 'Christianized eudaimonism' in which forgiveness is a disinterested, aneconomic act offered because 'one is *already* receiving the infinite divine charity' and amounting to 'the unqualified return of this gift in the very act of receiving'. Thus, one gives because one has *already* received and not *in order* to receive. This is the pure forgiveness of God (2003: 62), mediated through human beings who are already the recipients of that forgiveness and have received the capacity to forgive. In contrast, those who forgive out of their own resources without recourse to divine forgiveness engage in an economy of exchange.

and debits (whether moral or causal): this idea destroys the very idea of gift and grace. Integral to the idea of gift and grace is forgiveness, for the creditor must forgive the debt that arises from the gift if the gift is truly to be a gift. Jesus makes clear that the only obligation is to forgive and to go on forgiving if one is to be forgiven oneself. Even here, there is a contradiction, for, according to Derridean thought, if debt poisons the gift, then, in recognising that one has to forgive in order to be forgiven, one also has to recognise that the duty to forgive is causally linked to the expectation of receiving forgiveness.[5] Derrida recognises this contradiction and for him '*any* presence of the gift draws it into an economy of exchange' (Caputo in Caputo and Scanlon, 1999: 212).

Derrida's view that 'there is only forgiveness, if there is any, where there is the unforgivable' (2001: 32–3) offers an ideal of forgiveness that is unattainable. If forgiveness is forgiving the unforgivable, it will be impossible.[6] Forgiveness of the unforgivable transcends the 'heritage' of the concept of forgiveness that we have received and cannot be 'the object of a theoretical statement' but 'exceed[s] the order of presence, the order of being, the order of consciousness' (Derrida in Kearney 2001: 53). True forgiveness, Derrida says, is a 'pure and unconditional' gift[7] and has meaning only with reference to itself so that, according to the ordinary grammar of its discourse, it is 'madness of the impossible' (Derrida 2001: 32f., 39, 45). It is a concept about which Derrida admits he does 'not know' and has 'no knowledge'; he 'cannot speak of it in a theoretical fashion' but he can 'think' or (though he does not use this word) dream about it (Derrida in Kearney 2001: 53). Even so, the existential demand altruistically to forgive remains and human beings must continue to seek to do the impossible.

Derrida's 'pure and unconditional' forgiveness is an impossible and an unattainable ideal. Nevertheless, as Derrida describes it, it is wonderfully attractive and, I would want to add, it models, anticipates and reflects divine forgiveness. Even if we only partly attain that sort of forgiveness, it is still better than not attaining it at all. Despite Derrida's theoretical reservations, forgiving the forgivable does remain a species of forgiveness.

---

[5] In Milbank's words, Derrida seeks to purge certain concepts of religious elements – elements that have to do with reward and punishment, for example – so as to make them 'purer and more religious' (Kearney 2001: 64).

[6] In contrast, and applying what Marion says, the gift of impossible forgiveness has *already* been given, and faith is to see and practise what is invisible but now possible (Caputo in Caputo and Scanlon 1999: 186, 203, 205).

[7] So also Enright *et al.* 1998: 48 but not necessarily as 'pure and unconditional'.

Christian theology also sometimes takes another approach. A view commonly held is that what characterises forgiveness and distinguishes it from other sorts of response to wrongdoing is that it is an act of love, offered when one would have expected in its place revenge, hatred or bitterness.[8] (On this basis, the dead cannot forgive because they cannot love any longer.)[9] Such an act of love is to practise the forgiveness of God – to imitate the pattern of forgiveness that we see in Jesus and that is at the heart of the Christian gospel. The living can forgive, and when the living forgive they practise the dominical command to love other people. In doing so, they model and mediate to others God's unconditional love towards – and forgiveness of – human beings. Jones (1995) describes such forgiveness as 'embodying' divine forgiveness through participation in the sacramental life of the church.[10]

That God is forgiving has been strongly attacked as illogical and absurd by Minas (1975).[11] In so doing, she seeks to limit forgiveness to being an interpersonal phenomenon and not one that is imitative of or has its origin in an attribute of God. Minas argues that 'possession of divine attributes logically precludes conditions which are necessary for forgiveness' and that it is 'possession of distinctly human, non-divine characteristics that makes forgiveness appropriate for human beings' (1975: 138). Minas' arguments are complex, and the following is a summary.

Minas points out that forgiveness is impossible for a being predicated as having 'perfect moral sense, a perfect moral will, perfect knowledge, and perfect benevolence'. According to Minas, a being with perfect moral sense cannot retract or modify a previous moral judgment, and neither can such a being not take into account a wrong done. In addition, if forgiveness is remitting a punishment, we have to ask 'why God makes laws that he knows he is going to override'. Third, since an omniscient being cannot forget anything, it would not be possible for a divine being to forget feelings of resentment towards a sinner – and, anyway, feelings of resentment are particularly human and petty. Lastly, why should a divine being need to forgive since such a being's 'very perfection should make

---

[8] This idea is anticipated in Aristotle's idea of 'equity' (see *Rh.* i, 13, 1374a25–1374b25 in Barnes 1984), 'the sort of justice that goes beyond the written law . . . [and] bids us to be merciful to the weakness of human nature . . .'.

[9] Benn (1996: 378) suggests that there may be 'quasi-forgiveness' by people who, though not directly victims of wrongdoing, have been affected by it. It arises if 'third parties, whilst not [at] all condoning what was done, overcome the indignation they feel on behalf of those directly wronged'.

[10] Such a view appears to have nothing to offer those outside the sacramental worship of the Christian church.

[11] Swinburne (1989: 87, n. 8) refuted Minas' arguments. See also Drabkin 1993.

him immune from the kind of injury which makes forgiveness appropriate'? Minas' conclusion is that it is morally and logically absurd for a divine being to forgive sins – and at one point she refers to a divine being who forgave as being like 'a practical joker', since such a being prescribes punishments for sin in the perfect foreknowledge that they would be remitted.

There is considerable force to Minas' arguments but, in relation to her third and fourth points, two observations can be made. First, *forgetting* feelings of resentment (which Minas says God does when God forgives) is different from *abandoning* feelings of resentment. Second, while it is true that one cannot envisage God being injured (and so needing to forgive), one can envisage God being offended by – and so forgiving – human wrongdoing.

As for Minas' first point, the assumptions that with God there can be no backwards causation and that God cannot change the past or its moral status presuppose that God is no different from human beings. A similar point is made more generally by Meirlys Lewis (1980) who says that to predicate divine forgiveness on our conceptions of human forgiveness (as Minas does) is simply mistaken. The 'criterion of intelligibility' sets the limits of what is logically possible, and Lewis argues that this is 'unnecessarily prescriptive' when it comes to God (Lewis 1980: 236). She argues that Christian forgiveness is not 'an extension of conditional, arbitrary, temporal forgiveness': its source is God, whose forgiveness, like God's love, is unconditional, unchanging, always applicable as the model for human conduct. In other words, 'there are forms of forgiveness which do not presuppose mutability, selfishness, limitations of knowledge and power, feelings of anger, pride, revenge, retaliation, the necessity for rational justification, as conditions for the possibility of forgiveness'. There is, she argues, always an obligation to forgive other human beings that is 'determine[d] and define[d]' by 'the relation between God and the world', a relation that is characterised by unconditional divine forgiveness of human sin. Lastly, Drabkin (1993: 234f.) argues that there is a genus of forgiveness 'fully open to God' that Minas does not take into account, namely forgiveness without resentment. Drabkin says this is characterised by God 'giving up . . . suffering for rejoicing on the occasion of a person's repentance'.

Milbank (2003) takes up a question similar to Minas' fourth reason for the impossibility of divine forgiveness, namely, how can God forgive human beings if God, unlike the human victims of suffering, is beyond all suffering? God is not (and cannot be) a victim and so cannot be wronged in the way a human being can.[12] Milbank's answer to the question is that in Jesus Christ there is 'the only imaginable site' of the resolution of the difficulty. As the 'unique sovereign victim' he became 'capable of representing all suffering and to forgive on behalf of all victims[,] . . . able to forgive, unlike other human beings, at the very original instance of hurt without a single jolt of rancor'. What we have in Christ is '*not* God forgiving us (since he has no need to) but humanity forgiving humanity' (2003: 61f.) – and through him, humanity acquires the capacity to forgive humanity.[13]

### FORGIVENESS REVISITED

In this book, I have argued that forgiveness has at least two attributes. The first is that forgiveness is a moral response to wrongdoing. The second is that forgiveness is a person-to-person phenomenon: one does not forgive groups, and neither do groups forgive.[14] This is probably as much as one can say confidently. These attributes do not define forgiveness, tell us how someone forgives or say how one recognises forgiveness when it has occurred. They only describe the minima of what ought to be present if we are to say that we recognise that forgiveness has taken place. And even if the two attributes I have identified *are* in evidence, it does not necessarily mean that forgiveness has taken place.

I have also argued that it is probably mistaken to speak of forgiveness as something that is clear-cut[15] or even the end-point of a process.[16] It is possible to forgive one day and not the next. It is better to regard forgiveness as something that develops and admit that there are ebbs and flows in one's capacity to forgive. One can be forgiving *and* unforgiving at the same time. There are diverse routes to the point when one begins the process of forgiveness and there are diverse ways of developing, enhancing and revisiting one's forgiveness. The process may begin for most unattractive

---

[12] If we say God can be affronted or offended (if not harmed) we could say God is wronged and so a victim. It does, however, seem something of a divine over-reaction if the sole reason for the atoning work of Christ were the fact that God has been affronted or offended.

[13] For a critique of Milbank's views as to why forgiveness is possible, see Dooley 2001: 136–45.

[14] There is often – but not always – a third attribute, namely, that forgiveness is a bilateral process.

[15] Pettigrove (2004a: 204) makes a similar point when considering whether it is possible to forgive an unrepentant wrongdoer. Sometimes, he argues, it *is* right to forgive an unrepentant wrongdoer. He says, 'Within a consequentialist framework, it will be largely an empirical matter whether one ought to forgive or not. Sometimes it will be objectionable . . . at other times, forgiving the unrepentant will promote the better outcome'.

[16] Haber (1991: 6f., 51) thinks that the process of overcoming resentment does not need to be complete for forgiveness to take place. What is necessary is for the victim to have at least a sincere intention to overcome resentment towards the wrongdoer.

reasons – self-interest, moral weakness, compromise, even the desire to hurt, and so on – and with most unattractive actions, but these can lead to better actions and new motives in the course of time.[17] The process of forgiving involves psychological, spiritual and intellectual change and the process, which involves personal growth, is as important as forgiveness itself. Many would say that forgiveness is like a journey that is never completed; and even those who would say they have forgiven may sometimes need to forgive more or to forgive anew. For example, a woman who has been unable to bear children because of the negligence of a surgeon may have forgiven the surgeon for the fact that she will remain childless; she may need to revisit her grief and forgive once again when in later years she realises that, unlike her contemporaries, she will also not be a grandparent.

In addition, much of the discussion about forgiveness is simplistic, not doing justice to the complexity of the issues – philosophical, moral, relational and spiritual – with which forgiveness intersects. Forgiveness is a complex, multi-layered process, a medley of discrete, heterogeneous phenomena that apply (in varying degrees) situationally. Even within specific systems of thought, forgiveness may be complex. Puka (2005: 136) wrote, 'Rather than being a simple virtue, forgiveness is a complex psychology dividing into several cognitive systems that evolve in several developmental phases much like the grieving process does.' What amounts to forgiveness in one situation may not be forgiveness in another; and what satisfies one person as forgiveness may well not satisfy another. The test whether there is forgiveness is *not* whether victim and wrongdoer undergo and complete certain formulaic processes but whether the attributes I have identified are present and whether the victim *intends* to forgive the wrongdoer and, to the victim's own satisfaction, *does* so. Forgiveness is recognisable when certain results from it are in evidence, and there is no other way – except by this pragmatic criterion – to establish whether forgiveness has or has not taken place. What Derrida calls 'heterogeneous forms of remission' in contrast to 'pure or unconditional forgiveness' (2001b: 45) may in fact be species of forgiveness though not forgiveness as he defines and describes it. Forgiveness is recognisable when it occurs[18] – and forgiveness occurs through a

---

[17] Murphy (2003: 15) rightly criticises Tutu's description of forgiveness ('waiving one's right to revenge') as being broad enough to include actions that are founded not on moral virtue but, for example, on selfish motives. What Murphy does not appear to take into account is that what at first was done for selfish reasons can, in the course of time, open the way to other actions and reactions – even to morally virtuous actions and reactions – and to forgiveness.

[18] Intuition can confirm this: Bennett 2003: 141.

medley of different ways and by degree, so long as the two attributes I have identified are in evidence.[19]

One also has to recognise the limited extent of human forgiveness. Human forgiveness does not – and cannot – undo the past or free people both from the consequences of what they have done and from what Arendt calls 'the predicament of irreversibility'. Human forgiveness and the process of which it is part do not exculpate the wrongdoer. If we hold that forgiveness addresses the wrongdoing, forgiveness betrays the integrity of one's initial reactions to the wrongdoing, leaves the past unaltered and compromises one's former response to the violation of the moral order.

Interpersonal forgiveness is part of a series of experiences that have to do with moving on from the past and offering hope for the future.[20] Hieronymi (2001: 550f.) is right, for example, when she suggests that an apology *can* undermine resentment because, in accepting an apology, a victim 'in some way ratifies, or makes real, the offender's change of heart' and 'agrees to bear in [his or] her own person the cost of the wrongdoing and to incorporate the injury into [his or] her life without further protest and without demand for retribution'. In such a situation, the victim may forgive – or may not.

Of course, none of these effectually addresses the problem of past wrongdoing: only atonement can do this. Interpersonal forgiveness is therefore different from divine forgiveness: its effects are psychosocial – being both restorative and humanitarian (Thomas 2003) *but not more* – and they do not and cannot undo or put right the past.

I therefore reject a prescriptive view of forgiveness that stipulates that certain criteria should or should not always be present, though I would want to insist that the two attributes of forgiveness that I have identified are at least present in *some* form if the term 'forgiveness' is to have any meaning and substance. Biggar (2001: 215) concludes, after a magisterial review of literature on forgiveness in the twentieth century, that forgiveness comes 'in two parts'. First, the victim unilaterally and unconditionally overcomes vindictive resentment. This is followed by '"absolution" . . . that is, the moment when the victim declares he will no longer view the wrongdoer in the light of his misdeed and that their relationship may proceed as before'. The second stage (which is conditional) 'depends upon the wrongdoer's demonstration of sincere repentance'. It is not that Biggar is mistaken in describing forgiveness in this way; it is that forgiveness – or something akin to what Biggar regards as forgiveness – may also come by other routes.

---

[19] Scobie and Scobie (1998) seek to avoid the pitfall of being too specific first by offering a 'general definition' that is not based on one approach or model and, second, by postulating 'an integrated model of forgiveness' that does not claim to be comprehensive.

[20] See Pettigrove 2004b: 383–6.

Typically, what people call 'forgiveness' is an amalgam. Forgiveness is possible even when what is also present compromises the 'purity' of the two identity markers of forgiveness that I have identified. O'Shaugnessy (1967: 344, 351) is right when he says that what is important is 'what forgiving means for the *forgiver*' (and see also Neblett 1974) – and, I would want to add, so long as the two attributes are present in some recognisable form. This is the kind of forgiveness that Derrida (2001a: 32, 27, 45) describes as not 'pure' but 'confounded . . . with related themes: excuse, regret, amnesty, prescription' and containing 'confusions which reduce forgiveness to . . . amnesia, to acquittal or prescription, to the work of mourning or some political therapy of reconciliation, in short to some historical ecology'. This sort of forgiveness is not 'impossible' forgiveness, but forgiveness that can restore relationships, heal troubled communities and bring about peace and reconciliation. It *is* compromised forgiveness – but to deny that it is a form of forgiveness, albeit pragmatic, is to limit the expression of grace that ultimately underpins the many different forms that forgiveness can take and the many different routes by which people come to forgive.[21] Such forgiveness is an alloy – but better than hatred and resentment, and all that goes with them. In the nature of things, people cannot, *pace* Derrida, do the impossible.

Haber (1991: 40–53) rightly argues that to attempt to define the meaning of forgiveness based on the presence of certain 'necessary and sufficient conditions' will fail. Forgiveness, he suggests, is a complex phenomenon and it is not possible to reduce what we mean by forgiveness to a formulaic definition. Haber bases his approach to forgiveness on a linguistic model, namely, that forgiveness is a 'performative utterance'.[22] Thus forgiveness occurs when words such as 'I forgive you' (or similar) are said with the intention of forgiving 'according to the rules of the expression' in appropriate circumstances and when the person to whom they are spoken believes that forgiveness has taken place.[23]

The fact is that it is impossible to delineate any set of necessary and sufficient conditions that will always identify an action or attitude to be

---

[21] Murphy in Murphy and Hampton 1988: 24; but compare Haber (1991) whose view is that this amounts to condoning. Haber thinks the only ground of forgiveness is the wrongdoer's repentance and repudiation of the deed.

[22] So also Swinburne (1989: 84f.). Cf. Bennett (2003: 135) who says that 'what forgiveness consists in is the change in our attitude towards the offender rather than the utterance of the words "I forgive you"'. Cf. also Pettigrove 2004b: 379–82.

[23] An example of a 'performative utterance' is the making of marriage vows in a church: saying the vows effects the marriage, not signing the marriage registers. Logically speaking, therefore, a woman who wishes to change her surname on marriage to that of her husband should sign the marriage register in her new name (since by then she will already be married). In personal correspondence with the Marriage Registrar for England and Wales I have been informed that this is not regarded as 'good practice'!

forgiveness.[24] One can only stipulate certain attributes that are minima, but even if they are present they do not guarantee that forgiveness will have taken place. There are also phenomena (such as apologies by individuals or groups, and pardons) that are not forgiveness in the way I have identified forgiveness but which are akin to forgiveness. These phenomena have some characteristics that overlap with forgiveness but also some points of difference. Wittgenstein calls such similarities and points of contact in phenomena 'family resemblances' (1968: 32e). In my view, there is a medley of concepts – of which forgiveness is one – that are clearly related to one another but which are also distinguishable. Some of the other concepts in the 'family' may share some of the features of forgiveness and produce outcomes that are different from forgiveness but akin to it. One thinks here of reconciliation between groups of people, for example. At best, there will be some recurring features in many of the concepts in this 'family' of phenomena, even though not all the phenomena will share at least one common feature. I think it is to these other concepts in the 'family' that Murphy refers when he speaks of 'less morally rich' definitions of forgiveness (Murphy 2003: 15).[25]

We can see the range of concepts in the following examples. One response to wrongdoing may be no more than to acknowledge to oneself that one has been hurt or offended, and then to put the hurt to one side. Here we probably have no more than an internal psychological and emotional change because putting aside hurt may not necessarily be for moral reasons. Another kind of response may be to accept an apology and then to choose to forget about the wrongdoing.[26] The basis of one's choice may be moral (for example, that it is right to accept and act on apologies that have been made with integrity)[27] or simply pragmatic (for example, that there is no point in continuing to hold a grudge or be resentful), or one may treat the apology as repentance and choose to forgive.[28] Yet another response is

---

[24] Haber 1991, and see in Scobie and Scobie 1998 the 'general definition' of forgiveness that sets out 'an integrated model of forgiveness' that does not claim to be comprehensive.

[25] See also Worthington (2005: 557) who concludes that 'forgiveness has not one but several definitions'.

[26] Cf. Scobie and Scobie (1998: 386, 389f., 398) who conclude that 'trivial and minor offences', that is, where 'there is no serious disruption to the relationship . . . and no significant damage', should be dealt with by apology, which in their terminology is different from forgiveness. Forgiveness is required, they argue, only where there is 'conflict in the relationship and individuals have ceased to co-operate to reduce the tension': but the absence of conflict and lack of co-operation may be because the victim has unilaterally forgiven the wrongdoer.

[27] Hampton in Murphy and Hampton 1988: 41f. denies that such a response is forgiveness.

[28] Cf. Richards (1988: 79) who says that forgiveness which is no more than an 'act of mental hygiene' (e.g., deciding to rid oneself of disruptive feelings caused by not forgiving through professional help) is not forgiveness at all.

in the form of a reciprocal process by which the wrongdoer acknowledges the wrongdoing and asks for forgiveness and, in consequence, the victim forgives. Reconciliation and a restored relationship may then result. Here forgiveness is concerned with the restoration of relationships and the possibility of communion in the future through a process that involves exploring actions and feelings. Finally, there is the response of forgiveness in the face of appalling wrong and without the repentance of the wrongdoer. This is 'unconditional' forgiveness, popularly believed to be exemplified in the life of Jesus, and especially in his words of forgiveness on the cross. In this case, the victim chooses not to let the wrongdoing and its effects intrude into how the victim views the wrongdoer, and the victim is committed to re-establishing a relationship with the wrongdoer. Ironically, this is no different in form from the first example given above: what is different is the question of degree and intent.

There can be no such response of forgiveness where the victim or victims are dead. In the twentieth century particularly, there has been obscenity of wrongdoing that has been brought to human attention – the 'pure positive horror . . . and radical evil'[29] of the Gulags, the concentration camps of Nazi Germany, the killing fields of Cambodia and Rwanda, and so on. The victims of these monstrous atrocities do not – and cannot – forgive because they have 'vanished' (Milbank 2003: 30): gassed, burned, shot, starved and disposed of in makeshift graves or left to rot in open air.[30] Those who survived may be traumatised and broken and so unable to forgive. Others who survived may want to forgive but cannot find or identify the perpetrators of evil against them because, so very often, the wrongdoers have moved on to anonymous, faceless lives, hiding their wicked past and covertly protected by communities tainted with the guilt of tacit complicity. At best, the forgiveness the victims intend remains expressed only in their minds and among their friends and communities: most importantly, it will not have been communicated to the perpetrators of the wrongs, and to this extent remains inchoate, incomplete and deficient.

We cannot force forgiveness into a mould. It is a family of rich, complex and multiform phenomena. Usually forgiveness coexists with what debases and compromises it. Nevertheless, forgiveness, in its Derridean 'pure' form,

---

[29] The term 'radical evil' is a term first used by Kant to refer to the propensity not to do what duty requires and not to follow the moral law, and is now used to refer to evil that arises, not from the pursuit of some good, but from evil perversely pursued for its own sake and as an end in itself.

[30] Compare Horsbrugh (1974: 274) (and Haber (1991: 45) who agrees) who thinks that one can forgive on behalf of a victim if one is intimately associated with the victim.

*can* be glimpsed at and, perhaps more often than we think, even almost attained.

Even if we cannot precisely define forgiveness and say what it is, forgiveness *is* recognisable when it takes place. We can probably say that to ask for forgiveness is to appeal to the victim to believe in what the (now repentant) wrongdoer can become. To forgive in response to such an appeal is an act of love that offers hope for the future.

It is undeniable that what is commonly recognised to be forgiveness can transform or liberate a person. Certainly, there can be changes that victims regard as being for the better. North (1987: 500) describes the transformation that comes from forgiveness: 'What is annulled in the act of forgiveness is . . . the distorting effect that . . . wrong has upon one's relations with the wrongdoer and perhaps with others' and (as she adds in 1998: 20) also with oneself.

Anecdotal examples of this abound, of which two follow. The first concerns Stephen Metcalf who (along with about two thousand other people) was interned in Weihsien (now Weifang) in China by the Japanese in 1943–5. One of the other internees was Eric Liddell, a former athlete who in the Olympic Games of 1924 in Paris won a gold medal in the 400 metres track event. Metcalf said of Liddell, 'The best thing he gave me was his baton of forgiveness. He taught me to love my enemies, the Japanese, and to pray for them.'[31] The second is about Martin Jenco OSM, a Roman Catholic priest serving as Director of Catholic Relief Services in Beirut. Jenco was kidnapped and imprisoned by Shiite Muslims in Beirut in 1985–6. In his autobiography, he wrote, 'Having forgiven, I am liberated. I need no longer be determined by the past' (Jenco 1995: 135).

Equally, forgiveness can transform and liberate a wrongdoer. For example, Eric Lomax (Lomax 1996) became convinced that Nagase Takashi's repentance was genuine and this helped to generate friendship between Lomax and Nagase that eventually led to forgiveness and friendship.[32] Lomax's forgiveness helped 'release' Nagase from the burden of his guilt and shame that he had carried for much of his life after the Second World War.

At best, human forgiveness – that is, forgiveness that cannot absolve another from guilt and that does not result from sin being atoned – may have these results: relief for the wrongdoer from a recollection of past wrongs that is painful, recovery and restoration for the victim from a recollection of past hurts that is painful, and reconciliation of both wrongdoer and victim. One is left with the 'four r's' – relief, recovery, restoration and reconciliation.

---

[31] *Daily Telegraph*, August 18 2005, p. 15.     [32] On Lomax, see pp. 73–4, 76–7 and 107 above.

Even then, the fourth 'r', reconciliation, may not always be appropriate or applicable and sometimes, in the case of 'unilateral forgiveness' (forgiveness by the victim of a wrongdoer who has not repented), there may be no relief for the wrongdoer, because the wrongdoer is not troubled about the wrongdoing. Apart from these peripheral observations – which are about the effect or consequences of forgiveness – we can probably say little more with confidence. In other words, forgiveness is recognisable when it occurs, though both the process by which one gets there, precisely what forgiveness is and what results from forgiveness are not easy to define and may not even be capable of unitary definition or description. It is, as I have said above, a psychosocial phenomenon – but not *only* that, because it *also* mirrors and is imitative of the model of divine forgiveness that the gospel discloses.

Relief, inner peace and transformed and reordered relationships can come other than through forgiveness. Forgetting, excusing, collusion, denial and condoning may also produce the same effects. Forgiveness is not only about feeling better: it is about addressing the moral issues that caused the unforgiveness. The fact of the morally wrong acts and the ensuing guilt that arises from having done them need to have been addressed if the term 'forgiveness' is to be a moral – rather than simply a relational, existential – term.

# CHAPTER 10

# Afterthoughts

The ancient world – whether Jewish or Gentile – gave little thought to the ethics of forgiveness. Plutarch and Seneca alone among pre-Christian writers discussed forgiveness and even Aristotle did not list forgiveness as a virtue.[1] In the Hebrew Scriptures, though God was forgiving, forgiveness was not enjoined as a human virtue or duty.

The place and significance of forgiveness changed as a result of the influence of the Christian gospel. Christians understood forgiveness to be integral to the Christian gospel and an attribute of God that they ought to model in their relations with other people. One of the great ethical achievements of the New Testament and the Christian church was to establish forgiveness as a moral virtue. Throughout the two millennia of the Christian era and until very recently, thought, discussion and critical reflection about forgiveness principally took place in the context of Christian theology. Christians had the 'market niche' when it came to forgiveness.

A significant change occurred in the second half of the twentieth century. The Christian understanding of forgiveness was no longer always the starting point for discourse about forgiveness. Some who reflected on forgiveness – Anne C. Minas is an example in Minas 1975 – specifically distanced themselves from the Christian traditions about forgiveness. Christians lost the 'market niche' on the subject in this period. People remained interested in the impact of forgiveness (or non-forgiveness) on their personal relationships (perhaps more so than ever as 'quality of life issues' became important in western Europe and the United States) but much less interested – if interested at all – in the significance of forgiveness from a God-ward perspective. Issues to do with forgiveness also became of political and public interest, and some regarded forgiveness as a virtue that concerned relationships between groups as well as individuals.

The most significant contribution to the recent understanding of forgiveness has come, not from Christian theologians, but from philosophers

[1] According to Haber 1991: 3.

and psychologists who have generally sought to work from a non-religious standpoint. The result is that the Christian voice in the development of understanding about forgiveness is now largely mute and not regarded as significant in academic discourse. The significant work of Jones (1995) on forgiveness has not been given much regard among those in secular disciplines. This is because Jones' book makes its most cogent contribution to those who are within the Christian church and has little to say to those who are not active within it. It is also because, as Watts (in Watts and Gulliford 2004: 4–6) argues, Jones is over-critical of the extra-biblical approaches to and interpretations of forgiveness that Jones terms 'therapeutic forgiveness'.

Psychologists have alerted a widespread audience to the fact that sometimes people will need psychological therapy if they are to be in a position to choose whether to forgive. It is simplistic to say that victims should forgive because to forgive is a moral good: the psychological trauma of having been wronged may disable a victim from being able to forgive. Psychological therapy may help victims to explore what is an appropriate moral response to trauma and so help bring victims to the point when they may wish to forgive. Despite what some psychologists appear to be suggesting, forgiveness is not a goal in therapy.

Philosophers have helped to uncover the complexity of forgiveness. As a result of their work in the last half century in particular, we cannot now say that one should always forgive. There are times when it is wrong to forgive and there are times when one cannot forgive.

It is undeniable that Archbishop Tutu has made a profound contribution to establishing the place of forgiveness in public discourse both through his work in chairing the Truth and Reconciliation Commission in South Africa and in his subsequent books and articles on forgiveness. However, forgiveness was an incidental consequence of some of the work of the Commission and its place the subject of considerable debate and even disagreement during the course of the hearings of the Commission. Tutu's writings on forgiveness express his conviction that there is 'no future without forgiveness' but it cannot be taken that the Truth and Reconciliation Commission demonstrates that assertion. The theological basis of Tutu's own reflection on forgiveness has also come in for considerable criticism by Christian theologians.

### FORGIVENESS AS AN IDEAL

This book, in revisiting the idea of forgiveness, seeks to affirm that to forgive is a moral good – but not always and not necessarily. Forgiveness can present a moral dilemma that brings into question the rational character of a deontologically derived morality.[2] When it comes to forgiveness, context, timing and inclination are also important. For example, an over-eager rush to forgive means that one may fail to seek justice for the oppressed or to take seriously the fact that the wrongdoer has wronged the victim. The result of hasty forgiveness has been that some have colluded with wrongdoing, and failed to speak out against evil or to seek justice because they thought that to forgive was the better way. The incidental but tragic result is that, when forgiven, the guilty appear free from blame and moral responsibility, even though, objectively speaking, they remain guilty.

Forgiveness can only properly take place if it is expressed as a person-to-person moral response to wrongdoing. This means that one does not ignore, waive or deny the fact that the victim has been violated. To forgive is not the only way to respond to wrongdoing: one may also, for example, be resentful or even vengeful. Surprisingly, not all unforgiving responses to wrongdoing are morally wrong (for example, in some situations, resentment may be a moral virtue), and some responses that are not forgiving can eventually lead to forgiveness.

Within the Christian church, there has often been a drive to urge people to forgive because to forgive is a surpassing moral ideal. Forgiveness gives people, as Tutu (1999: 35) rightly says, 'resilience, enabling them to survive and emerge still human, despite all efforts to dehumanise them'. Such forgiveness takes as its paradigm the life of Jesus.

It is also true to say that many people of Christian faith feel immensely guilty if they are unable to forgive those who have wronged them. This is particularly the case in the early stages of the process of forgiving. Such people think that to forgive is a moral duty and that they are failing in their moral duty as Christians if they fail to forgive. Those with sensitive consciences may also fear that God will not forgive them their sins if they do not also forgive others, as the Lord's Prayer is sometimes interpreted to suggest.

This is not entirely correct. The Christian's duty – and I suggest the duty of all people – is to strive to attain a moral ideal, the ideal to forgive. This is so, whether or not the wrongdoer is repentant. It is not enough (as it were) to fold one's arms and to say, 'I have been grievously wronged. It is too hard to forgive'. Rather, one should say, 'I have been grievously wronged. It is hard to forgive but I shall strive, as best I can, to become able to forgive.' It seems to me that God requires no more of people than that they should

---

[2] See the discussion of Porter 1995, pp.183–6, below.

seek to do all they can to forgive. For some, it will not take much to become able to forgive. For others it may take most of a lifetime. A few, even if they have participated in the sacramental life of the church (as Jones (1995) suggests they should if they are to forgive) and have received psychological therapy, will never be able to forgive because they are too violated or broken. This latter group will not face the sentence of divine unforgiveness because they have done what they could to forgive.

### FORGIVENESS AS SPECTRUM OF RESPONSES

Those who reflect on forgiveness have tended to see forgiveness as a discrete phenomenon that can be recognised or identified when certain identity markers are present. I have rejected this view and have argued that forgiveness comprises a variety of different responses to wrongdoing. Forgiveness can be identified by its effects (and some of these I discussed in chapter 9), though the effects that forgiveness brings can also come in other ways and from other forms of human behaviour. What marks out forgiveness as different from other expressions of human behaviour is that it is the result of certain kinds of moral responses to wrongdoing. Apart from that, the fact is that interpersonal forgiveness is no more than a psychosocial phenomenon and it is not necessarily related to repentance or atonement.

### FORGIVENESS AND THE KINGDOM OF GOD

God forgives because it is in God's essential being to forgive. Human forgiveness has its prototype in divine forgiveness and is imitative of God. I suggest that people want to forgive – and believe that to forgive is a moral good – because human beings have been made in the image of God.

According to the New Testament, divine forgiveness is a gift of the kingdom of God that may be partially experienced in the present, as a prolepsis of what is to come. It is, at best, a foretaste of future realities. Christians, who will have already experienced something of God's eschatological forgiveness, are to live out, model and practise that forgiveness before the watching world. It is evidence that the kingdom has come in the person of Jesus Christ but has yet to be fully established.

According to Luke especially, eschatological forgiveness is part of God's *aphesis* – God's liberating and freeing redemptive work. To forgive is to be part of God's redemptive work that includes the moral transformation of human relationships and society; it is not just to put right particular acts of wrongdoing on a person-to-person basis. To forgive is an expression of 'the

Lord's favour' because it is part of God's work to vindicate the broken and oppressed, to establish peace and justice and to restore the whole created order (Luke 4:18f.) To forgive, therefore, is to participate in the completion of the work of the cross.

Interpersonal forgiveness is a poor imitation of divine forgiveness because, as Derrida says, it can never be 'aneconomic' and because it does not – and cannot – undo the past or free people from the consequences of what they have done. The extent that human forgiveness bears the imprint of its prototype is the extent to which human beings can glimpse at – and have a foretaste of – the divine forgiveness that will have its consummation at the *eschaton*. To forgive is therefore an evangelistic, kerygmatic act that points to what is at the heart of the Christian gospel.

Of course all people, whether Christians or not, can forgive because they have been made in God's image. When people forgive, they are responding to the grace of God that is common to all and thereby participate in God's reconciling work in the world.

FORGIVENESS AND JUSTICE

Simon Wiesenthal said, 'I am someone who seeks justice, not vengeance. My work is a warning to the murderers of tomorrow, that they will never rest. When history looks back I want people to know that the Nazis weren't able to kill millions of people and get away with it.'[3] Vengeance *is* destructive and (*pace* Murphy) I can find no moral justification for it. But to seek justice when there has been wrongdoing is wholly laudable. And to seek justice and to eschew vengeance when there has been wrongdoing is not all that one can do. One can also seek to forgive.

In my view, it is undeniable that there is sometimes a conflict between seeking justice and forgiving. To seek justice means that one remembers the wrongdoing and strives to have it put right. To forgive means that one renounces one's right to seek justice and to have the wrong put right. To say that one has forgiven and, at the same time, to insist that the wrongdoer remains culpable and accountable for the wrongdoing is to emasculate forgiveness in its richest expressions. Jesus submitted to the cross and renounced his right to 'more than twelve legions of angels' who could have righted the wrong he was suffering. In this respect, he waived his right

---

[3] http://dailysally.blogspot.com/2005/09/simon-wiesenthal-justice-not-vengeance.html – accessed 28 May 2006.

to justice and surrendered to the depraved cruelty of his murderers and those who stood with them, praying for God's forgiveness for them.

We cannot resolve – in logic or in practice – the conflict between seeking justice and forgiving without appeal to a higher ethic. The Christian answer to the conflict – and this is the only answer of which I know that faces and addresses the antinomy – is that there is eschatological justice with God. One can forgive, confident in the knowledge that God will vindicate the oppressed at the *eschaton*. Even if one cannot forgive (this has to do with thoughts and attitudes that result in a particular sort of behaviour) one can still forbear to avenge (this has to do with behaviour), as the gospel enjoins.

Does God insist that personal moral accountability and moral culpability remain, even if a victim has forgiven the wrongdoer? If it is so, the internal coherence and logic of forgiveness are impossible to understand, for God will continue to hold people responsible for actions or omissions for which others have forgiven them. Yet there are indications in Scripture that this may be the case, as the idea of the judgment of works – even for those who have been forgiven their wrongdoing – seems to suggest. These observations reinforce the suggestion I made earlier that human forgiveness is no more than psychosocial in its effects and that it is unconnected with the idea of atonement.

### FORGIVENESS AS A PERSONAL RESPONSE

A surprising fact is that the New Testament sees forgiveness as personal and relational even though, on the whole, identity and personality were understood in collective terms in that period. Tutu's attempt to fuse the African idea of *ubuntu* with forgiveness goes further than the New Testament could have done but did not. It gave theological justification to the idea that individuals could forgive wrongdoing by groups, but the result has been that such 'forgiveness' has sometimes not been forgiveness at all. I take the view that groups cannot forgive or be forgiven and that individuals cannot forgive groups – because the encounter is not person-to-person – though it is possible to engage in ways that are akin to forgiveness, repentance and so on. The result can be a pardon and reconciliation.

In revisiting forgiveness for the twenty-first century, it is with wrongdoing by groups that more work has to be done. We need to recognise that one cannot forgive groups but only specific individuals within groups – and so recognise that there are many people who have been wronged and who are, to borrow Tutu's phrase from a different context, 'trapped in victimhood'.

THE FUTURE OF FORGIVENESS

Nietzsche's strictures that forgiveness is for the weak and feeble can no longer be taken to be self-evident. Forgiveness is today widely recognised as a moral good that is important both in public discourse and for personal practice. There are, I suggest, two reasons for this.

The first is that people recognise that unforgiving thoughts and feelings can be personally and communally destructive. Such thoughts and feelings *can* change and be changed, and unforgiveness resolved. Psychological interventions, especially using the principles of cognitive behaviour therapy, sometimes expedite that process of change. People now recognise that they do not have to be unforgiving and, if they forgive, the quality of their lives (and even health) is likely to improve.

The second reason is that people now believe that they have 'human rights' – whether as individuals or as part of a group – and that those who disregard or violate their rights can be held accountable. People sometimes think, feel and behave in an unforgiving way when they believe that their rights have been disregarded or violated.

Forgiveness will have a future only if it remains a moral response to wrongdoing. Many of the North American models of 'forgiveness interventions' run the risk of detaching forgiveness from ethics. If they succeed, forgiveness will become little more than pragmatic and narcissistic self-indulgence – what Jones terms 'therapeutic forgiveness' – and a mechanism to increase one's sense of happiness and well-being, sometimes at the expense of moral integrity. Provided forgiveness remains rooted in ethics, and especially if its practice is enriched by the benefit of psychological insights, forgiveness may continue to transform individuals and communities and offer a foretaste of future divine realities.

SOME WIDER ISSUES

The issues and questions raised in this book, and some of the methods used to explore those issues and questions, intersect with some wider issues to do with ethics that are being explored among philosophers and ethicists.

Hollenbach (2002), for example, has argued that the idea of the 'common good' – formulated by Aristotle and developed by Augustine, Aquinas and Loyola in the context of the Christian tradition – can and should be adapted and integrated into the value systems of modern communities. Hollenbach's starting point is Aristotle's, namely, that the 'good life of a single person and the quality of the common life persons share with one another in society are linked. Thus the good of the individual and the common good are inseparable' (Hollenbach 2002: 3).

Hollenbach rightly observes that the philosophical individualism of the enlightenment has reversed the order of Aristotle's philosophy so that the good of the individual now comes before the good of the community to which the individual belongs. The modern individualistic approach has per-haps most famously been popularly summarised by the former British Prime Minister, Mrs Margaret Thatcher, in an interview in a popular woman's magazine in 1987. Mrs Thatcher said,

I think we've been through a period where too many people have been given to understand that if they have a problem, it's the government's job to cope with it. 'I have a problem, I'll get a grant.' 'I'm homeless, the government must house me.' They're casting their problem on society. And, you know, there is no such thing as society. There are individual men and women, and there are families. And no government can do anything except through people, and people must look to themselves first. It's our duty to look after ourselves and then, also to look after our neighbour. People have got the entitlements too much in mind, without the obligations. There's no such thing as entitlement, unless someone has first met an obligation. (Thatcher 1987)

The result is a modern individualism that is not disciplined by the needs of others or corrected by a shared narrative of universal values. Hollenbach calls this phenomenon, in the title of his first chapter, 'The eclipse of the public'. One result is that each person has the right to hold views on morality and to act in ways that may be idiosyncratic, selfish or perverse and even incidentally detrimental to the good of others so long as those views and actions are 'tolerant' and compatible with the ideas of pluralism and respect for diversity on which modern society is predicated.

Rather than pluralism and the detached tolerance that goes with that, Hollenbach argues that there are some goods that can only be known in common, of which one is the good of community life itself. There is, he argues, a place for 'solidarity', that is, social and collective values, social forms and community life which (particularly taking up ideas in the writings of Pope John Paul II) express human interdependence and constitute 'the common good'.

In Hollenbach's view, people should commit themselves to the common good and actively seek to participate in promoting and achieving it. The result will be that there will be greater 'participation' (an important, recur-ring word in Hollenbach's book) in human society. He seeks to formulate what the common good is, whatever religious or other worldviews people may hold, and advocates that, to reach that point, differing views must be heard and explored.

Hollenbach argues that religion has an important contribution to make to the idea of what the common good may be and (despite some of the lessons of history) religion is not necessarily a threat to the common good. He writes this of Archbishop Tutu and his work with the Truth and Reconciliation Commission, for example:

> Tutu's struggles [to seek a peaceful path to a truly common justice in South Africa] rose simultaneously from his religious faith and from a conviction that the good of each person is integrally connected with the good of all. His opposition to Apartheid – apartness – is the very antithesis of the notion that religion is essentially divisive. Tutu's Christianity . . . is the root of commitment to a public good that is truly common. (Hollenbach 2002: 98)

Hollenbach explores the common good on a macro level, in the contexts of poverty in inner cities, consumerism and the global inequalities between rich and poor. Though Hollenbach does not ask this question, it is worth reflecting whether forgiveness might be a social and collective value that should be recognised as part of society's common good.[4]

To establish what the common good comprises, Hollenbach says one must engage in 'an intellectual endeavour' that 'calls for serious thinking by citizens about what their distinctive understandings of the good imply for the life of a society made up of people with many different traditions. It is a form of solidarity, because it can only occur in an active dialogue of mutual listening and speaking across boundaries of religion and culture' (Hollenbach 2002: 137 and see 152–9). Hollenbach (2002: 137–70) calls the pursuit of such a shared vision 'intellectual solidarity'.

In my view, forgiveness is part of the common good. To forgive is a moral good that benefits individuals and, on the basis of Aristotle's reasoning adapted by Hollenbach, it is a good that will benefit society. Even if it is not possible, strictly speaking, for there to be forgiveness where there has been structural wrongdoing, it is undeniable that expressions of regret and remorse, steps to right the wrongs and so on (these are akin to forgiveness on a person-to-person basis) also contribute to the common good. In contrast, unforgiveness dislocates relationships and fractures human interdependence and solidarity – and these violate the common good. Unforgiving

---

[4] Hollenbach (2002: 79–86) regards human and social relationships as good in themselves but does not refer to them in relation to forgiveness. Although he says that 'the good realized in the mutual relationships in and through which human beings achieve their well-being' (p. 82) is an important aspect of the common good, the principal application of this theoretical work on the common good is worked out socio-politically, in relation to poverty and justice.

people are often detached, bitter, isolated and in conflict with others – and so undermine the common good.

This book has had the incidental effect of contributing to (what Hollenbach calls) 'intellectual solidarity' about forgiveness as a common good, because it explores the nature of forgiveness, the effects of failing to seek forgiveness and the social effects of forgiveness. It seeks to do so with the deliberation, reciprocity and civility that Hollenbach enjoins.

Hollenbach also argues that, when it comes to the common good, there *can* be 'a dynamic interaction between the biblical faith handed on . . . through the centuries of the Christian tradition and the intelligence that is a preeminent manifestation of the *imago Dei* in all human beings' (Hollenbach 2002: 154f.). This is certainly true when it comes to reflection about forgiveness. In my view, there is a place for a distinctively Christian voice and vision in the debates. There is also a place for other views and approaches, especially because, as we have observed, discourse on forgiveness is no longer the preserve of Christians alone but is now the discourse of many people, whether of faith or no faith. The result of the dialogue has been that, in the 'dynamic interaction' to which Hollenbach refers, the Christian tradition has preserved its distinctive voice, has been refined and enriched, and has contributed to the understanding that others, from different traditions, hold.

An important contribution to Christian ethics has also been made by Porter (1995). Porter argues that neither a deontological (Kantian) approach (that is, that some kinds of actions are never morally justified) nor a consequentialist (utilitarian) approach (that is, that the morality of a specific act is determined by the overall balance of good *versus* bad consequences that it produces) is right. The better approach is to regard moral thinking as analogical (Porter 1995: 44–8) and, in that context, to ask whether a certain case counts as moral or immoral. In relation to murder, for example, the right approach is to ask whether a particular kind of action amounts to murder[5] rather than whether the action is an exception to the rule against murder. Porter concludes that our interpretations of a particular moral concept 'must be guided by inspection and reflection on the actual usage of the concept, and not used to determine in advance what counts as a moral concept, and what does not . . . The complexities of our most important concepts

---

[5] An example of this process from the world of science is that in August 2006 scientists declared that Pluto is no longer to be regarded as a 'planet'. This is because (according to the latest scientific definition of a planet) Pluto is not a celestial body that is in orbit around the sun that (i) has sufficient mass for its self-gravity to overcome rigid body forces so that the body assumes a nearly round shape and (ii) has cleared the neighbourhood around its orbit.

will generally outstrip our efforts at interpretation' (Porter 1995: 48). This process can be 'excruciatingly difficult' (p. 75).

In practical terms, when it comes to the moral notion of forgiveness, I have not taken a deontological approach and neither have I taken a strictly consequentialist approach (that is, I have not sought to evaluate all the benefits and drawbacks of forgiving in a particular instance). Rather, in seeking to analyse forgiveness, I have explored the different levels of ambiguity that may arise when people believe they should forgive others, and sought to analyse the ambiguities from a variety of methodological starting points. We *can* 'think morally . . . without committing ourselves to the strait-jacket of a narrow and reductionist concept of morality' (Porter 1995: 66). The same is true when we think of the sorts of wrongdoing that give rise to forgiveness: not all acts that a victim regards as morally wrong are necessarily so, and it is sometimes necessary to take into account a variety of considerations in order to determine whether a particular act is in *that* case morally wrong and so forgivable. As Porter (1995: 68) says, in many situations there is a conflict of moral duties. In each such case, what we must do is to consider 'the ways in which we . . . negotiate these conflicts at the level of individual judgment'. We may in the process be mistaken, misunderstand or fail in moral judgment.

How can one know which are the right criteria to use in the analogical process of moral reflection – and how can we know when someone, using the analogical process, makes a palpably wrong moral judgment, as opposed to a moral judgment made in good faith but on which wise and right-thinking people might not have unanimity? (An example of the latter that I have explored in this book is whether Wiesenthal should have forgiven Karl – and see also Scarre 2005). The issue does not concern a person's cognitive capacities or their competence to make moral judgments. Rather, it concerns a person's 'capacities for sensibility and perception' and 'empathy and awareness of others' (Porter 1995: 78, 80). (So if, for example, there is defect of character, a person's 'perceptions would be dulled or distorted in such a way that [the] construal of situations, and [the] construal of the options . . . would be systematically warped' – Porter 1995: 79.)

The answer, according to Porter (1995: 110f.), who develops the thought of Aquinas, is that, based on a normative account of human nature, it is possible to 'make distinctions of priority, and even validity, among the different considerations which inform our basic moral notions'. To this end, she argues that the moral virtues – even though they may sometimes be indeterminate or even ambiguous – must inform the process of moral reasoning that is governed by moral rules. Like moral rules, moral virtues also provide criteria by which to evaluate human actions and to inform human moral choices. They amount to 'goodness in action' (Porter 1995: 167) and, together with moral rules, cohere to establish what amounts to good action.

Porter reformulates Aquinas' account of moral virtues. She observes that, for Aquinas, 'the warmer, less determinate capacities for care and responsiveness do not have a central role' (1995: 183) because Aquinas is more concerned about the (self-regarding) moral virtues of self-restraint and courage. There is a place for moral virtues such as the capacity to care for others and the desire for the common good, which, Porter says, are 'other-regarding virtues' (1995: 188) and related to the virtues as Aquinas describes them.

Porter agrees with Aquinas that the self-regarding virtues are essential if a moral agent is to act at all. This has important implications when it comes to acts of vengeance and retribution. For example, if people do not control or restrain themselves (that is, do not demonstrate the self-regarding virtue of temperance as Porter interprets it) and pursue acts of vengeance, there is little chance that they will also be able to demonstrate other-regarding virtues, such as compassion and forgiveness, whether in relation to particular wrongs or generally. As Porter (1995: 171f.) says,

an agent who did not possess these [self-regarding] qualities at all would be able to perform discrete actions, but [the agent] would not be able to do most of the things that involve sustaining a course of activity; the fulfilment of role responsibilities, the pursuit of aims that can only be attained by a series of actions, participation in most social actions, promising, contracting, all these would be prohibitively difficult.

Although Porter does not specifically discuss the place of forgiveness among the virtues, her reformulation of the virtues leaves a place for the virtue of forgiveness. One who forgives has 'forgivingness', a quality of character that often incorporates empathy, mercy and compassion towards a wrongdoer and, because of its societal implications, implicitly has regard for the common good. This is a virtue, in the sense that Porter describes the virtues. The virtue of 'forgivingness' critically appraises the moral duty to strive to forgive and in dialectical encounter with the duty will evaluate the choices that the wrongdoers make.

Porter also suggests that the virtue of 'justice' that Aquinas describes might today be restated as being 'fairness' and 'integrity'. Fairness and integrity 'have in common a willingness, indeed an insistence, on construing one's own good in the context of some wider good, which is valued more than one's own immediate interests and desires' (Porter 1995: 193). Such willingness and insistence express the longing for justice that many wronged people feel.

Porter (1995: 194–6) recognises the dilemma – even contradiction – that many experience between the competing claims of the virtues of fairness and integrity, on the one hand, and the 'other-regarding' virtues, on the other.[6] There is, she says, no simple formula: the 'diverse ideals' must be balanced through 'intelligent action in situations of tension'. Beyond, that, she offers no help. In my view, we are left certainly more morally attuned but no wiser as to what it is morally right to do.

FINALLY

Properly understood, forgiveness is a gift, albeit an elusive gift.

A naïve and simplistic approach to forgiveness robs the concept of its moral richness and its transformative power. To engage with the complexity of forgiveness is to engage with an ideal that affects people – wrongdoers, victims and even onlookers – relationally, psychologically, morally and spiritually. One can probably never completely forgive but, in the process of seeking to forgive, individuals and communities can be enriched and changed.

In setting out the urgency and moral cogency of the task of forgiveness, I have sought to add to and broaden our understanding of what it may mean to forgive, even if some of the complexities and ambiguities of forgiveness remain unresolved. A world without forgiveness will be an impoverished world; a world with an impoverished notion of forgiveness will also be an impoverished world. A world that forgives will have a foretaste of the *aphesis* of God and will be incomparably the better for it.

---

[6] In contrast, Lévinas (1969) would argue that at the moment when a person encounters 'other', that person would know what is the appropriate moral response. Ethics is thus the result of encounter and is a response to the 'alterity' of the other. Lévinas is concerned not so much with what it is right to do in a particular situation (the contents of ethics) as what is ethical, and he derives the idea of what is ethical from the encounter with the 'other'. For Lévinas, therefore, there are no rigid moral obligations but obligations that arise from encounter.

# Bibliography

Adams, Marilyn M. 1991. 'Forgiveness: A Christian Model', *Faith and Philosophy* 8: 277–304.

Affinito, Mona Gustafson 2002. 'Forgiveness in Counseling: Caution, Definition and Application' in Lamb and Murphy 2002, pp. 88–111.

Ansorge, Dirk 2000. 'God between Mercy and Justice: The Challenge of Auschwitz and the Hope of Universal Reconciliation' in Bemporad *et al.* 2000, pp. 77–90.

Appleby, R. Scott 2000. *The Ambivalence of the Sacred. Religion, Violence, and Reconciliation.* Lanham, MD and Oxford: Rowman & Littlefield Publishers, Inc.

Aquino, K., Grover, S. L., Goldman, B. and Folger, R. 2003. 'When Push Doesn't Come to Shove. Forgiveness in Workplace Relationships', *Journal of Management Enquiry* 12: 209–16.

Arendt, Hannah 1958. *The Human Condition.* Chicago: University of Chicago Press.

 1968. *Eichmann in Jerusalem: A Report on the Banality of Evil.* New York: Viking Press.

Asch, Solomon Elliott 1946. 'Forming Impression of Personality', *Journal of Abnormal and Social Psychology* 41: 1230–40.

 1951. 'Effect of Group Pressure upon the Modification and Distortion of Judgments' in Harold Steere Guetzkow, *Group Leadership and Men.* Pittsburgh, PA: Carnegie University Press (1951), pp. 177–90.

Audra, E. and Williams, Aubrey (eds.) 1961. Alexander Pope, *Pastoral Poetry and an Essay on Criticism*, in *The Poems of Alexander Pope*, Volume I of 'The Twickenham Edition of the Poems of Alexander Pope'. London: Methuen.

Barber, Louise, Maltby, John and Macaskill, Ann 2005. 'Angry Memories and Thoughts of Revenge: The Relationship between Forgiveness and Anger Rumination', *Personality and Individual Differences* 39: 253–62.

Barnes, Jonathan (ed.), 1984. *Rhetoric. The Complete Works of Aristotle. The Revised Oxford Translation*, translated by W. Rhys Roberts. Guildford: Guildford University Press. (Volume II, pp. 2152–269; Bollingen Series LXXI.2.)

Barrett, Charles Kingsley 1991. *The Epistle to the Romans*, 2nd edition. Black's New Testament Commentaries. London: A & C Black.

Bash, Anthony and Bash, Melanie 2004. 'Early Christian Thinking' in Watts and Gulliford 2004, pp. 29–49.

Baumeister, Roy F., Exline, Julie Juola and Sommer, Kristin L. 1998. 'The Victim Role, Grudge Theory and Two Dimensions of Forgiveness' in Worthington 1998c, pp. 79–104.

Beauchamp, Tom L. and Childress, James F. 2001. *Principles of Biomedical Ethics*, 5th edition. New York and Oxford: Oxford University Press.

Bemporad, Jack, Pawlikowski John T. and Sievers, Joseph 2000. *Good and Evil after Auschwitz: Ethical Implications for Today*. Hoboken, NJ: KTAV Publishing House Inc.

Benn, Piers 1996. 'Forgiveness and Loyalty', *Philosophy* 71: 369–83.

Bennett, Christopher 2003. 'Personal and Redemptive Forgiveness', *European Journal of Philosophy* 11: 127–44.

Berry, Jack W. and Worthington, Everett L. 2001. 'Forgiveness, Relationship Quality, Stress while Imagining Relationship Events, and Physical and Mental Health', *Journal of Counseling Psychology* 48: 447–55.

Biggar, Nigel 2001. 'Forgiveness in the Twentieth Century. A Review of the Literature, 1901–2001' in McFadyen and Sarot 2001, pp. 181–217.

Bole, William, Christiansen, Drew and Hennemeyer, Robert T. 2004. *Forgiveness in International Politics: The Alternative Road to Peace*. Washington, DC: US Conference of Catholic Bishops.

Boon, S. D. and Sulsky, L. M. 1997. 'Attributions of Blame and Forgiveness in Romantic Relationships: A Policy-Capturing Study', *Journal of Social Behavior and Personality* 12: 19–44.

Burnside, Jonathan and Baker, Nicola 1994. *Relational Justice. Repairing the Breach*. Winchester: Waterside Press.

Calhoun, Cheshire 1992. 'Changing One's Heart', *Ethics* 103: 76–96.

Campbell, Catriona, Devlin, Roisin, O'Mahony, David, Doak, Jonathan, Jackson, John, Corrigan, Tanya and McEvoy, Keith 2006. *Evaluation of the Northern Ireland Youth Conference Service. NIO Research and Statistical Series: Report No. 12*. Produced by the Statistics and Research Branch of the Northern Ireland Office (Criminal Justice Policy Division): Belfast, Northern Ireland.

Caputo, John D., Dooley, Mark and Scanlon, Michael J. (eds.) 2001. *Questioning God*. Bloomington and Indianapolis: Indiana University Press.

Caputo, John D. and Scanlon, Michael J. (eds.) 1999. *God, the Gift and Postmodernism*. Bloomington: Indiana University Press.

Carmichael, Kay 2003. *Sin and Forgiveness. New Responses in a Changing World*. Aldershot, Hants: Ashgate.

Cassese, Antonio 2003. *International Criminal Law*. Oxford: Oxford University Press.

Cherry, Stephen 2004. 'Forgiveness and Reconciliation in South Africa' in Watts and Gulliford 2004, pp. 160–77.

Cose, Ellis 2004. *Bone to Pick. Of Forgiveness, Reconciliation, Reparation and Revenge*. New York: Washington Square Press.

Craig, W. J. (ed.) 1964. *The Complete Works of William Shakespeare*. London, New York and Toronto: Oxford University Press.

Davies, William David 1965. *Paul and Rabbinic Judaism. Some Rabbinic Elements in Pauline Theology*. London: SPCK. (First published 1948.)

Davies, William David and Allison, Dale C. 1991. *A Critical and Exegetical Commentary on the Gospel According to Saint Matthew*. Edinburgh: T. & T. Clark. Volume II (Commentary on Matthew VIII – XVIII).

Davis, Colin 1996. *Levinas. An Introduction*. Notre Dame: University of Notre Dame Press.

de Gruchy, John W. 2002. *Reconciliation: Restoring Justice*. London: SCM Press.

Denny, Norman (ed.) 1980. *Les Misérables* by Victor Hugo, translated and with an introduction by Norman Denny. Harmondsworth: Penguin.

Derrida, Jacques 2001a. *On Cosmopolitanism and Forgiveness*, translated by Mark Dooley and Michael Hughes with a Preface by Simon Critchley and Richard Kearney. London and New York: Routledge.

2001b. 'To Forgive' in Caputo *et al*. 2001, pp. 21–51.

Dooley, Mark 2001. 'The Catastrophe of Memory' in Caputo *et al*. 2001, pp. 129–49.

Downie, R. S. 1965. 'Forgiveness', *Philosophical Quarterly* 15: 128–34.

Drabkin, Douglas 1993. 'The Nature of God's Love and Forgiveness', *Religious Studies* 29: 231–8.

Duff, R. Antony 2001. *Punishment, Communication, and Community*. New York and Oxford: Oxford University Press.

Dunn, James D. G. 1988. *Romans 1–8*. Word Biblical Commentary, Volume 38A. Dallas: Word Books.

2003. *Jesus Remembered*. Christianity in the Making, Volume I. Grand Rapids: W. B. Eerdmans.

Durham, M. S. 1990. 'The Therapist and the Concept of Revenge: The Law of Talion', *Journal of Pastoral Care* 40: 131–7.

Ehrman, Bart D. (ed.) 2003a. *Lost Scriptures: Books that did not make it into the New Testament*. New York: Oxford University Press.

2003b. *Apostolic Fathers (Early Christian Collection)*, Volume II, edited and translated by Bart D. Ehrman. Loeb Classical Library. Cambridge, MA: Harvard University Press.

Elizondo, Virgil 1986. 'I Forgive But I Do Not Forget' in Floristan and Duquoc 1986, pp. 103–16.

Enright, Robert D. and Coyle, Catherine. T. 1998. 'Researching the Process Model of Forgiveness within Psychological Interventions' in Worthington 1998c, pp. 139–61.

Enright, Robert D. and Fitzgibbons, Robert P. 2000. *Helping Clients Forgive: An Empirical Guide for Resolving Anger and Resolving Hope*. Washington, DC: APA Press.

Enright, Robert D., Freedman, Suzanne and Rique, Julio 1998. 'The Psychology of Interpersonal Forgiveness' in Enright and North 1998, pp. 46–62.

Enright, Robert D. and the Human Development Study Group 1996. 'Counseling within the Forgiveness Triad: On Forgiving, Receiving Forgiveness, and Self-Forgiveness', *Counseling and Values* 40: 107–26.

Enright, Robert D. and North, Joanna (eds.) 1998. *Exploring Forgiveness* (with a foreword by Archbishop Desmond Tutu). Madison, WI: University of Wisconsin Press.

Exline, Julie Juola, Baumeister, Roy F., Bushman, Brad. J., Campbell, W. Keith and Finkel, Eli. J. 2004. 'Too Proud to Let Go: Narcissistic Entitlement as Barrier to Forgiveness', *Journal of Personality and Social Psychology* 87: 894–912.

Exline, Julie Juola, Worthington, Everett L., Hill, P. and McCullough, Michael. E. 2003. 'Forgiveness and Justice: A Research Agenda for Social and Personality Psychology', *Personality and Social Psychology Review* 7: 337–48.

Falls, Margaret M. 1987. 'Retribution, Reciprocity, and Respect for Persons', *Law and Philosophy* 6: 25–51.

Farrant, F. 2006 *Out For Good: The Resettlement Needs of Young Men in Prison.* London: Howard League for Penal Reform.

Farrow, T. F. D., Zheng, Y., Wilkinson, I. D., Spence, S. A., Deakin, J. F. W., Tarrier, N., Griffiths P. D. and Woodruff, W. R. 2001. 'Investigating the Functional Anatomy of Empathy and Forgiveness', *Neuroreport* 12: 2433–8.

Fiddes, Paul S. 1989. *Past Event and Present Salvation: The Christian Idea of Atonement.* London: Darton, Longman and Todd.

Fincham, Frank D. 2000. 'The Kiss of the Porcupines: From Attributing Responsibility to Forgiving', *Personal Relationships* 7: 1–23.

Fitzgibbons, Richard 1998. 'Anger and the Healing Power of Forgiveness: A Psychiatrist's View' in Enright and North 1998, pp. 63–74.

Fitzmyer, Joseph A. 1993. *Romans: A New Translation with Introduction and Commentary.* The Anchor Bible, Volume 33. New York and London: Doubleday.

Flanigan, B. 1998. 'Forgivers and the Unforgivable' in Enright and North 1998, pp. 95–105.

Floristan, Casiano and Duquoc, Christian (eds.) 1986. 'Forgiveness', *Concilium* 184. English Language editor: Marcus Lefébure. Edinburgh: T & T Clark (1986).

*Forgiveness in Conflict Resolution: Reality and Utility* 1998. Four volumes of Proceedings of Colloquia. Published by the Woodstock Theological Center. Washington, DC: US Conference of Catholic Bishops.

Fowler, Alastair (ed.) 1971. *Paradise Lost* by John Milton. Harlow: Longman.

Freedman, Suzanne, Enright, Robert D. and Knutson, Jeanette 2005. 'A Progress Report on the Process Model of Forgiveness' in Worthington 2005, pp. 393–406.

Fürer-Haimendorf, Christoph von 1979. *South Asian Societies: A Study of Values and Social Controls.* London: East-West Publications (1979).

Garrard, Eve 2002. 'Forgiveness and the Holocaust', *Ethical Theory and Moral Practice* 5: 147–65.

2003. 'Forgiveness and the Holocaust' in Garrard and Scarre 2003, pp. 231–45.

Garrard, Eve and McNaughton, David 2002. 'In Defence of Unconditional Forgiveness', *Proceedings of the Aristotelian Society* 103: 39–60.

Garrard, Eve and Scarre, Geoffrey Francis (eds.) 2003. *Moral Philosophy and the Holocaust*. Aldershot, Hants: Ashgate.

Gavrielides, Theo 2005. 'Some Meta-Theoretical Questions for Restorative Justice', *Ratio Juris* 18: 84–106.

Gillon, Raanan 1994. 'Medical Ethics: Four Principles Plus Attention to Scope', *British Medical Journal* 309: 184–8.

Girard, Michelle and Mullet, Étienne 1997. 'Propensity to Forgive in Adolescents, Young Adults, Older Adults, and Elderly People', *Journal of Adult Development* 4: 209–20.

Gladstone, William Ewart (ed.) 1995. *The Works of Joseph Butler*, Volume II, 'Sermons'. Bristol: Thoemmes Press, pp. 136–67.

Golding, Martin P. 1984–5. 'Forgiveness and Regret', *Philosophical Forum* 16: 121–37.

Gopin, Marc 2000. *Between Eden and Armageddon. The Future of World Religions, Violence and Peacemaking*. Oxford and New York: Oxford University Press.

Gorringe, Timothy 1996. *God's Just Vengeance. Crime, Violence and the Rhetoric of Salvation*. Cambridge: Cambridge University Press.

Govier, Trudy 1999. 'Forgiveness and the Unforgivable', *American Philosophical Quarterly* 36: 59–75.

2002. *Forgiveness and Revenge*. London and New York: Routledge.

Gregor, Mary (ed.) 1996. *The Metaphysics of Morals. Practical Philosophy*. Translated and edited by Mary Gregor with an Introduction by Roger J. Sullivan. New York: Cambridge University Press.

Gunton, Colin 1988. *The Actuality of the Atonement. A Study of Metaphor, Rationality and the Christian Tradition*. Edinburgh: T & T Clark.

Haber, Joram Graf 1991. *Forgiveness*. Savage, MD: Rowman and Littlefield.

Hieronymi, Pamela 2001. 'Articulating an Uncompromising Forgiveness', *Philosophy and Phenomenological Research* 62: 529–54.

Hirsch, Andrew von 1976. *Doing Justice. The Choice of Punishments: Report of the Committee for the Study of Incarceration*. Introduction by William Gaylin and David J. Rothman. New York: Hill & Wang.

Hollenbach, David J. 2002. *The Common Good and Christian Ethics*. New Studies in Christian Ethics, 22. Cambridge: Cambridge University Press.

Hollingdale, R. J. (ed.) 1969. *Thus Spoke Zarathustra: A Book for Everyone and No One* by Friedrich Nietzsche. Translated with an Introduction by R. J. Hollingdale. Harmondsworth: Penguin.

Holmgren, Margaret R. 1993. 'Forgiveness and the Intrinsic Value of Persons', *American Philosophical Quarterly* 30: 341–52.

2002. 'Forgiveness and Self-Forgiveness in Psychotherapy' in Lamb and Murphy 2002, pp. 112–35.

Hong, Howard V. and Hong, Edna H. (eds.) 1995. *Søren Kierkegaard's Writings. 16, Works of Love*. Edited and translated with Introduction and Notes by H. V. Hong and E. H. Hong. Princeton: Princeton University Press.

Hooker, Morna D. 1959. *Jesus and the Servant. The Influence of the Servant Concept of Deutero-Isaiah in the New Testament*. London: SPCK.

1990. *From Adam to Christ. Essays on Paul*. Cambridge: Cambridge University Press.

1991. *The Gospel According to St. Mark*. Black's New Testament Commentaries. London: A. & C. Black, 1991.

Horsbrugh, H. J. N. 1974. 'Forgiveness', *Canadian Journal of Philosophy* 4: 269–89.

Hughes, Paul M. 1997. 'What is Involved in Forgiving?', *Philosophia* 25: 33–49.

Hutchens, Benjamin C. 2004. *Lévinas. A Guide for the Perplexed*. New York and London: Continuum.

Jankélévitch, Vladimir 1986. *L'Imprescritible: Pardonner? Dans l'honneur et la dignité*. Paris: Seuil.

1996. 'Should We Pardon Them?', *Critical Enquiry* 22: 549–72.

Jenco, Lawrence Martin 1995. *Bound to Forgive. The Pilgrimage to Reconciliation of a Beirut Hostage*. Notre Dame: Ave Maria Press.

Jeremias, Joachim 1971. *New Testament Theology*, Part One: *The Proclamation of Jesus*. London: SCM.

Johnston, Douglas and Sampson, Cynthia (eds.) 1995. *Religion, the Missing Dimension of Statecraft*. Oxford: Oxford University Press.

Jones, L. Gregory 1995. *Embodying Forgiveness. A Theological Analysis*. Grand Rapids: W. B. Eerdmans.

Kaminer, Debra, Stein, Dan J., Mbanga, Irene and Zungu-Dirwayi, Nompumelelo 2000. 'Forgiveness: Towards an Integration of Theoretical Models', *Psychiatry* 63: 344–57.

Kearney, Richard 2001. 'On Forgiveness. A Roundtable Discussion with Jacques Derrida. Moderated by Richard Kearney', in Caputo *et al.* 2001, pp. 52–72.

Klawans, Jonathan 2000. *Impurity and Sin in Ancient Judaism*. New York and Oxford: Oxford University Press.

Kolnai, Aurel 1973–4. 'Forgiveness', *Proceedings of the Aristotelian Society* 74: 91–106.

Konstam, Varda, Marx, Fern, Schurer, Jennifer, Lombardo, Nancy B. Emerson and Harrington, Anne K. 2002. 'Forgiveness in Practice: What Mental Health Counselors are Telling Us' in Lamb and Murphy 2002, pp. 54–71.

Kornfield, Jack 2002. *The Art of Forgiveness, Lovingkindness and Peace*. New York: Bantam.

Kroll, Una 2000. *Forgive and Live*. Edinburgh: Continuum.

Kübler-Ross, Elizabeth 1970. *On Death and Dying*. London and New York: Tavistock/Routledge.

Kurzynski, M. J. 1998. 'The Virtue of Forgiveness as a Human Resource Management Strategy', *Journal of Business Ethics* 17: 77–85.

Lacey, Nicola 1998. *State Punishment. Political Principles and Community Values*. International Library of Philosophy. London: Routledge.

Lamb, Sharon 2002. 'Women, Abuse and Forgiveness: A Special Case' in Lamb and Murphy 2002, pp. 155–71.

Lamb, Sharon and Murphy, Jeffrie G. (eds.) 2002. *Before Forgiving: Cautionary Views of Forgiveness in Psychotherapy*. New York: Oxford University Press.

Lang, Berel 1994. 'Forgiveness', *American Philosophical Quarterly* 31: 105–17.

Langer, Ellen 2001. 'Well-Being. Mindfulness versus Positive Evaluation' in Snyder and Lopez 2001, pp. 214–30.

Lawler, Kathleen A., Younger, Jarred W., Piferi, Rachel L., Billington, Eric, Jobe, Rebecca L., Edmondson, Kimberley and Jones, Warren H. 2003. 'A Change of Heart: Cardiovascular Correlates of Forgiveness in Response to Interpersonal Conflict', *Journal of Behavioural Medicine* 26: 373–93.

Lawler, Kathleen A., Younger, Jarred W., Piferi, Rachel L., Jobe, Rebecca L., Edmondson, Kimberley and Jones, Warren H. 2005. 'The Unique Effects of Forgiveness on Health: An Exploration of Pathways', *Journal of Behavioral Medicine* 28: 157–67.

Lévinas, Emmanuel 1968. *Quatre Lectures Talmudiques*. Paris: Les Editions de Minuit.

1969. *Totality and Infinity: An Essay on Exteriority*, translated by A. Lingis. Martinus Nijhoff Philosophy Texts, Volume I. The Hague: Martinus Nijhoff Publishers.

1990. *Difficult Freedom: Essays on Judaism*, translated by S. Hand. Baltimore: Johns Hopkins University Press.

1998. *Entre Nous. On Thinking of the Other*, translated by M. B. Smith and B. Harshaw. New York: Columbia University Press.

Lewis, Clive Staples 1995. *Mere Christianity*, revised and amplified edition, with a new introduction. London: Fount.

Lewis, Meirlys 1980. 'On Forgiveness', *Philosophical Quarterly* 30: 236–45.

Lin, W., Mack, D., Enright, Robert D., Krahn, D. and Baskin, T. 2004. 'Effects of Forgiveness Therapy on Anger, Mood and Vulnerability to Substance Use among In-Patient Substance-Dependent Clients', *Journal of Consulting and Clinical Psychology* 72: 1114–21.

Lofthouse, William Frederick 1906. *Ethics and Atonement*. London: Methuen.

Lomax, Eric 1996. *The Railway Man*. London: Vintage Press.

Löschnig-Gspandl, Marianne 2003. 'Corporations, Crime and Restorative Justice' in Weitekamp and Kerner 2003, pp. 145–60.

Macaskill, Ann 2002. *Heal the Hurt: How to Forgive and Move On*. London: Sheldon Press.

Mackintosh, Hugh Ross 1927. *The Christian Experience of Forgiveness*. London: Nisbet.

Malina, Bruce J. 2001. *The New Testament World: Insights from Cultural Anthropology*, 3rd edition, revised and expanded. Louisville: Westminster John Knox Press.

Mandela, Nelson 1994. *Long Walk to Freedom. Autobiography of Nelson Mandela*. Boston: Little Brown.

Marshall, Tony F. 1999. *Restorative Justice: An Overview*. London: Home Office, Research Development and Statistics Directorate.

Martin, David 1997. 'Collective National Guilt. A Socio-Theological Critique' in Lawrance Osborn and Andrew Walker (eds.), *Harmful Religion. An Exploration of Religious Abuse*. London: SPCK.

McCullough, Michael E., Pargament, Kenneth I. and Thoresen, Carl E. 2000. *Forgiveness: Theory, Research and Practice*. New York: The Guilford Press.

McCullough, Michael E., Rachal, Kenneth Chris, Sandage, Steven J., Worthington, Everett L., Brown, Susan Wade and Hight, Terry L. 1998. 'Interpersonal Forgiving in Close Relationships II. Theoretical Elaboration and Measurement', *Journal of Personality and Social Psychology* 75: 1586–603.

McCullough, Michael E. and Witvliet, Charlotte van O. 2001. 'The Psychology of Forgiveness' in Snyder and Lopez 2001, pp. 446–58.

McCullough, Michael E. and Worthington, Everett L. 1999. 'Religion and the Forgiving Personality', *Journal of Personality* 67: 1141–64.

McCullough, Michael E., Worthington, Everett L. and Rachal, Kenneth Chris 1997. 'Interpersonal Forgiving in Close Relationships', *Journal of Personality and Social Psychology* 73: 321–36.

McFadyen, Alistair I. and Sarot, Marcel (eds.) 2001. *Forgiveness and Truth*. The Society for the Study of Theology: Explorations in Contemporary Theology. Edinburgh and New York: T & T Clark.

McGary, Howard 1989. 'Forgiveness', *American Philosophical Quarterly* 26: 343–51.

McGinn, Colin 1997. *Ethics, Evil and Fiction*. Oxford: Clarendon Press.

McLaughlin, Eugene, Fergusson, Ross, Hughes, Gordon and Westmarland, Louise 2003. *Restorative Justice. Critical Issues*. London: Sage Publications.

McManus, Jim and Thornton, Stephanie 2006. *Finding Forgiveness. Personal and Spiritual Perspectives*. Chawton, Hants: Redemptorist Publications.

Milbank, John 2003. *Being Reconciled. Ontology and Pardon*. London: Routledge.

Miles, Siân (ed.) 1986. *Simone Weil: An Anthology*. London: Virago.

Milgram, Stanley 1963. 'Behavioural Study of Obedience', *Journal of Abnormal and Social Psychology* 67: 371–8.

Minas, Anne C. 1975. 'God and Forgiveness', *Philosophical Quarterly* 27: 138–50.

Moberly, Robert Campbell 1901. *Atonement and Personality*. London: John Murray.

Moore, Michael 1998. *Placing Blame: A Theory of Criminal Law*. Oxford: Clarendon Press.

Morris, Alison and Young, Warren 2000. 'Reforming Criminal Justice. The Potential of Restorative Justice' in Strang and Braithwaite 2000, pp. 11–33.

Moule, Charles Francis Digby 1998. *Forgiveness and Reconciliation and Other New Testament Themes*. London: SPCK.

Mullet, Étienne, Barros, José, Frongia, Loredena, Usaï, Veronica, Neto, Félix and Shafighi, Sheila Rivière 2003. 'Religious Involvement and the Forgiving Personality', *Journal of Personality* 71: 1–19.

Mullet, Étienne, Girard, Michelle and Bakhshi, Panul 2004. 'Conceptualizations of Forgiveness', *European Psychologist* 9: 78–86.

Mullet, Étienne, Neto, Félix and Shafighi, Sheila Rivière 2005. 'Personality and its Effects on Resentment, Revenge, Forgiveness, and Self-Forgiveness' in Worthington 2005, pp. 159–81.

Murphy, Jeffrie G. 1978a. 'Kant's Theory of Criminal Punishment' in Murphy 1978b, pp. 82–92.

  2003. *Getting Even: Forgiveness and Its Limits*. New York: Oxford University Press.

2005. 'Forgiveness, Self-Respect and the Value of Resentment' in Worthington 2005, pp. 33–40.

Murphy, Jeffrie G. (ed.) 1978b. *Retribution, Justice, and Therapy*. Boston, MA: Reidel.

Murphy, Jeffrie G. and Hampton, Jean 1988. *Forgiveness and Mercy*. Cambridge: Cambridge University Press.

Murphy, Liam B. 1993. 'The Demands of Beneficence', *Philosophy and Public Affairs* 22: 267–92.

Nagel, Thomas 1986. *The View from Nowhere*. New York and Oxford: Oxford University Press.

Neblett, William R. 1974. 'Forgiveness and Ideals', *Mind* 83: 269–75.

Neu, Jerome 2002. 'To Understand All Is to Forgive All – or Is It?' in Lamb and Murphy 2002, pp. 17–35.

Nikolić-Ristanović, Vesna 2003. 'The Possibilities for Restorative Justice in Serbia' in Walgrave 2003, pp. 239–54.

Nolland, John 1989. *Luke 1–9:20*. Word Biblical Commentary, Volume 35A. Dallas: Word Books.

North, Joanna 1987. 'Wrongdoing and Forgiveness', *Philosophy* 62: 499–508.
    1998. 'The "Ideal" of Forgiveness' in Enright and North 1998, pp. 15–34.

Novitz, David 1998. 'Forgiveness and Self-Respect', *Philosophy and Phenomenological Research* 58: 299–315.

O'Shaugnessy, R. J. 1967. 'Forgiveness', *Philosophy* 42: 336–52.

Panichas, George A. (ed.) 1981. *The Simone Weil Reader*. New York: Dorset Press.

Pargament, Kenneth I. and Rye, Mark S. 1998. 'Forgiveness as a Method of Religious Coping' in Worthington 1998c, pp. 59–78.

Pearsall, Judy and Hanks, Patrick (eds.) 2003. *Oxford Dictionary of English*, 2nd edition, edited by Catherine Soanes and Angus Stevenson. Oxford: Oxford University Press.

Perelman, Sidney Joseph 1970. *Baby, It's Cold Inside*. London: Weidenfeld and Nicolson.

Pettigrove, Glen 2003. 'Apology, Reparations and the Question of Inherited Guilt', *Public Affairs Quarterly* 17: 319–48.
    2004a. 'Unapologetic Forgiveness', *American Philosophical Quarterly* 41: 187–204.
    2004b. 'The Forgiveness We Speak. The Illocutionary Force of Forgiving', *Southern Journal of Philosophy* 42: 371–92.

Pokrifka-Joe, Todd 2001. 'Probing the Relationship between Divine and Human Forgiveness in Matthew' in McFadyen and Sarot, 2001, pp. 165–72.

Porter, Jean 1995. *Moral Action and Christian Ethics*. New Studies in Christian Ethics, 5. Cambridge: Cambridge University Press.

Puka, Bill 2005. 'Forgoing Forgiveness' in Lamb and Murphy 2002, pp. 136–52.

Ramsey, Boniface (ed.) 2005. *The Works of Saint Augustine: A translation for the 21st century. Part 2, Letters. Volume IV, Letters 211–270, 1\*–29\**, translation and notes by Roland Teske. Hyde Park, NY: New City Press.

Redlich, E. Basil 1937. *The Forgiveness of Sins*. Edinburgh: T & T Clark.

Reiff, Mark R. 2005. *Punishment, Compensation and Law: A Theory of Enforceability.* Cambridge: Cambridge University Press.

Reiss, S. and Havercamp, S. M. 1998. 'Toward a Comprehensive Assessment of Fundamental Motivation: Factor Structure of the Reiss Profiles', *Psychological Assessment* 10: 97–106.

Richards, Norvin 1988. 'Forgiveness', *Ethics* 99: 77–97.

2002. 'Forgiveness as Therapy' in Lamb and Murphy 2002, pp. 72–87.

Roberts, Paul 1998. 'On the Preconditions and Possibilities of Criminal Law Theory', *South African Journal of Criminal Justice* 11: 285–301.

Roberts, Robert C. 1995. 'Forgivingness', *American Philosophical Quarterly* 32: 289–306.

Robinson, James M. (ed.) 1971. *The Future of our Religious Past. Essays in Honour of Rudolf Bultmann*, translated by Charles E. Carlston and Robert P. Scharlemann. London: SCM Press.

Rowe, Christopher and Broadie, Sarah (eds.) 2002. *Aristotle: Nicomachean Ethics*, translation (with Historical Introduction) by Christopher Rowe; Philosophical Introduction and Commentary by Sarah Broadie. Oxford: Oxford University Press.

Rye, Mark S., Pargament, Kenneth I., Ali, A., Beck, G. L., Dorff, E. N., Hallisey, C., Narayanan, V. and Williams, J. G. 2000. 'Religious Perspectives on Forgiveness' in McCullough *et al.* 2000, pp. 18–40.

Sanders, Edward P. 1976. *Paul and Palestinian Judaism.* London: SCM Press.

1985. *Jesus and Judaism.* London: SCM Press.

Scarre, Geoffrey Francis 2003. 'Moral Responsibility and the Holocaust' in Garrard and Scarre 2003, pp. 103–16.

2004. *After Evil. Responding to Wrongdoing.* Aldershot, Hants: Ashgate.

2005. 'Excusing the Inexcusable? Moral Responsibility and Ideologically Motivated Wrongdoing', *Journal of Social Philosophy* 36: 457–72.

Schabas, William A. 2004. *An Introduction to the International Criminal Court*, 2nd edition. Cambridge: Cambridge University Press.

Scobie, E. D. and Scobie, G. E. W. 1998. 'Damaging Events: The Perceived Need for Forgiveness', *Journal for the Theory of Social Behaviour* 29: 373–401.

Shriver, Donald W. 1995. *An Ethic for Enemies: Forgiveness in Politics.* New York and Oxford: Oxford University Press.

Smedes, Lewis B. 1984. *Forgive and Forget: Healing the Hurts We Don't Deserve.* New York: HarperCollins.

Smith, Douglas (ed.) 1996. *On the Genealogy of Morals. A Polemic: By Way of Clarification and Supplement to My Last Book 'Beyond Good and Evil'* by Friedrich Nietzsche, translated with an introduction and notes by Douglas Smith. Oxford and New York: Oxford University Press.

Smith, Tara 1997. 'Tolerance & Forgiveness: Virtues or Vices?', *Journal of Applied Philosophy* 14: 31–41.

Snyder, C. R. and Lopez, Shane J. (eds.) 2001. *Handbook of Positive Psychology.* New York and London: Oxford University Press.

Stegemann, Ekkehard W. and Stegemann, Wolfgang 1999. *The Jesus Movement. A Social History of its First Century*, translated by O. C. Dean. Edinburgh: T & T Clark.

Stendahl, Krister 1976. *Paul among Jews and Gentiles and Other Essays*. Philadelphia: Fortress Press.

Strang, Heather and Braithwaite, John (eds.) 2000. *Restorative Justice: Philosophy to Practice*. Aldershot, Hants: Ashgate.

Strawson, Peter F. 1968a. 'Freedom and Resentment' in Strawson 1968b, pp. 71–96.

Strawson, Peter F. (ed.) 1968b. *Studies in the Philosophy of Thought and Action*. London, Oxford and New York: Oxford University Press.

Sullivan, Dennis, Tifft, Larry and Cordella, Peter 1998. 'The Phenomenon of Restorative Justice: Some Introductory Remarks', *Contemporary Justice Review* 1: 7–20.

Sussman, David 2005. 'Kantian Forgiveness', *Kant-Studien* 96: 85–107.

Swinburne, Richard 1989. *Responsibility and Atonement*. Oxford: Clarendon Press.

Talbott, Thomas B. 1993. 'Punishment, Forgiveness and Divine Justice', *Religious Studies* 29: 151–68.

Taylor, Joan E. 1997. *John the Baptist within Second Temple Judaism*. London: SPCK.

Taylor, Vincent 1941. *Forgiveness and Reconciliation. A Study in New Testament Theology*. London: Macmillan.

Temple, William 1924. *Christus Veritas. An Essay*. London: Macmillan.

Thackeray, Henry St. J., Marcus, R., Wikgren, A. and Feldman, L. H. (eds.) 1926–65. *Josephus: Works*, 9 volumes, Loeb Classical Library. London: Heinemann.

Thatcher, Margaret 1987. Interviewed in *Woman's Own*, 31 October 1987.

Thomas, Laurence 2003. 'Forgiving the Unforgivable?', in Garrard and Scarre 2003, pp. 201–30.

Thompson, Laura Yamhura, Snyder, C. R., Hoffman, Lesa, Michael, Scott T., Rasmussen, Heather N., Billings, Laura S., Heinze, Laura, Neufeld, Jason E., Shorey, Hal S., Roberts, Jessica C., Roberts, Danae E. 2005. 'Dispositional Forgiveness of Self, Others, and Situations', *Journal of Personality* 73: 313–59.

Thomson, Judith Jarvis 1971. 'A Defense of Abortion', *Philosophy and Public Affairs*: 1: 47–66.

Thyen, Hartwig 1971. '*Baptisma metanoias eis aphesin hamartion*' in Robinson 1971, pp. 131–68.

Tombs, David and Liechty, Joseph (eds.) 2005. *Explorations in Reconciliation: New Directions in Theology*. Aldershot, Hants: Ashgate.

Turner, Nigel 1963. *A Grammar of New Testament Greek* by James Hope Moulton, Volume III: Syntax of the Moods and Tenses of New Testament Greek. Edinburgh: T & T Clark.

Tutu, Desmond 1999. *No Future Without Forgiveness*. London: Rider.

Vermes, Geza (ed.) 1987. *The Dead Sea Scrolls in English*, 3rd edition, translated by Geza Vermes. Sheffield: Sheffield Academic Press.

Volf, Miroslav 1996. *Exclusion and Embrace: A Theological Exploration of Identity, Otherness and Reconciliation*. Nashville: Abingdon.

Wade, Nathaniel G. and Worthington, Everett L. 2005. 'In Search of a Common Core: A Content Analysis of Interventions to Promote Forgiveness', *Psychotherapy: Theory, Research, Practice, Training* 42: 160–77.

Walgrave, Lode (ed.) 2003. *Repositioning Restorative Justice*. Cullompton, Devon: Willan Publishing.

Watts, Fraser N. and Gulliford, Elizabeth Z. 2004. *Forgiveness in Context: Theology and Psychology in Creative Dialogue*. London and New York: T & T Clark.

Webb, Robert L. 1991. *John the Baptizer and Prophet. A Socio-Historical Study*. JSNT Sup 62. Sheffield: JSOT Press.

Weitekamp, Elmar G. M. and Kerner, Hans-Jürgen (eds.) 2003. *Restorative Justice in Context. International Practice and Directions*. Cullompton, Devon: Willan Publishing.

Wiesenthal, Simon 1998. *The Sunflower: On the Possibilities and Limits of Forgiveness. With a Symposium edited by Harry James Cargas and Bonny V. Fetterman*, revised and expanded edition. New York: Schocken Books.

Willemsens, Jolien. 2003. 'Restorative Justice: A Discussion of Punishment' in Walgrave 2003, pp. 24–42.

Wilson, J. 1988. 'Why Forgiveness Requires Repentance', *Philosophy* 63: 534–5.

Wittgenstein, Ludwig 1968. *Philosophical Investigations*, translated by G. E. M. Anscombe, 2nd edition. Oxford: Blackwell.

Witvliet, C. van O., Phipps, K. A., Feldman, M. E. and Beckham, J. C. 2004. 'Posttraumatic Mental and Physical Correlates of Forgiveness and Religious Coping in Military Veterans', *Journal of Traumatic Stress* 17: 269–73.

Wohl, Michael J. and Branscombe, Nyla R. 2005. 'Forgiveness and Collective Guilt Assignment to Historical Perpetrator Groups Depend on Levels of Social Category Inclusiveness', *Journal of Personality and Social Psychology* 88: 288–303.

Wolfendale, Jessica 2005. 'The Hardened Heart: The Moral Dangers of Not Forgiving', *Journal of Social Philosophy* 36: 344–63.

Worthington, Everett L. 1998a. 'Empirical Research in Forgiveness: Looking Backward, Looking Forward' in Worthington 1998c, pp. 321–39.

1998b. 'The Pyramid Model of Forgiveness: Some Interdisciplinary Speculations about Unforgiveness and the Promotion of Forgiveness' in Worthington 1998c, pp. 107–37.

2001. *Five Steps to Forgiveness: The Art and Science of Forgiving*. New York: Crown Publishers.

Worthington, Everett L. (ed.) 1998c. *Dimensions of Forgiveness. Psychological Research and Theological Perspectives*. Laws of Life Symposia, Volume I. Philadelphia and London: Templeton Foundation Press.

2005. *Handbook of Forgiveness*. New York; Hove: Routledge.

Worthington, Everett L. and Scherer, Michael 2004. 'Forgiveness is an Emotion-Focused Coping Strategy that Can Reduce Health Risks and Promote Health Resilience: Theory, Review and Hypotheses', *Psychology and Health* 19: 385–405.

Wright, Martin 2003. 'Is It Time to Question the Concept of Punishment?' in Walgrave 2003, pp. 3–23.

Wright, Nicholas Thomas 1996. *Jesus and the Victory of God*, Christian Origins and the Question of God, Volume II. London: SPCK.

Yandell, Keith E. 1998. 'The Metaphysics and Morality of Forgiveness' in Enright and North 1998, pp. 35–45.

Zehr, Howard 1990. *Changing Lenses. A New Focus for Crime and Justice.* Scottdale, PA and Waterloo, Ontario: Herald Press.

Zehr, Howard and Mika, Harry 2003. 'Fundamental Concepts of Restorative Justice' in McLaughlin *et al.* 2003, pp. 40–3.

## PAPAL DOCUMENTS

Bull of Indiction of the Great Jubilee of the Year 2000, *Incarnationis mysterium,* www.vatican.va/jubilee_2000/docs/documents/hf_jp-ii_doc_30111998_bolla-jubilee_en.html (29 November 1998).

*Memory and Reconciliation: The Church and the Faults of the Past,* www.vatican.va/roman_curia/congregations/cfaith/cti_documents/rc_con_cfaith_doc_20000307_memory-reconc-itc_en.html (December 1999).

## LAW REPORTS

Attorney-General of Israel *v.* Adolf Eichmann, 36 *ILR* 5–342 (1968).

DPP *v.* Kent and Sussex Contractors Ltd [1944] KB 146–59.

R. *v.* Bow Street Metropolitan Stipendiary Magistrate, and others, *ex parte* Pinochet Ugarte (Amnesty International and others intervening) (no. 3) [1999] 2 All ER 97–192.

White and Others *v.* Chief Constable of South Yorkshire and Others, 2 *AC* 455–511 (1999).

## WEBSITES

http://dailysally.blogspot.com/2005/09/simon-wiesenthal-justice-not-vengeance.html

http://news.bbc.co.uk

http://news.bbc.co.uk/1/hi/england/beds/bucks/herts/4968534.stm

http://news.bbc.co.uk/1/hi/magazine/4522173.stm

http://news.bbc.co.uk/1/hi/magazine/5016536.stm

http://news.bbc.co.uk/1/hi/uk/5105328.stm

http://news.bbc.co.uk/1/hi/world/africa/4534196.stm

http://news.bbc.co.uk/go/pr/fr/-/hi/uk/4726915.stm

http://news.findlaw.com/hdocs/iraq/tagubarpt.html

www.abc.net.au/7.30/content/2006/s1647727.htm

www.abc.net.au/cgi-bin/common/printfriendly.pl?

www.abc.net.au/pm/content/2006/s1645748.htm

www.amnestyusa.org/news/document.do?
id= 80256DD400782B84802570590039A155

www.bbc.co.uk/go/pr/fr/-/hi/world/asia-pacific/4749467.stm

www.bridge-builders.org

www.ddaymuseum.org/about/news_032204.html

www.forachange.co.uk/index.php?stoid=143

www.forgivenessinstitute.org

www.forgiving.org

www.foxnews.com/story/0,2933,188008,00.html
www.icc-cpi.int
www.ictr.org
www.iirp.org
www.ipsnews.net/news.asp?idnews=29789
www.iraatrocities.fsnet.co.uk/enniskillen.html
www.pbs.org/eliewiesel/resources/reagan.html
www.pficjr.org
www.publicintegrity.org/docs/AbuGhraib/Abu21.pdf
www.relationshipsfoundation.org
www.restorativejustice.org
www.sc-sl.org/
www.theforgivenessproject.com
www.theforgivenessproject.com/stories/andrew-rice
www.timesonline.co.uk/article/0,,3–2236871.html
www.timesonline.co.uk/article/0,,22989–2073010.html
www.timesonline.co.uk/article/0,,6–2074741.html
www.timesonline.co.ukwww.cyc-net.org/today/2000/today000328.html
www.un.org/icty/
www.vatican.va/jubilee_2000/docs/documents/hf_jp-ii_doc_30111998_
    bolla-jubilee_en.html
www.vatican.va/roman_curia/congregations/cfaith/cti_documents/rc_con_
    cfaith_doc_20000307_memory-reconc-itc_en.html

## NEWSPAPERS

*Church Times*
17 February 2006

*Hadoar*
3 February 1995: 3

*Daily Telegraph*
18 August 2005

*Guardian*
18 December 1995

*The Times*
30 July 2005
7 March 2006
28 March 2006

# Indexes

## INDEX OF AUTHORS

## INDEX OF PAPAL DOCUMENTS

## INDEX OF SCRIPTURE PASSAGES

# INDEX OF OTHER PRIMARY SOURCES

## ARISTOTLE